Ukrainian Vignettes

Ukrainian Vignettes

Essays on a Culture
at War

Mitja Velikonja

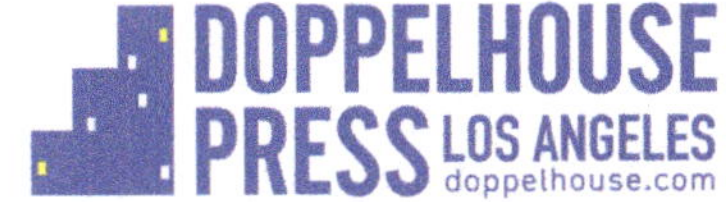

Mitja Velikonja
Ukrainian Vignettes
Essays on a Culture at War
Translated by Sonja Benčina

First published as

Mitja Velikonja
UKRAJINSKE VINJETE
Eseji o kulturi bližnje vojne

Miš založba
Miš d. o. o.
Gorjuša 33
1233 Dob pri Domžalah
info@miszalozba.com
www.miszalozba.com

All photos by Mitja Velikonja taken in Ukraine in May, August and September 2023, and June 2024.

Cover design: Carrie Paterson
Book design: Carrie Paterson, based on Miš book design by Žiga Valetič

Cover image: Uzhhorod, June 2024.
Following pages, left to right:
Paste-up on a shack, Kyiv, June 2024.
"Be Brave Like Ukraine" socks, Uzhhorod, September 2023.

Publisher's Cataloging-in-Publication Data

Names: Velikonja, Mitja, author. | Benčina, Sonja, translator.
Title: Ukrainian vignettes : essays on a culture at war / by Mitja Velikonja.; translated by Sonja Benčina.
Description: Includes bibliographical references. | Los Angeles, CA: Doppel-House Press, 2025.
Identifiers: LCCN: 2025933244 | ISBN: 978-1-954600-27-0 (paperback) | 978-1-954600-34-8 (ebook)
Subjects: LCSH Street art--Ukraine. | Mural painting and decoration, Ukrainian--21st century. | Russian Invasion of Ukraine, 2022. | Ukraine--Foreign relations--21st century. | BISAC HISTORY / Europe / Ukraine | ART / Art and Politics | ART / Essays | ART / Graffiti and Street Art
Classification: LCC ND2768.U37 .V45 2025 | DDC 751.7/3/094771--dc23

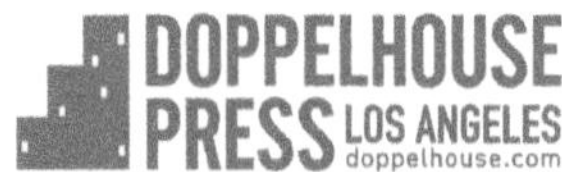

TABLE OF CONTENTS

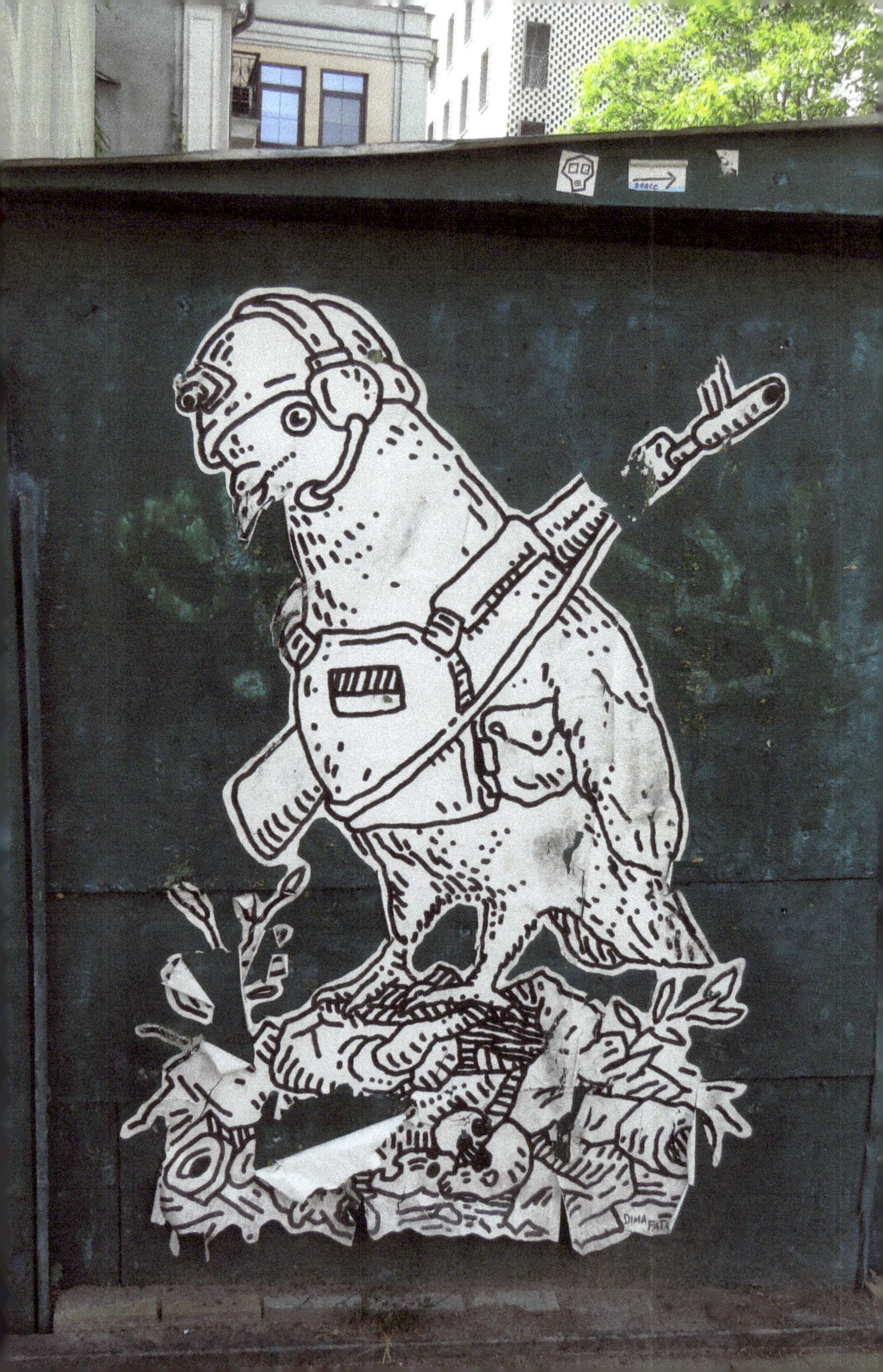
ВРАСС
DIMA

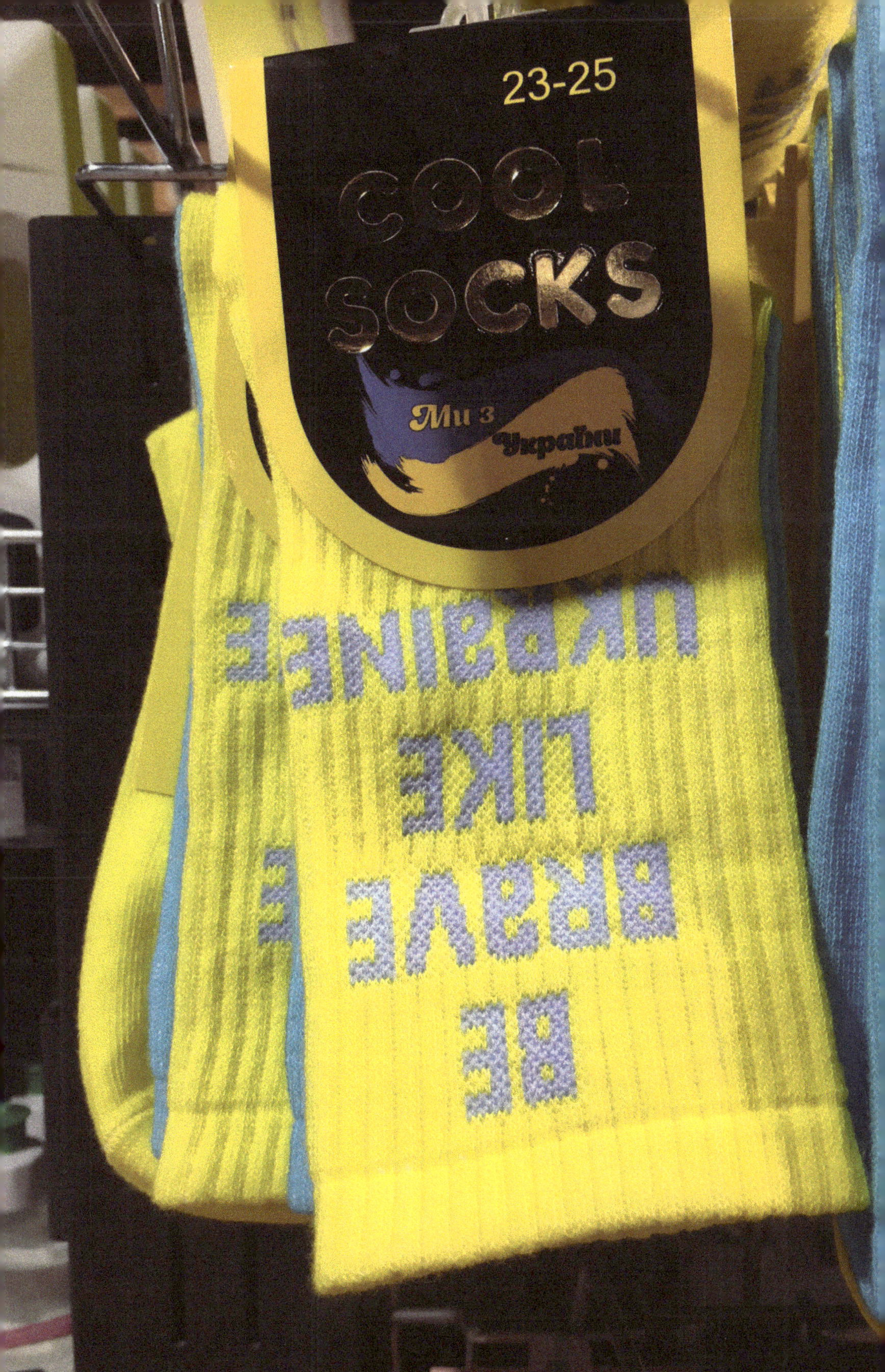
23-25
COOL
SOCKS
Ми з Україна
UKRAINE
LIKE
BRAVE
BE

FOREWORD

by Milan Subotić

In the imagination of the "Lord of War," Russian President Vladimir Putin — for whom, as one of his associates says, "time flows differently, because he lives in a history book" — the current war conflict is not only a continuation of the Second World War and the collapse of the Soviet Union as "the greatest geopolitical catastrophe," but also a series of events from the distant past in which, to use Andreas Kappeler's metaphor, the Ukrainian "younger brother" repeatedly tried to break away from the tight embrace of the Russian "elder brother." Therefore, it is understandable that Putin often repeats that "we did not start the war, we are only trying to end it."[1]

The extradordinary length of the war leads to its "normalization" in Russia and elsewhere, which, among other things, is reflected in the loss of interest in news reports about it and its disappearance from the front pages of newspapers and breaking reports of electronic media into the background. After dramatic images of the war in the Middle East, analyses of the American elections, or anticipations of the unfolding of crises in Georgia and Moldova, the war in Ukraine is often sidelined.

Nevertheless, at least within the framework of academic life, the war, despite all the horrors, led to a "collateral gain," materialized in the creation of entire libraries of books, a series of study programs and scientific

---

1 Answers to the questions of journalist Pavle Zarubin, Kremlin.ru/events/president/news, February 14, 2024; Also: Session of the discussion club "Valdaj," October 5, 2023 (http://kremlin.ru/events/president/news/72444).

gatherings dedicated to the history of Ukraine and Ukrainian-Russian relations. One of the books that would most likely not have been written without the war is Mitja Velikonja's book, *Ukrainian Vignettes*.

Unlike numerous historians, political scientists and geopolitical analysts, the author of this book is a professor at the department of cultural studies whose research focus is on the former Yugoslav countries, the Balkans and Central Europe, and is not an expert on Russian and Ukrainian studies. Therefore, he already points out in the introduction that the book he wrote is "far from being a scholarly treatise, much less a historical study or a study or a study of the current situation in Ukraine" (30). However, the modesty in defining the theoretical ambitions and limitations of the author's academic specialization, which, at first glance, appear to be a shortcoming, represent the virtue of this book because it allows Velikonja to formulate his view and interpretation of the war against Ukraine *out of the box*, i.e. beyond the usual and already established interpretive canons.

In accordance with this is the genre characteristic of the book, its "hybrid" essayistic form, in which the travelogue-literary record is combined with theoretical passages and the author's critical questioning of his own theoretical and political point of view. The result, according to Velikonja, is "barefoot culturalology" in which the researcher looks at his immediate experience in a war-torn country through the prism of the autobiographical method and self-reflection.

There are two main consequences of such an approach. The first is to avoid the temptation of "essentialization," which sees eternal, unchanging essences in the states, nations, and cultures of the two conflicting parties, and reduces them to homogeneous entities that are depicted in black and white. Before the Russian aggression in 2022, Ukrainian historian Andriy Portnov had warned against widespread essentialist reduction in the interpretation of the Russian-Ukrainian conflict and about whether or not we are even capable of thinking about Ukraine beyond concepts of 'identity', 'history', and 'clash of civilizations', while neglecting analyzes of the interests of political elites, class relations, the re-traditionalization of society, the power and influence of oligarchic groups, i.e. all that is commonly referred to as the social context of the "post-socialist transition" in the East.[2] Although Mitja Velikonja primarily deals with the phenomenon of culture during the war in Ukraine, his answer to this question is affirmative — he advocates a "materialist craft" according to which ethno-politics is the consequence, but not the cause, of real-politics, the politics of practical interests.

Another consequence of the author's approach is avoiding the trap of "exoticization" of the research subject, by which the researcher-outsider pretends to give final answers and discover the true nature of life phenomena that remain opaque to the "natives," whom he treats paternalistically. In contrast, Velikonja carefully listens to the voices, reads the texts, and observes the images created in the everyday wartime life of his Ukrainian hosts in order to better understand and interpret them "from below," without pre-adopted position and acceptance of official interpretations. Nevertheless, the key factor in avoiding the exoticization of the war in Ukraine is the author's experience of the disintegration of Yugoslavia. During his recent trips to Ukraine, therefore, he often experienced *déjà vu*, the recognition of a series of analogies with those pre-war and wartime events in which his former homeland disappeared.

The reader of his book will probably be surprised by the whole series of the author's critical comments on Ukrainian ethno-nationalism and the cultural production that forms and supports it, and on the politics of the history of the Ukrainian authorities, which, especially during the presidential terms of Yushchenko and Poroshenko, rehabilitated fascist movements and parties such as the Organization of Ukrainian Nationalists and the Ukrainian Liberation Army from the Second World War. The iconography in which Stepan Bandera and Roman Shukhevych are the central figures and role models of a significant part of today's generations, and the members of extreme-right movements, organizations, and militias are national heroes, does not meet the sympathy of our author. Understanding the war as a

2 Portnov, Andriy (2015): "On Decommunization, Identity, and Legislating History, From a Slightly Different Angle," *Krytyka* (May 2015).

context that feeds extreme ethno-nationalism and Ukrainian chauvinism does not justify them, and only remembering their defensive, reactive character in relation to Russian imperial nationalism only partially explains them. Also, Velikonja's criticism is caused by a confrontation with Russian cultural heritage ("Pushkinopad"), which, like the symbolism of extreme right-wing political groups, only helps to make Putin's "fight against neo-Nazism" a "self-fulfilling prophecy" for the Russian and a part of the European public.

The aforementioned criticisms of Ukrainian reality and culture represent a departure from the influential genre of travel writing by members of the European left who in the past — searching for the "promised land" in the form of a "political pilgrimage" — often uncritically sought and found their own utopia in different places, from the Soviet Union, China, and Cuba to Yugoslavia. In his view of the Russian-Ukrainian War, Velikonja does not romanticize Ukraine, although he adopts the key positions of the discourse of the contemporary Left — a critique of the policy of neoliberalism and the ideology of ethnic nationalism.[3] Accepting this "diagnosis" of the situation, which does not concern only the post-socialist "transition" countries, it is difficult to avoid the impression that the contemporary Left remains unclear in the selection and offer of "remedies" that can help us.

The author does not pretend to discover such "medicine" in his book. Velikonja's analysis of the culture of war is based on the rejection of authoritarianism and his aversion to collectivism that reduces individuals to mere members of the nation, state, church, or party. In the background of this analysis, hope still simmers in him that a society based on the values of freedom, solidarity, social justice, and equality is possible, and that a culture of peace is not necessarily doomed to retreat and be defeated. At the same time, this hope is accompanied by the author's skepticism fueled by the historical

---

3 "Neoliberalism is dominated by obsessive individualism, ethnonationalism by tribal inwardness — but always and everywhere, they act solidly together, complementing each other... Neoliberalism creates class differences, nationalism levels them ethnically. In short, what neoliberalism impoverishes materially, ethnonationalism ideologically justifies" (78).

   Ukrainian Vignettes: Essays on a Culture at War

experience of the 20th century, in which the culture wars continued even after the end of armed conflicts. In this regard, the example of the author's former homeland is illustrative, where three decades after the bloody, war-torn disintegration, peace is still a temporary state that can be most accurately expressed by the title of the Yugoslav film *See You in the Next War* (1980).

Will Ukraine, after the end of the war, have the strength and will to avoid the long-term negative consequences of the culture of war, regardless of the possible loss of territorial integrity? This question remains open, as well as the possibility of a democratic transformation of Russia, during which the country would finally be freed from imperial nationalism and its aspiration to expand the borders of the "Russian world." Or are these questions completely irrelevant when raised in the shadow of the threat of nuclear catastrophe as the key trump card of the Russian advocates of war? The future remains unclear, and with all the critical remarks about the ethno-nationalism of the Ukrainian culture of war, we can conclude with Velikonja that at least the basic fact of the present is that "Russia is occupying parts of the Ukraine, not the other way around; in every aspect, the former is stronger than the latter, while the latter struggles to put up a fight" (37). That is enough to take a stand towards the war, so that, like the author of this book, we feel a "critical affection (36)" ... "of an independent yet engaged observer, whose affection doesn't win over judgement" (251).

Milan Subotić
"From the Road in Ukraine"
Peščanik
November 16, 2024

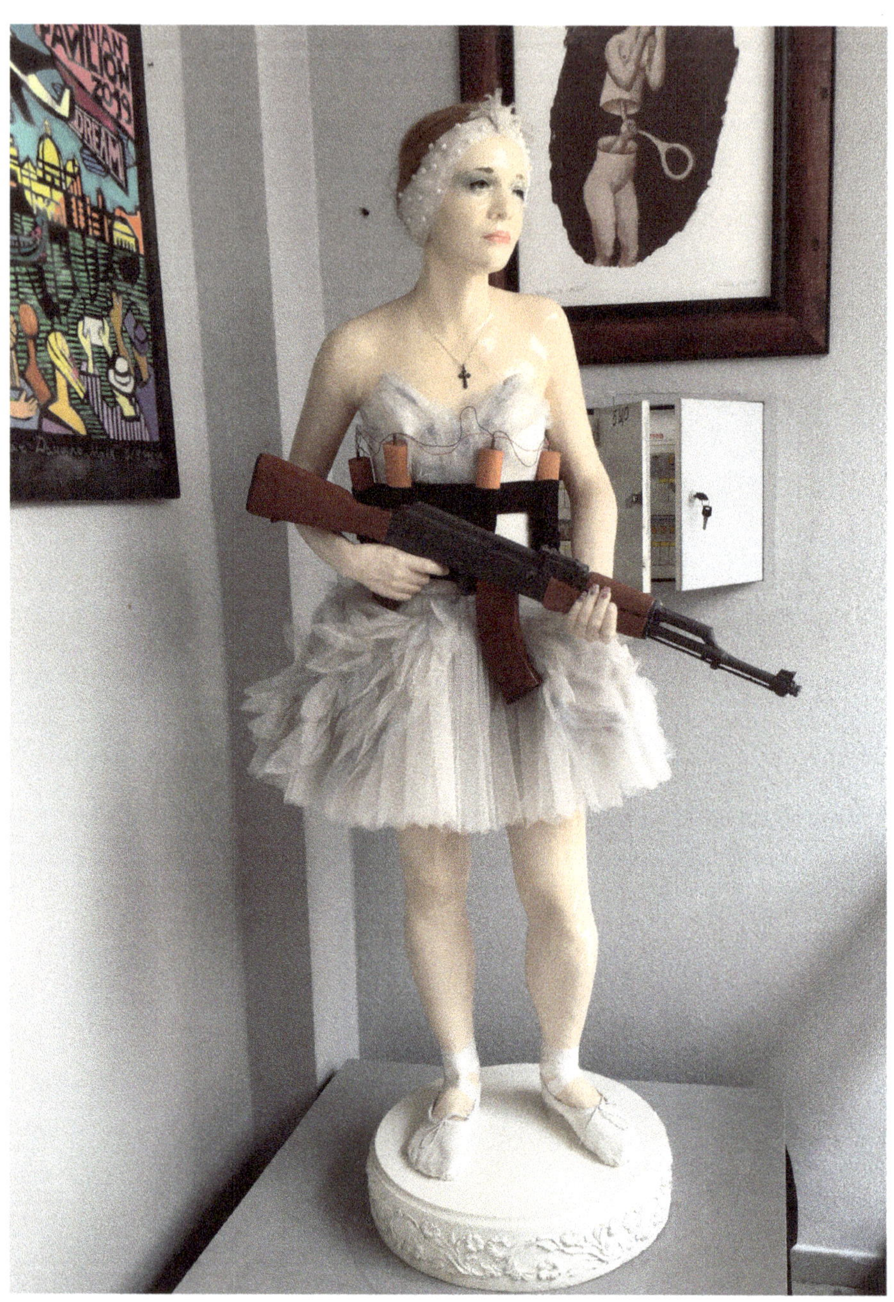

Vasyl Tsagolov, mixed media sculpture, Kyiv, May 2023.

"You're a true Kyivan now!" my host responds when I squint into the slanted morning light and utter a sleepy, long *"Of couuurse,"* following his question of whether I could get any sleep during the night.

"Around twenty of them were intercepted over the city tonight," he continues. *"Luckily, no victims and no greater damage."*

My laughter is bitter, it reaches daylight through my morning haze and heavy eyelids. It feels good and sad at the same time. Just like any day on my journey through the land of war, Ukraine.

I.

FOYERS OF WAR

> *"For it is precisely on a trip, in the morning, in a strange city, before the second cup of coffee has begun to work, that you experience most palpably the oddness of your banal existence."*
> —*Andrzej Stasiuk,* On the Road to Babadag, 2011.[1]

A few days after the invasion, in March 2022, I received a letter from an academic publishing house in Odesa asking me if I would be interested in publishing a Ukrainian translation of my book on political graffiti. First, I thought it was an internet scam — being a typical, already aging child of the analogue era, I am easy prey. But the tone of the editor's letter together with the serious and concrete proposals that followed convinced me otherwise: they really wanted for my book to speak in their language. When I finally asked him, in a roundabout and almost apologetic way, how it was that they were interested in publishing my book while the war was beginning to rage, his calm reply was: "We just want a normal life, do what we know and love to do."

Later, I found this same stubbornly personal and intimate, yet strongly political stance — this "just an ordinary desire to live like a human being," to quote Kyiv-born Mikhail A. Bulgakov[2] — burning in almost every person I met for an arranged interview or a random chat, in everyone who was pouring their experiences of war onto paper, the internet, canvas, staves, stages, walls, into galleries, and onto their own bodies. I found it everywhere.

"It's hard but I keep doing what I did before," a Kyiv-based jewelry designer told me when she handed me a parcel to take to her friend from Ljubljana. When she learned about my journey, a dance teacher who now lives between Kyiv and Ljubljana took out her phone to show me three months of productions with children's groups that she leads: "We dance even when there's wars," she added, laughing, as if her every swipe pushed away dark thoughts and worries.

"We still lecture in hybrid mode: after one disaster, the Covid pandemic, we were hit by another, Putin's invasion," my Ukrainian colleagues told me. And in the same reservedly proud breath, they emphasized: "But we don't give up!"

In Mykola Semena's preface to a collection of his articles (2018), the Crimean veteran journalist, since charged by Russian authorities, wrote that he had no other option during the occupation but to continue doing what he had always been doing. All of these and many other virtuous people that I met before, during and after my two trips to Ukraine in 2023 and 2024 use their defiant anger not to fake normalcy, but to nurture normalcy, creating it in abnormal conditions. They do not strive to avoid reality. They resist reality to preserve their dignity. They do not deny or ignore the war — their "war drive," or "war mode" directs their lives and creativity with such deep conviction that they go beyond the war. This, in short, is called bravery — and I understood my trips there mostly as support for their courage.

In these utterly unusual circumstances, the editor of the Odesa publishing house and I began the mundane process of publishing a book: translation, corrections and additions, agreements on the go, technical questions, selection of images, new explanations and clarifications.

I soon realized how highly professional the publishing house, the editor, and his colleagues were: the combination of procedural routine and the recognizable, hard-to-miss enthusiasm of everyone involved was extremely productive. It helped overcome the logistic nightmares of which the publishing houses and the authors based in the peaceful parts of the world have no idea: frequent internet outages (making Skype and Zoom practically impossible), power outages (for a few months, Odesa was left without electricity; during this time, people used diesel generators, which caused an enormous noise in the city), weak phone signal (accompanied with the roar of the said generators in the background), production congestion due to states of emergency (i.e. shelling), Russian occupation of one of the printing companies, a lack of paper and other raw materials, searching for expatriated and dispersed experts willing to write a foreword, etc., etc., etc.

However, with strong nerves, by including improvisation into your plans, and with even more commitment than usual, everything can be done. My hands were shaking from excitement when I could finally hold the published book: hardcover, beautiful design, numerous color photos of various sizes. Truth be told, my hands shake every time I receive one of my books fresh from the printer: each one is like my first one, each time the first time.

Once published, a book should be presented to the academic, expert, and wider public of the country. Again, this would normally not be a problem: wherever I published a translation, I did a presentation — almost everywhere I did it live, even during the pandemic I somehow managed. Yet this time, I knew not how, nor where, nor with whom — I only knew that I was going. In a wartime situation, especially in the feverish anticipation of the *spring offensive* that both sides were predicting, this seemed impossible at first.

I say seemed, because a few connections later, I reached relevant, more than interested, and incredibly enterprising individuals and institutions willing to host book events and lectures. The publishing house employed its own channels and even printed out flyers and posters for this occasion turning a few of the most interesting photos from the book into postcards.

This was a first for me, too. It took maybe a few days to arrange everything: posts in media, on webpages, and on social media (this I could follow vicariously) were ahead of schedule. I shared their enthusiasm from afar and there was never a moment where I thought I would not go there, into a war state for the first time in my life: you cannot say no to such people with such invitations in such tones. My loved ones offered worried understanding, while a wider circle paired their surprise at the translation and the astonishment at my plan with certain moralizing comments: is it appropriate, is it right, at a time when the people there are bleeding, that we discuss a new book and that I give lectures there?

The first time I went to Ukraine was in May of 2023; helped by the kind and efficient team of the Slovenian embassy, I presented my book on political graffiti and lectured at universities and institutes in Odesa, Kyiv, and Lviv. Three months later, in August and September 2023, I went again, this time to the far West of the country, to Uzhhorod. Next spring, in June 2024, I came again because my second book was translated at the same publishing house — this one on nostalgia for Yugoslav leader Josip Broz Tito. So again, I lectured and presented my book at universities, galleries, and libraries in Uzhhorod, Odesa, Mykolaiv, and Kyiv, and visiting few other places, among them Drohobych, Chornomorsk, and Berehove.

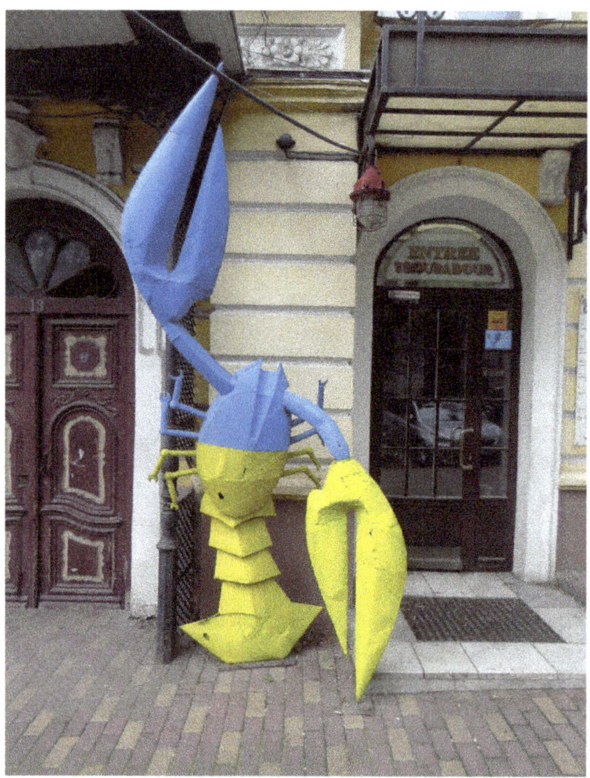

Odesa, May 2023.

   Ukrainian Vignettes: Essays on a Culture at War

On these trips, I could only really approach and learn about two of the innumerable bubbles of their environment — academia and art. Professors and researchers, students and librarians, university chancellors and presidents, gallery employees and artists, curators and journalists — the usual. Yet, strewn between these were encounters with other curious characters; for example, the postcard seller who told me, when he learned where I was coming from, that he used to drive trucks through Ljubljana and that he always used to stop at a *Zlatko* who made him excellent *jaja na oko* (Serbo-Croatian for fried eggs; as he kept repeating the phrase, it was obvious that he liked the eggs as much as he did saying it — in any case: thanks to the unforgettable unknown Zlatko!). During this limited time, I tried to see, hear, experience, talk and think through as many things as possible.

And had I stayed longer, I would do even more. I prefer to live abroad than to travel — this enables me to put down at least a few small roots. Gradually, the foreignness unlocks. Every time I return from abroad, the ideas that I carry with me multiply — this is probably the purpose of travel. To be able to start anything new, you must always leave first, kick yourself out of your comfort zone if need be — home lulls you to sleep.

My first trip to Ukraine was the most powerful experience of my life. Usually, you can describe an experience as either good or bad, sad or beautiful, pleasant or unpleasant — but what I lived there and then was everything at once. In Ukraine, the two all-encompassing yet mutually radically exclusive realities were always running into each other. In a completely Brechtian way, they were interrupting each other's illusion: in every moment, in every place, in every gesture and at every step, in every situation and with every person, they were together, tightly connected in an ever-changing tense and conflicting cohabitation.

On the one hand, and I first realized this in Kyiv, the first stop on my trip: nobody could ignore the rush of the sunny spring. The city was bursting with life: as the trees grew greener, the city filled with people joyously chatting in bars, lovebirds hugged on park benches, children squealed on playgrounds and filled candy stores with laughter, students went to school or ditched it, street artists and musicians provided entertainment to passers-by, cliques and families gathered on terraces, likeably reckless teenagers on e-scooters slalomed among the crowd scaring people. And as far as the academic side of my visit was concerned: I had perfectly normal debates with my colleagues and students about mutually interesting topics, exchanging experience, contacts, knowledge, and book titles. My book presentations and lectures were well-promoted, visited, extremely inspiring; the journalists were interested, I gave out statements and interviews. Coffee was good and food tasted amazing, spring flowers were sold at each step — this is a beautiful custom that I also encountered elsewhere in Eastern Europe. The pulse of every city that I visited was more than ordinary — like there was no war.

However — and this is also what the Kyiv mayor, former boxing champion (and, by the way, PhD!) Vitali Klitschko bitterly summarized at a reception during that time — this appearance is merely a deceptive illusion, a giant lie: war is definitely raging! This is the other side that everyone is always thinking about. His city — and the entirety of Ukraine — is in the state of war, the front rages a few hundred kilometers ~~away from~~ *close* to Kyiv, its inhabitants fearing night raids, fearing day raids. Above the streets bursting with spring and home to boisterous youth until early evening, anti-aircraft warfare is striking down weaponized drones during the night. The unfortunate city has for months been the target of various deadly projectiles; with a strict curfew imposed, city life is domesticated between the hours of midnight and 5 a.m. Sirens and explosions regularly pierce the dark silence — at night, their whining is even more prominent. You can never avoid patrols of men, but also young people, female and male, armed to their teeth, peering grimly at you from under their different helmets. Absolutely every aspect of life is under a state of war, a state of gloom — yet at the same time a state of life and hope. In this schizophrenic atmosphere, I always felt the surrealism of liveliness dividing into morbidity, peace into war, bitterness into beauty, *Eros* into *Thanatos*, as if the blossoming May days amalgamated with emergency calls *Mayday-Mayday-Mayday*.

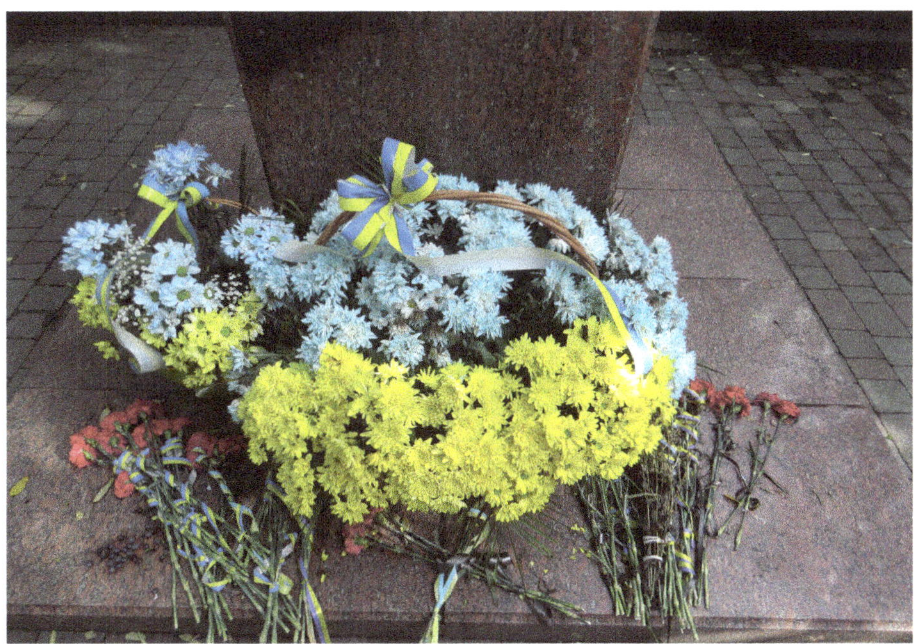

Uzhhorod, September 2023.

The second constant and prevalent feeling I got while traveling across the planes behind the Carpathians, but also before and after, when I was reading/browsing through/listening to various works on recent Ukrainian history and the present, was *déjà vu*. My musings were incessantly interrupted by "Hang on — we've already seen and lived all of this."[3] Parallel to my direct and indirect Ukrainian experience, I was also reflecting on the post-Yugoslav experience that I lived intimately: the collapse of the economy, the fall of the federation, irredentist ideologies, ethnic incitement by dividing the people into *ours* and *yours*, the strong attacking the weak, the conversion of the communists in power into nationalists in power, the drumming that we are *Europe* (while the other side isn't), calling each other *fascists* and *Nazis*, the politics of dehumanizing ethnic groups and the subsequent *cleansings*, the waves of refugees fleeing in every direction, the militarization of society, the rise of new military-political oligarchs and tycoons, the insidious interests of nearby or global superpowers, the triumph of historical revisionism, the

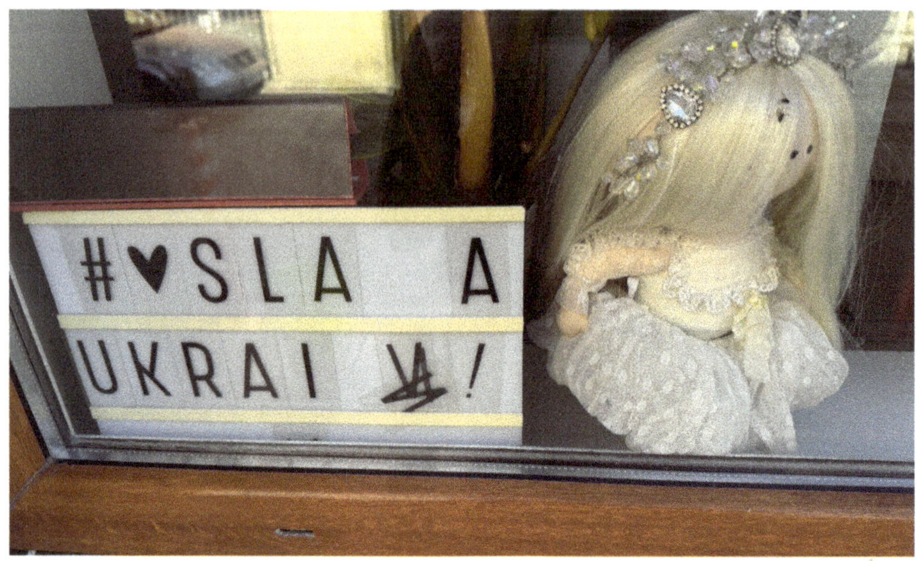

"Glory to Ukraine!" Uzhhorod, June 2024.

neo-traditionalization of society with a re-clericalization and new patriarchy. And all the while, the legal theft of formerly common goods (euphemistically called *privatization*) and the consequent pauperization of the majority and the immense enrichment of a very narrow elite.

The Balkan Wars were another bloodbath, in which the innocents again suffered the most while war supporters on all sides enriched themselves; again the killings, the prosecutions, the torture, the rape, the theft of children in front of the cameras of the world's public. And again, the resistance against all of this: not just against the attackers, but also against one-mindedness, nationalism, the militarist psychosis on one's own side. Being aware of the limitations of so-called Yugo-splaining — simplified understanding the contemporary social developments through the lens of the collapse of Yugoslavia — I could not *not notice* similarities between certain events, processes, personalities, even phrases, which I encountered in Ukraine, either in person or indirectly, with those of *our region* (a popular euphemism for the post-Yugoslav space, Yugosphere in words of British reporter Tim Judah) from the loooong 1990s, which have unfortunately continued in one form or another until today, in all three decades that have followed.

I started preparing for my journey to Ukraine a few months before — when it became clear that, despite all the obstacles, the Ukrainian translation of my book really would be published. I admit, in my nerdy-nerd way, I began reading every accessible historical and current studies on this part of Eastern Europe, the books of old and new authors of Ukrainian literature (from Nikolai Gogol to Iryna Shuvalova and Kateryna Babkina). I followed related webpages, watched countless documentaries, coverages, and clips. I read newspaper articles, and listened to testimonies from the battlefields and the rear. From the beginning, I felt ashamed of how little I knew and even more surprised at the fact of how little attention Ukrainian literature, science, history, language, cinema, music, and other arts have received so far; how few translations we have in Slovenian and English and in other languages I speak. Unfortunately, it was the war that brought this closer to us, brought it to the fore — which is not only wrong and unjust, but also very sad. We should have come to all this, we should have known much more about all this without the present tragedy.

Even though I am a teacher by profession, I still prefer learning from others to teaching. While surrounded with all these secondary resources, I spent a lot of time talking to the Ukrainian women living in Slovenia — because of martial law, men are hardly allowed to cross the border. For a couple of years now, every class that I teach at my home Department for Cultural Studies and at the Academy of Fine Arts is attended by at least one student from Ukraine. Each with their own story: from the first one, who, immediately after the beginning of the war, rescued her frail grandmother from the bombs so that she could receive normal medical treatment here in Slovenia, to the most recent, whose words are simultaneously a mixture of joy at the resumption of her interrupted studies and her first paid jobs, and concern for the fate of those close to her who had to stay behind.

My trip to Ukraine was led by the absolute freedom of the unexpected: I have never experienced real war; I cannot imagine its monotonous cruelty. I was present in a situation that was completely unknown to me. Whatever I do know, I know second-hand: from the testimonies of those who survived, from books, films, documentaries, exhibitions, plays, photographs, and music. The idea of writing a book of essays or illustrated sketches was only born once I was in the country. If my book had not been translated into Ukrainian, I never would have gone there and I never would have started writing.

The loudest publicists of war are war experts and political analysts; their perspective is mainly systemic, institutional, geopolitical, and geostrategic, or, in schematic terms, *top-down*. On these pages, I am interested in the exact opposite viewpoint, the personal one, *bottom-up*, the experience of war that I was able to encounter among the people there in those long and sunny days of two Ukrainian late springs and one late summer. The subjective, not the objective side of war; the prejudicial stories of people rather that the even more prejudiced politics of the state or the national historiography; the "people's perspective" in Howard Zinn's way rather than the official, normative one. I was reminded of what Paolo Rumiz, the Trieste-based journalist and author, wrote in his novel-travelogue *Like Horses Asleep on Their Feet*: places "can only be understood if you sleep over and try to catch the voices released by darkness."[4] What an old anthropologist told me as a young culturologist more than thirty years ago: "No field work means no real research, only more or less office gossip!" And the former Polish dissident, editor, and publicist Adam Michnik: "Anyone who wants to talk about hell, must descend into it himself."[5] A first-hand, unfiltered experience is much more valuable and much more motivational than anything you might read or see on computer- and TV screens.

Driven by my curiosity, I spent my free days roaming these cities and towns, their well-lit and side streets. I investigated certain districts and edges in more detail, others barely so and faster. I was an observer, interlocutor, reader, photographer, listener, bookworm. And I was curious, nosey, tempted. I wandered around with my eyes, ears, and camera lens open, I never took the same road back to be able to hear and experience more, to be able to be lost further. A note-taker and a reflector. To use humanities newspeak, I was doing barefoot culturology, which combines *lived experience* with self-reflections, the auto-ethnographic method that has become popular again. I was searching, but also just finding: most things simply came to me. I was meeting extremely different people and, as I was interested in their sides of the stories, I mainly listened to them. I generally like to listen more than I do talking — I follow human anatomy that gave a person two ears and only one mouth (even though some act as if they had the opposite number of these appendages). All my experience on the road was regularly and carefully absorbed in my small booklet of fast impressions that I filled in Slovenian, English, and my home Gorica dialect. Later, during the ceasefire between my fleeting perceptions and the accumulating feelings, I transcribed these eager scribbles and scrabbles together with what was supposed to be sketches and drawings into my traveler's diary.

I kept taking photos of everything (and everyone) that I found symptomatic, irritating, prominent, beautiful and astonishing, bad and worse, problematic and inspiring, every *studium* and every *punctum*, to follow Roland Barthes' terms. My smart phone helped me with fast translations, Google Translate with longer texts, and local people for the especially important writings: more than with any subject matter I have been interested in so far, I realized *the limits of my world through the limits of my languages*. I sadly speak neither Ukrainian nor Russian, I banked a little Polish during the two semesters I spent in Krakow, which came in extremely handy. I was able to read the Ukrainian Cyrillic alphabet by knowing the Serbian one — which I was taught long ago, during a semester of *Serbo-Croatian Language* in Grade five (I still remember the shrill diction of our otherwise diligent teacher conjugating verb *be: ću ćeš će, ćemo ćete će* ...). But the texts of Ukrainian journalists, literary authors, and academics are relatively rarely written in the languages I do speak.

My experiences were strong and concentrated — not in the least due to sleepless nights interrupted by the alarms that prolonged every day or turned one day into two. So many new and unexpected things happened at once that it was difficult to get a sober grip on them, question them, form a critical opinion of them. Fast memories, that's it. Usually, when I return home from far away, I spend a few days in the grip of jet lag — more than the time difference, I believe to be hit by the cultural shock of coming into a new-old, home environment. This time, I was stricken by something similar, but it was due to the exceptionally intense experience across the Carpathians. At first, I pondered publishing my impressions as a feuilleton, a longer travelogue or weekend supplement of a newspaper. I was encouraged to do regular social media posts — but as I am slightly asocial, yet not sociopathic, I have no social media. My actual social network consists of live talks, over morning coffee or evening beers, on the phone, by email, or, as a last resort, hm hm, through telepathy.

When I came back the first time, however, I was so taken with the subject that I dived deeper in, investigating wider and further. I began reading and scanning everything that I could find on Ukraine in person or online. This enabled a necessary wider and more solid framework to my impressions and reflections. I have continued talking to the people I met there, to those who don't have much say during the war: Ukrainian intellectuals, artist, professors, students. I learn from them. Each has their own (pre-)story on these happenings and their own vision of the future. (During all these encounters, wanderings across the towns, and journeying through books, music, and images, I often thought of how I would experience them on the other side of the 800- or 900-kilometer-long frontline or even in Russia, from where there are very little reliable information, much less open opinions.)

My essays are grounded in intense and partly very emotional, but also in-depth and reasoned dialogues with all the people I met; in polylogues with the studies, novels, and media posts I read; and in, well, monologues, contemplations that I brainstormed all by myself while driving through endless Ukrainian plains. I constantly compared, confronted, changed, rejected, and upgraded my impressions and ponderings with the impressions and ponderings of others. Some of them slid into these lines all by themselves, while others made me work: I would need a scientific apparatus, methods, footnotes, more sources to process them properly.

Yet these essays also follow certain methodological lines. I believe myself

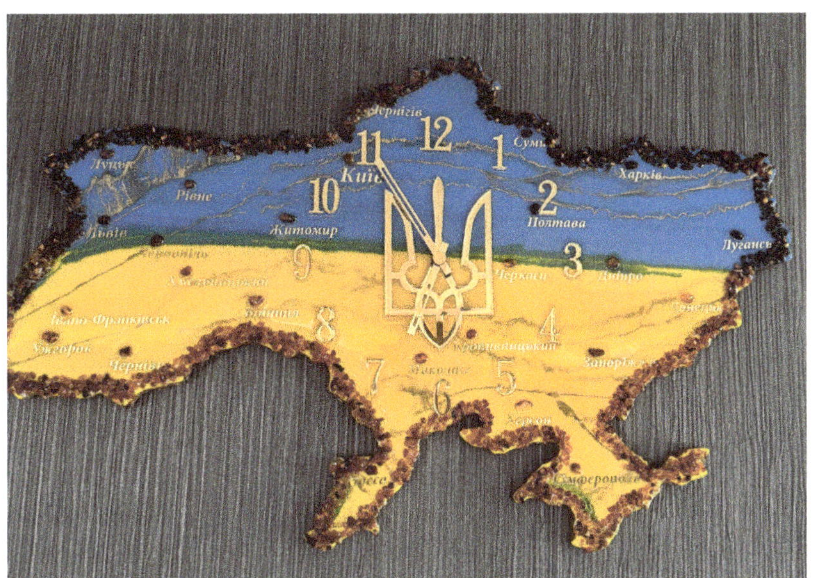

Uzhhorod, June 2024.

to be a follower of "heretical empiricism," as developed by Italian director, poet, and public intellectual Pier Paolo Pasolini in his book of the same title. These principles are based on the position in which the writer's presence and absence, closeness and remoteness, diving in and surfacing, spontaneity and reflexivity join in conflicting combinations. Pasolini defines this all-encompassing and simple, but constantly controversial coexistence of dualities in the foreword to the second edition of the book:

> "The two persons who wrote this book cohabit within a single author, who is slowly attempting to turn his ambivalence into two lives, all the while avoiding the extreme consequences of both these two lives. As a critic, this author neatly divides himself into two: a man who experiences, works and contemplates, and a man who is incapable of experiencing anything, who uses his work as a drug, and who cannot keep himself from acting."[6]

In other words, in my view, the main thing is to be aware of both, or rather all of these, before you start working.

This work is therefore far from being a scholarly treatise, much less a historical study or a study of the current situation. Contrary to those, the essayistic form and the personal touch in my writing enable me to express inductive and experiential opinions also on the subject matters that are not my specialty. I admit that there are shortcomings to this: I have no wider and deeper knowledge about the subject. However, I can think outside the ordinary, almost canonized interpretations, out of the box, and avoid the opinions of many researchers that can be surprisingly similar. I have written down my story, not a wider history of this situation.

While I was writing, I was reminded of the introduction that the Slovenian Christian-Socialist writer and partisan leader Edvard Kocbek published with his diaries from the war titled *Kamaradery*: "Many will see that they are neither merely an outside chronicle nor entirely a personal reflection. The diary joins event with contemplation; I write about what I discovered within things and people, about what had happened, especially in my immediate vicinity ..."[7] He continues that he can only depend on "what I establish with my senses, what I transpose in myself, process accordingly and valuate sensibly."[8]

My essays can marry contemplation with emotion; books with direct discussions; concrete events with the more general flashbacks from the past and the present; direct experience with previous knowledge; lived closeness with the remoteness conveyed through letters, pictures, and voices; immediate intuition with later thoughts — all the while constantly interrupting them with the plays on memory, associations, and analogies. The essay form allows me to reflect, not just describe: personal experience has immediately crushed all speculation and prejudice, but not my previous knowledge and imagination. At the same time, I can quickly, in a matter of months, react to certain events: I need a decade, even two of gathering and mulling over every possible relevant data to publish a sound scientific study. It took me a year from my first trip there to the last one — from May 2023 to June 2024 — to write this book which was then first published in Slovenian in August 2024 under the title *Ukrajinske vinjete — Eseji o kulturi bližnje vojne*[9] and immediately after in Serbian as *Ukrajinske vinjete — Zapisi o kulturi rata u susedstvu.*[10] The English version is slightly revised because of all the new information I gathered from that time on.

The main thread of the book, as I was able to develop it in such a short time and through ten interconnected essays — in the *ten circles of hell* of today's Ukraine — is the culture of war as I experienced it. The title and topic of every essay is war: *war war war.* By repeating this word, I try to create affect: I try to enforce discomfort, that uneasy feeling that I always felt there — to borrow the lyrics of the iconic Belgrade postpunk band Disciplina kičme: *sviđa mi se da ti ne bude prijatno, I love making you uncomfortable.* I repeat the word because war in Ukraine has usurped every area of social and private life of the inhabitants, including the cultural one: literature, music, everyday life, fashion, cinema, art and graffiti, advertising, media. Its *zeitgeist* is noticed on the street, seen on the inner and the outer walls, read between book covers and on posters, attracts in commercials, dominates in the news of various media, eats from the plate, is heard from guitars or the radio, and is reflected in everyday talk.

War changes everything, you can ask anyone who suffered and lived through it: in my case, my grandparents, who have been through two world wars; my parents, who survived one world war; *my* Bosnians and Ukrainians, who lived through one local but nevertheless total one; people in the Middle East, who are in an endless one. The war out there is war internally, too. It affects culture, arts, and everyday life — and everything in between: not just the content, but also the tone, techniques, expression, intensity. My Ukrainian journeys were full of people recounting how war changed their lives, their feelings, their thinking, their creativity; but straight after, they were already telling me how they are striving to put it all back in order or, in their words: "into a normal state."

As a *cultural studies scholar* during, before, and after my *working hours,* as a *researcher of culture,* which is what my official job description reads, but

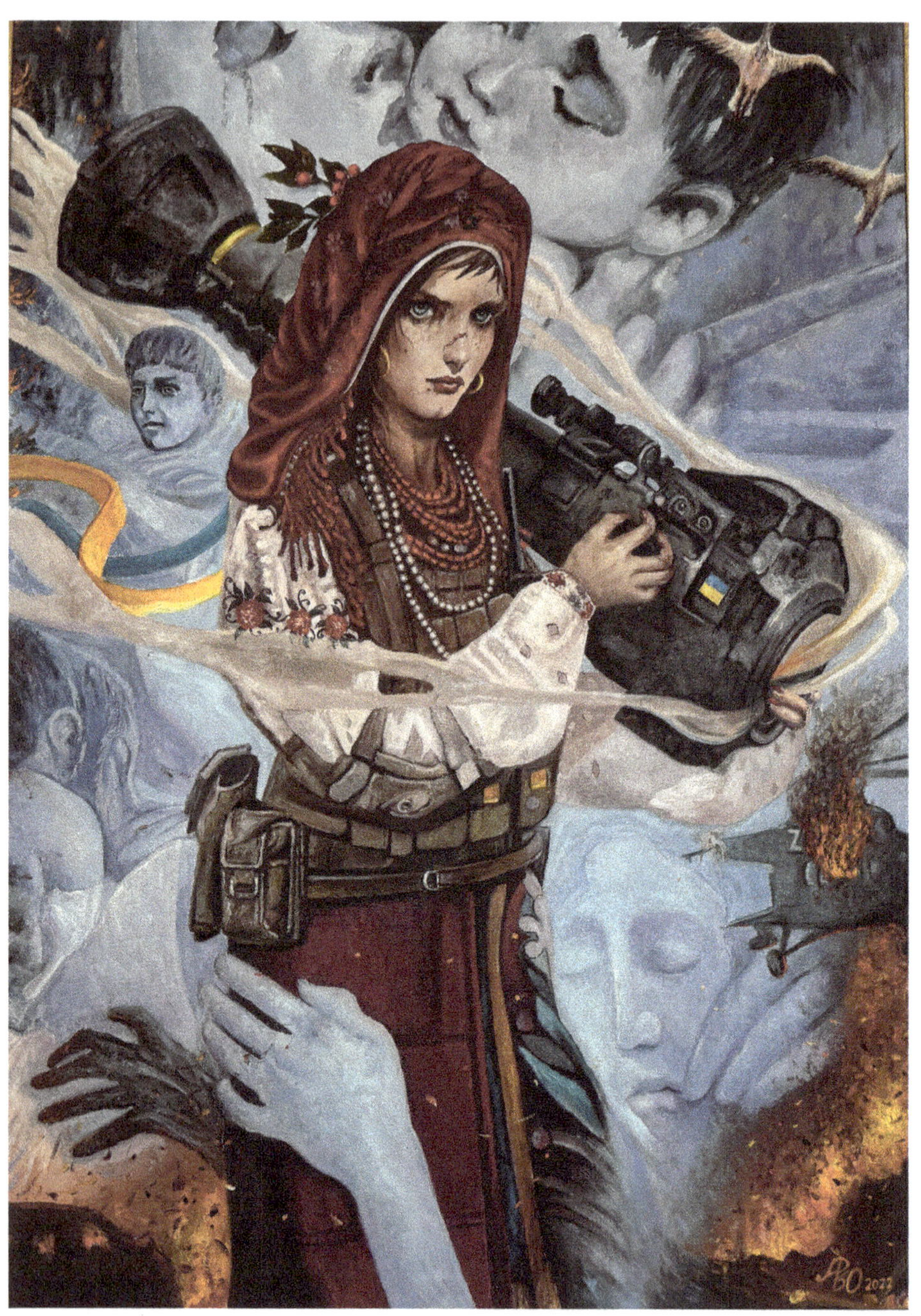

Painting on the wall of a university building, Uzhhorod, June 2024.

mostly as a lover and critic of culture, I use the form of the essay to address, firstly, the cultural interpretations of war, its metaphors, and the cultural reactions to it. As such, I deal with other aspects, the political and historical one, only insofar as they are directly related to culture and art. And secondly — and above all — I am concerned with the resistance that culture offers to war: how culture, in any of its varied forms, is becoming a broader strategy and a concrete version of resistance. In the words of a friend, with whom I was chatting over e-mail regarding this topic: "Resistance is called culture!"

Out of countless similar historical examples, I was reminded of Yugoslav partisan art and the diverse cultural life that helped contribute to the final victory against home and foreign fascism. Or of the brave Sarajevo people, who spent the entire three years and ten months of the siege developing an incredible, truly amazingly, innovative and rich cultural and artistic life ranging from theatre productions, concerts, and exhibitions to fashion shows and Miss Besieged Sarajevo contests. The people of resistance learned that culture, art, and science can also be weapons; they did not need Brecht to tell them this, but merely their own initiative, personal experience, and strong will.

However, when I was thinking about and then writing this book, I was constantly plagued by strong doubts, reservations, even blockages, which I had to anticipate, thoroughly confront and work through in a reflective and constructive way. To be honest, they haunt me still. First, is it even okay for me to write a book on the situation in Ukraine if I am not directly involved in it? Am I usurping something that fatally concerns them, the insiders, and not me, the outsider; that I am taking over the space, attention and work that belongs to them, the Ukrainians? Am I being a leisurely academic flaneur and voyeur at such a terrible time for them? I have certainly understood this and have been purposefully avoiding it: these essays speak of my perspectives, my experience, and my reflection on the Ukrainian present, not theirs. I do not write in their place or for them — they will have to do it, and they have busily been doing it themselves! They are loud: they write, draw, speak, sing, and record the war.

These lines have been put together in parallel and in connection to the existing views on the war that were created by the keyboards, quills, paintbrushes, voices, bodies, spray cans, guitars, and other means of expression of Ukrainians and all others, and I hope that they will serve in new dialogues themselves. In these essays, I am always developing a sympathetic, albeit intellectually unrelenting reflection towards the people there; a purely personal concern and at the same time, respect, not pity or patronage; sympathy, not romanticization or heroization; solidarity and support, not blind adherence.

In case I am reproached for writing my opinion on the war of others, I can offer a similar question: what has anyone to say about anything at any time; why are we doing what we are doing? I do it because I am — and have always been — interested in the complex societal events and the raw perspectives, their genesis, their present and future, the marginal, overheard, and suppressed views about them. And because I wish to publicly confront my reflections with the reflections of other people.

When I was beginning by research career and mentioned to a more experienced colleague that I plan to deconstruct Slovenian political myths, he laughingly told me: "The Academy of Sciences will be on your case in no time ..." I understood it as an encouragement not as a warning or a deterrent — after all, he went through the same thing a few years earlier. All the while, I have been dealing not only with controversial topics here in Slovenia (Balkanophobia; the new ideological single-mindedness called *Euro-Atlantic integration*; neoliberalism and ethnonationalism *à la slovène*; Yugonostalgia; and subcultures), but also in other environments. In the 1990s, the Balkan Wars encouraged me to research and to publish a book on the development of religious and national identities in another country torn by war, which is connected to Ukraine also by the graphically simple blue-and-white flag: I wrote *Religious Separation and Political Intolerance in Bosnia-Herzegovina* (2003, in Slovene in 1998). I have tackled the conflicting political ideology and secessionist rites of the Northern Italian secessionists, the *Padanians*, or the anti-Milošević movement Otpor!. As in these studies, the book of essays on the Ukrainian war states the same: this is my view, these are my feelings and reflections, while the main work of interpreting these dramatic events still awaits the Ukrainians.

The second query I had was whether I had any right to write about the war if I had not seen it up close, in the trenches, on the Ukrainian fields of death or on their equally bleeding rear. I can hear the sceptics saying that *this is not my war*, that *these are not my wounds*, why I am poking in it, that *I know nothing*, that it is easy to be clever from a safe distance, in the peaceful Slovenian Alpine bosom after three not lengthy trips to the parts of Ukraine that had actually not been the most targeted.

Let me repeat it to make it perfectly clear: these are not essays on the battlefields of the new *Eastern Front*, the third one in the past hundred and ten years, nor about military operations, about their geopolitical backgrounds, about diplomatic failures and successes, nor about direct experiences on the frontlines. I am interested in the cultural aspect of this tragedy, the militarization of culture, and cultural and artistic constructions of war. War does not begin when the first weapon goes off, nor does it end when it is silenced. The culture of the war is much deeper and longer-lasting, it precedes the conflict itself, and it also rears its ugly head after it — in all pores of social life. The post-Yugoslav present is a sad testimony to this fact: the war-ridden 1990s have continued over the next three decades of what can certainly be seen as peace, but also of poverty, divisions, emigration, hatred — and cultural struggle. Politics can also be the continuation of war with other means, to turn Clausewitz's famous aphorism upside down.

And for my third strong consideration: during my preparation and then the writing of the book, I was acutely — I can't tell you how much! — aware how sensitive this topic is. It is literally bloody serious stuff. At this very moment, as I write/you read these lines, people are dying on the frontline — which, in modern wars, includes both the first line of battle and the rear, both soldiers and civilians. It is a fact that every matter provokes as many opinions as there are people, but when talking about something as radical as the war, these opinions can only be painful or even more painful. It is perfectly clear to me that out of every explosion, the loudest is the one in my backyard; out of every wound, mine hurts the most; out of all the victims, we mourn ours the most. Many people I have met have lost their loved ones in battle or had them return home injured. Death has become a family member again.

In circumstances as dramatic as wars, my every reflection can be opposed with an x-number of different ones, while every information and example can provoke an x-times-ten opposing ones. This is why mine can, could, will, and must bother or hurt some of the readers. As with every conflict, this one also produces completely opposing opinions on *who started it, who is the victim and who the aggressor, who is right and who is wrong*, in this case even about its name. The entire world recognizes it as *war in Ukraine* — I would rename it into a more appropriate *war against Ukraine* (just like the one in Bosnia was actually *against Bosnia*) — except for the Kremlin and its apologists, who stick to the more modest, frankly misleading, definition of a *special military operation* in Ukraine (and, by extension, against the threat of the NATO alliance). Well, Putin did make a mistake once and called it by its real name, *war*. The Ukrainians, on the other hand, consistently refer to it as *war* or *full-scale aggression*.

I was finally persuaded to start writing despite these conundrums and reservations by a friend with whom I was wandering around the Tivoli Park in Ljubljana one June day after my first trip: he dispelled my embarrassment by saying: "If anyone, you can, after this experience and with all your new knowledge, you can write sensitive yet engaging essays on this difficult topic."

This is why I feel the need to emphasize my position from the very beginning. I wrote this book with great affection for the people there, the citizens of Ukraine — but with a critical affection. Not with an unconditional one, let me make it perfectly clear, with a critical affection. With thorough considerations and equally thorough concerns; honestly, with no embellishment. I have an entire spectrum of feelings towards and ideas about everything I experienced, saw, or heard there, towards everything I read before and after my travels there: agreement and support, understanding, but also reservations; when and where something disturbed me, I clearly state why I find them problematic and reject them. They must have a good reason, but I don't have to accept it as such. I'm not falling for the forced choice of being on the side of one country and one power or the other country, the other power. I have sympathies for no political entity as such, but, as always, take the side of the weak and the aggressed, the side of those who suffer — suffer here, there, and mostly in between. The side of regular people who are the only real victims of war. If prudent compassion and affinity for people is called bias, I am happy to accept that label.

On the whole, I have not a shred of doubt about this war. Despite a deafening cacophony of political opinions, conflicted historical interpretations, diametrically opposed media reports, and despite the complexity of the past and current situation, one thing is absolutely clear. Russia is attacking Ukraine, Ukraine is not attacking Russia. In words from the novel of the acclaimed and charismatic Ukrainian writer, poet, rocker and activist Serhiy Zhadan: "And the shells are coming from down there. And what don't you get about that? And what's so confusing about that?"[11] Russia is occupying parts of the Ukraine, not the other way around; in every aspect, the former is stronger than the latter, while the latter struggles to put up a fight. Even today, more than three years after the beginning of the war, there are interpretations like those during the war in Bosnia-Herzegovina: that *everybody shares some guilt and is a victim*; that *each has their own right*; that the attacked side *was looking for it* or even *caused or provoked it*. Attack is equated to self-defense as they are both supposed to be violent. Such equidistance is either the consequence of a Pilate-esque washing of the hands of those who should react decisively in such situations, or a convenient excuse by the attacker or their supporters. Such an attitude is not only dangerous, but above all deeply corrupt, since it consequently always favors the stronger and directly benefits them.

But much like nobody is the same on one side, neither is everybody the same on the other side. I can already hear a silent doubt creeping in: of course they are not the same, why do I even have to mention this? They are clearly not the same, but war distorts everything, states writer Sofia Andrukhovych in *State of War* (2023); war is constantly painting a black-and-white picture of the colorful world around us and turning people into *members of a nation*. This forced logic only accepts two sides in a war: the right and the wrong one, the good and the bad one, *our nation* and *their nation*, in her words, "either heroes or enemies, with no in-between."[12] This is why, in these essays and in general, I consciously reject any ethnic labels of either side in the war. I avoid any generalized — and in its essentialism, obsolete — understanding of nations, as well as equating them with the ideology and regime that rule in the given moment. I also avoid the reducing of the varied pasts of societies to the violently unified official histories of countries which are in fact more or less national mythologies.

I believe that what is happening in Ukraine today is not a war of one nation against another, a *battle of civilizations*, as essentialists and unilateralists would tendentiously have us believe since *the end of history*. There is no conflict among the people, but there is a conflict between political concepts or paradigms: between the pro-West, *pro-European* one, as their proponents call it, and the pro-Russian one. The situation is therefore similar to the recent history and present of many other East European and Balkan countries: Moldova, Serbia, Bulgaria, Belarus, Montenegro, and elsewhere. After

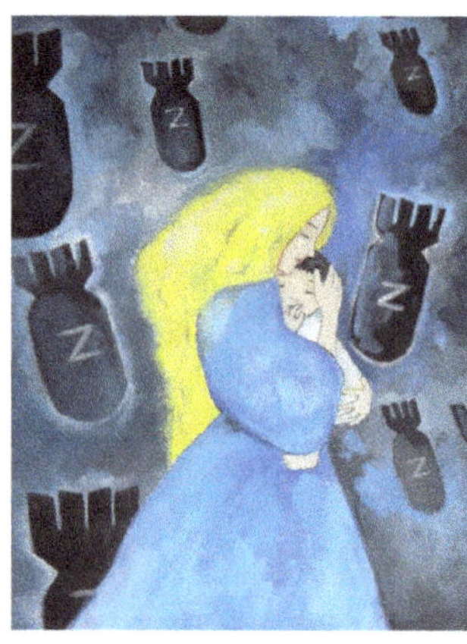
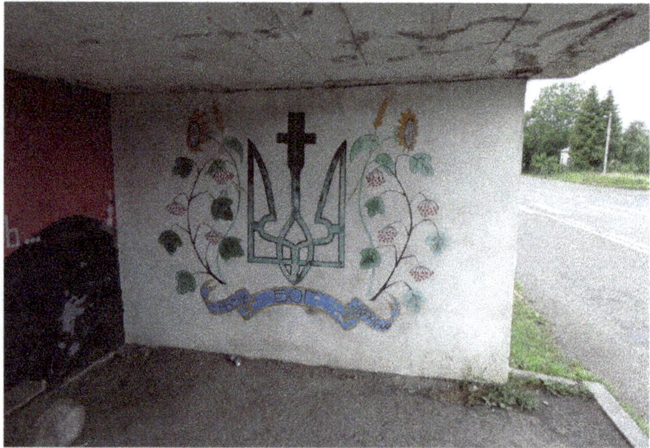

Left to right: painting from an exhibition by primary school kids, Uzhhorod, August 2023; mural near Drohobych, June 2024.

all, Russia has *Westernizers* and also *nationalists* who are drawn more to the East. "What are the conflicting interests of many Russians and Ukrainians in this war?" is the honest question critical Russian political analyst Ekaterina Schulmann asks in an interview (2023). Following the testimonies of numerous Ukrainians after the start of the war, in 2014, professor of Central European intellectual history at Yale University Marci Shore wrote (2017) that "this war was not a conflict between ethnicities, but a conflict between temporalities"[13]: — a forward-looking perspective and a nostalgic look back. Ukrainian Canadian historian Serhy Yekelchyk makes clear in the very introduction to his book (2020) that "this was not a clear-cut ethnic conflict, but also — or perhaps even primarily — a clash of different political models and concepts of citizenship masquerading as ethnic strife."[14]

During my Ukrainian travels, but also before and after them, I met people with a typically East-European mixed ethnic and linguistic background. Ukrainians who speak Ukrainian and Russian; Ukrainians who speak Russian and are learning Ukrainian; Ukrainian-Russians who are fluent in both languages or even combine them in a pidgin called *Surzhyk*; nationally undefined people who are indisputably on Ukraine's side in this conflict; and a majority with another one or two or more backgrounds (Polish, Belarusian, Jewish, Tatar, Slovakian, etc.). I heard, read, and know of specific cases of equally ethnically mixed situations on the other side of the front, which goes beyond the prevailing interpretations that this is a *war between Russians and Ukrainians*: pro-Russian Ukrainians, like parents who stayed behind in the occupied territories and whose children fled. Another situation equal to the one in the bloody Balkans of the 1990s when members of the same family often stood on different political shores, persistently interpreted as ethnic.

Faced with a war forced upon you, there is no means of staying neutral — but this of course does not mean that you have no reservations, no critical reflection or stance in taking the side of either state. I still understand the state as representing the interests, intentions, and goals of the ruling groups, not its citizens, the people. There is no social contract between one and the other — that is the liberal myth — but only coercion, direct or ideological. I therefore don't understand this war on a national, military, or narrowly political level but on a cultural one. On these pages, I explore culture as a battlefield and art as an armory: "reach for the book: it is a weapon" (the famous Brechtian idea) either for defense or for attack; a guitar as a "machine [that] kills fascists" (a sticker on Woodie Guthrie's guitar), the "pen that is mightier than the sword" (an old saying); "the mine fields of aesthetics" (the title of a book on the conflict on the Yugoslav literary left by Montenegrin writer and anti-war activist Jevrem Brković); the stanzas, paintings, notes, songs, voices as ideological state apparatuses (also a nod to Althusser); a "word of resistance" (the title of a book of poems by the Ljubljana-based Non-grupa from 2022); and "words that kill" (the title of a dark book of poems by Chicago-based author Vivid Vega).

This is how the locals put it: "art is our weapon" (project Taurus, former Ukrainian street artists); "I wish that poetry could really kill" (sharp speech by Ukrainian author and translator Halyna Kruk at the Berlin Poetry Festival in June 2022); "pen and brush are my weapons, the most humane weapons" (by Donetsk artist Sergii Zakharov, the *Ukraine's Banksy*, as *The Guardian* describes him); "writing contradicts death" (by poet and charismatic singer Serhiy Zhadan in his war diary); "culture is the shield of our identity and our borders" (by the dismissed minister of culture, Oleksandr Tkachenko); "street, book, and church" as the "Ukrainian battlegrounds" (a title to one the diary entries by famous author Andrey Kurkov); "thanks to literature, our anger will never die and will stay sharp" (by Kyiv-based writer Oleksandr Mykhed in the anthology *State of War*, 2023); or describing literature as "a form of national therapy" (by Ukrainian writer and public intellectual Oksana Zabuzhko). In short: I am interested in culture as a form of support and in culture as a form of resistance.

Along the way and even more so later, I had to put things in order, to bring *method to the madness* of this whole mass of impressions, events, information, experiences, opinions, feelings, and reflections. As every war

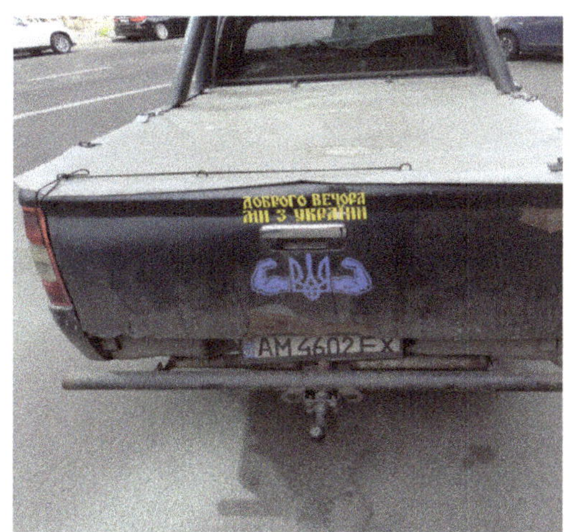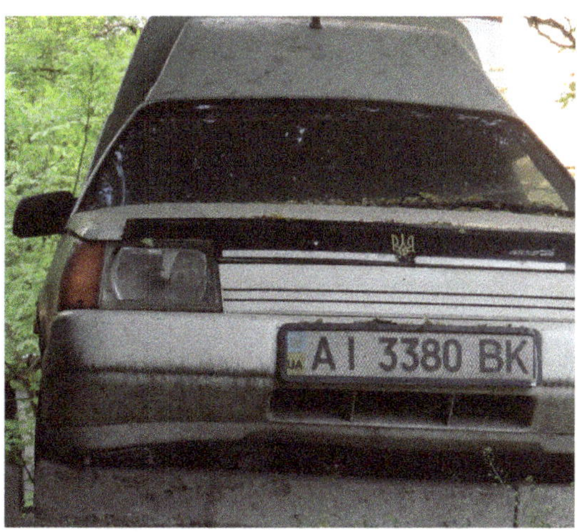

Left to right: Kyiv, May 2023; Kyiv, May 2023.

contains several wars, I arranged its dimensions into ten essays pertaining to everything I encountered on my two trips and everything I came up with in my head before and after them. Only together, they form a coherent whole. In every title, I am using the plural to show the whole tragic panorama and plurality of the effects of the war that I have experienced live or indirectly, with all their painful internal contradictions. I am deliberately intersecting the essays on my experiencing the situation in Ukraine, on the new (ab)normality there, by comparing it to the situations I am living here and elsewhere in the world, where I have traveled and worked — with our (ab)normalities. There are several areas where I have found surprisingly meaningful similarities, more analogies than differences, but also quiet continuities hidden behind loud discontinuities. The main two topics, or rather, the only two topics of these ten essays are the culture of war and the culture as resisting this same war.

An integral part of this book of essays are photographs that I took on my three travels: their visual language adds to the written word. If photos capture the contingencies, coincidences, and symptoms caught in the camera lens in the moment I pressed the shutter, the essays were written over a longer period of time, with reflections and reconsiderations. My camera was mostly

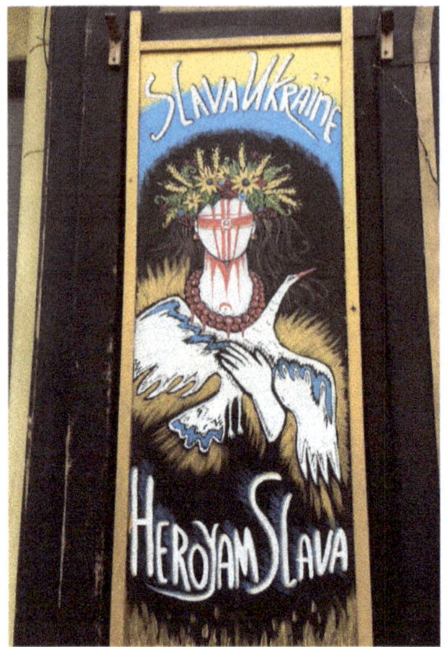

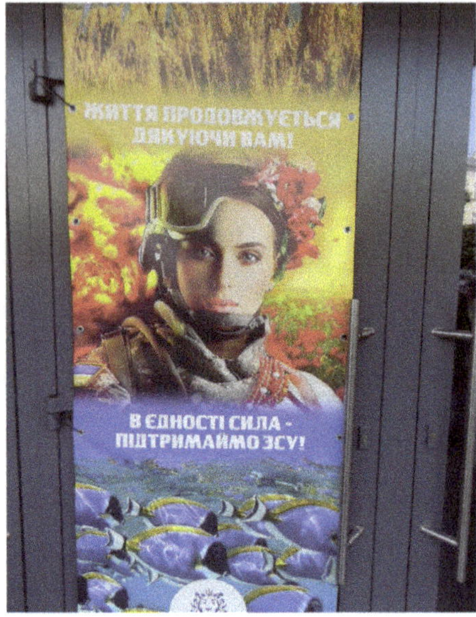

Left to right: "Glory to Ukraine – Glory to Heroes," Lviv, May 2023; Female model pictured half in uniform and half in folk dress, Lviv, May 2023.

trained on urban and pop-culture landscapes, less at the people themselves, because I find that too intrusive. However, both photos and words form visual sketches and must be understood as a whole — this is why the title of this book is *Ukrainian Vignettes*. The subtitle, *Essays on the Culture of a Nearby War*, sets a framework: I am writing on my experience of the culture of war — however nearby this war is, I haven't lived it directly. And, consequently, on the contemporary world that is constantly in an unannounced but permanent state of war. Wars are always just around the corner, whether we are aware of them or not.

NOTES

1 Stasiuk, Andrzej. *On the Road to Babadag*, 2011. 64.

2 Bulgakov, Mikhail A. *The Master and Margarita*, 2012. 56.

3 These same words were used by my comrade from the times of compulsory military service in Yugoslav Army back in the eighties, a Bosniak from Sarajevo, in his letter commenting on the Serbian edition of this book.

4 Rumiz, Paolo. *Like Horses Asleep on Their Feet*, 2016. 77.

5 Michnik, Adam. *Skušnjavec našega časa*, 1997. 111.

6 Pasolini, Paolo Pier. *Empirismo eretico*, 2014. 317–318.

7 Kocbek, Edvard. *Tovarišija*, 1972. 12.

8 Kocbek, 1972. 76.

9 Miš Publisher, Gorjuša, 2024.

10 XX vek Publisher, Belgrade, 2024.

11 Zhadan, Serhiy. *The Orphanage*, translated by Reilly Costigan-Humes and Isaac Stackhouse Wheeler, 2021. 153.

12 Andruhovich, Sofia. *State of War*, 2023. 21.

13 Shore, Marci. *The Ukrainian Night*, 2017. 220.

14 Yekelchyk, Serhy. *Ukraine: What Everyone Needs to Know®*, 2020. xv.

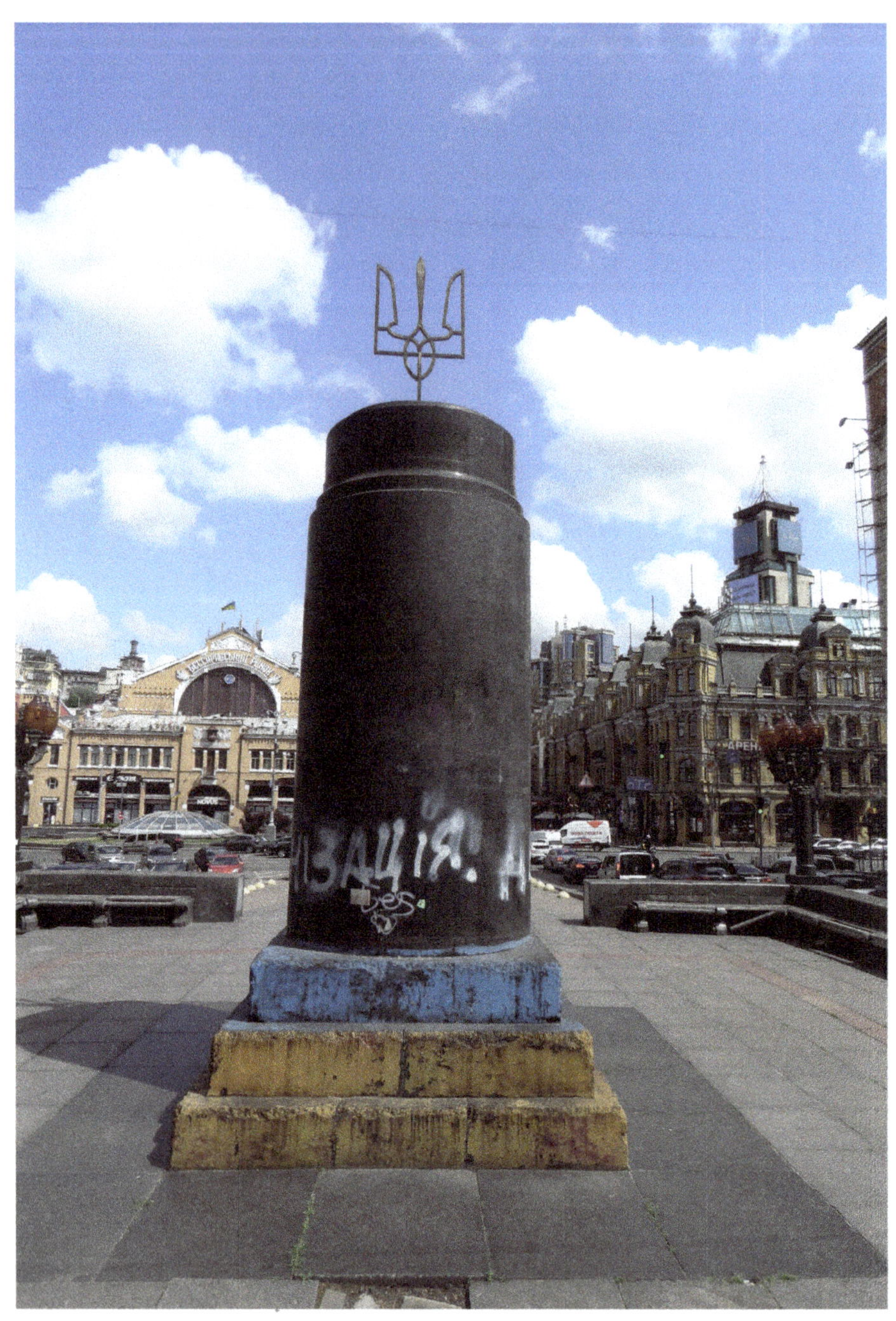

Remaining base of a toppled Lenin Statue with the Ukrainian national symbol on top and painted with the flag colors, Kyiv, June 2024.

II.

CITIES OF WAR

"… the steppe thorn of the sun doesn't let me see myself
but I'm there somewhere – in the ash heap of smoldering photos
I kiss some sky before it starts to burn."
Ukrainian poet Iya Kiva, excerpt from the poem "Ilya," 2022.[1]

I first realized I was going to a country at war when I was standing on a west Warsaw bus station platform for transit to and from Ukraine: the names of Ukrainian cities (Kyiv, Kharkiv, Lviv, Rivne, Ivano-Frankivsk, Vinnytsia, etc.) and those of Poland, the Czech Republic and Germany gave away the destinations. Airspace above the entire Ukraine had been hermetically closed since the start of the war, there were no flights there. When I sat on the bus to Kyiv — much like its neighbors, this one was also looking beat, a product of the 1990s, best case early 2000s — it dawned on me that I was in an exclusively female company: mothers with children, middle-aged women, teenagers, students. Of course, it's war, Ukrainian boys and men cannot travel. In contrast to fancy travelers on planes, these women were dressed modestly: the choice of public transport is also a class issue. It reveals the financial state of those using it. The second indicator of a *war state* that hit me on the bus was the seriousness of these passengers: again, the atmosphere differed completely from the vivacious and excited one on the planes. "War is a private men's club," I later read in the engaged first novel by Tamara Duda *Daughter*, "Women just get caught in the crossfire."[2]

With my legs, too long for bus rides, folded away, I noticed another man sitting down somewhere in the middle of the bus. Where I come from, this tattooed tough guy with a trim cut would be ironically called "Little Mouse." His rough stature, camo pants and bag gave away his robust profession. On our long ride, spotted with climbing off and back on the bus when we were crossing the border, I engaged him in a brief conversation — he was one of the rare ones who spoke English, well, Australian, as this was where he was coming from, but he never told me the reason for his journey. A mercenary, I guessed, this is a perfect opportunity for them — who else would hurry to Ukraine in times like these, apart from vultures, smelling blood and trying to sell their old stocks of weapons, constructors pushing their plans to rebuild before someone else gets there first, or populist politicians posing for a viral clip on their profile coming up to elections. He was the only *warrior* while the rest of us were more *worriers*, I mused during the 13 or 14 hours our journey took us without stopping as curfew was in force.

The first time I went there, we spent three hours at the border: the border police and the customs officers insisting that their slowness is a sign of thoroughness, but especially that our time is theirs and that they can have more than enough of it to do their work. In the same way that the former, dark carmine Yugoslav passport did once and the current, dark blue American one does now, my Slovenian or *European* passport made the procedure easier — but not the wait. On my return, entering Poland, we waited even longer, as if *Europe* wished to demonstrate its superiority and power of humiliating again (Andriy diarya often discussed this in his texts with characteristic sarcasm). The border police took great pain to go even through the motor of the bus; when one of them half wiggled his way into it, searching for God-knows-what, I exchanged grins and winks with the rest of the passengers, however tired we were from our travelling and climbing off and on the bus. Whatever he was searching for, the heat of the motor would long ago have cooked, fried, and roasted it — probably at the same time. As far as I am concerned, I have grown accustomed to opening my suitcases and seeing an *official* browsing through my underpants, socks, and books. An emigrant returning home to

Canada immediately spotted that I was a foreigner. "How can you tell?" I wondered earnestly. She calmly replied: "You're the only one here not frowning. I noticed it while we were getting on the bus."

On my second trip to Ukraine, to Uzhhorod, the Hungarian border police sadistically left us waiting in cars, parked in the smoldering sun, for an hour and a half. On that blazing hot asphalt, the thermometer read 41 degrees Celsius. Because they could, that's why, they were simply not there. With a weapon behind the belt, a uniform, and a mandate in the head, they are untouchable. When they finally show you mercy, they always make sure that it seems like they are doing you a giant personal favor. On the Ukrainian side, things went smoothly although the procedure was longer and had four steps: a soldier carrying a rifle does a personal check and writes a certificate; a police officer and a customs officer follow them, and then you are back with the soldier for another check and the collection of the certificate. Only one of their policewomen was quite curt with us. Her name tag said *Khuda*, and I thought, *Nomen est omen*, the name is a sign, as this would translate to *angry* in my mother tongue. Returning from my last trip, in mid-June 2024, I again waited for eight or nine hours before crossing the border to Hungary: later I calculated that their police and customs officers took approximately one hour to inspect every car in detail. You can imagine the feelings and condition of us passengers, standing for hours on the Ukrainian side of the border, with no sanitary facilities, water or food, and no garbage bins. "They hate Ukrainians, you know, because their Orban loves Putin," an old man whispered to me, a grandfather, taking his two grandchildren to the Dalmatian coast. He earned his pension by working in Poland in the construction industry.

The second time I felt the chills about the country I was going to, even though I was still hundreds of kilometers away from the front, was when I followed the ads and billboards along the road. Those in Poland were like every other country going into summer: selling beer, sun lotions, and new series of cheap Japanese and Korean cars. Across the border, however, I could almost exclusively see only those with war motifs: portraits of soldiers, appeals to support the regular army (with the slogan of *I believe in Ukrainian armed*

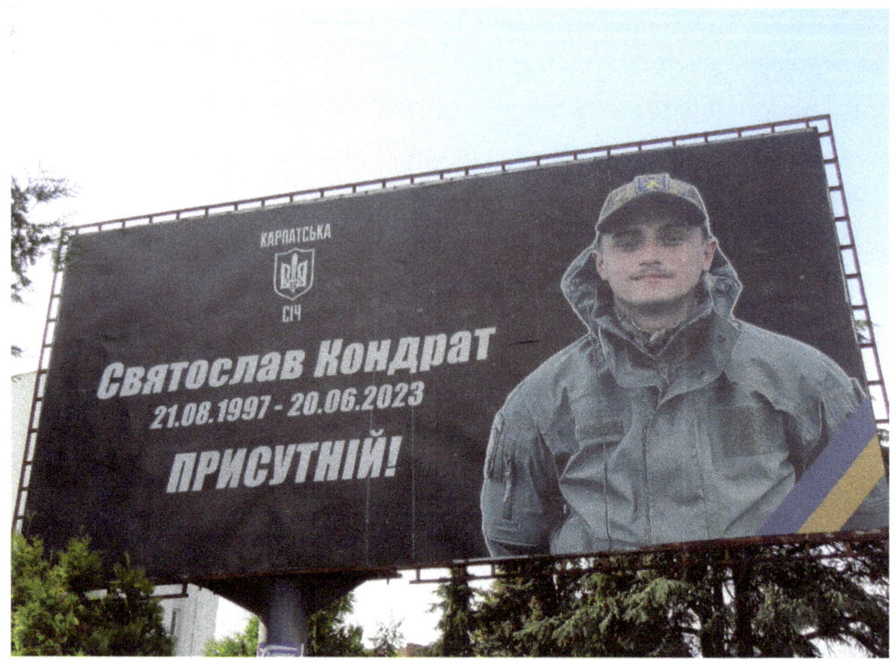

Fallen Soldier, Uzhhorod, September 2023.

forces!, a heart in Ukrainian colors, and, in the background, a commander pointing a Kitchenerian finger to say *This is your fight — Join our brigade*) or paramilitary units, appeals to protect the children and appeals to join veteran societies, with portraits of war invalids who continue living a proud life. Public buildings fly window-sized posters calling for victory (in Ukrainian and in English), depicting Ukraine in its internationally acknowledged borders, or supporting the fighters at neuralgic points on the front, for example in Azovstal. Two summarize them all: *Protect Ukraine together!* and *Join our lines!* The most moving are the portraits of fallen soldiers with their full names, years of birth and death, and inscription *Present!* (the same expression, *presente*, appears countless times also in the memorial complex of Redipuglia/Sredipolje, just across the Italian border, dedicated to tens of thousands of soldiers fallen in the Battles of Isonzo).

"The night in Ukraine is serene, / Stars glow in the translucent sky," wrote Pushkin in *Poltava*.[3] The nights in May that I spent on long rides had almost no middle phase between the dead of night and the bright of day. Suddenly, it dawned, the landscape turned to color, and I almost fell into the morning. The impression was that much stronger because there were no illuminated views of the towns on the road; in the best cases, the dark was only penetrated by small flickers — and the pale circle of the moon. "Of course, they cut the lights, fear of raids, and curfew," I pondered, half-asleep. Often in the middle of nowhere, improvised checkpoints dotted the roads and became more frequent on town arteries. They were usually very DIY: made from used car tires, metal drums, sacks of sand covered in nylon; some were in containers; a few rare ones were brick-built and masked with camo colors. "It's too early for Virilio's 'bunker archaeology,' I thought. "These are still in function, they guard against death." And I realized how privileged I was to only drive by. Next to them, as one can never be too careful, enormous concrete blocks stood in place of real anti-tank obstacles called *dragon's teeth*. Their grayness called out for color — and many of them really were painted in the Ukrainian blue-and-yellow color combination. A few times, we were stopped to be checked. Climbing on the bus yelling abrupt orders were young soldiers, boys, some yet to grow facial hair. In Ljubljana, these would be going to popular hang-out spots for young people like Zorica or Metelkova," I later noted in my journal. Others were waiting in nearby fortified checkpoints, attentive, ready to act if necessary.

Long waits on borders were followed by even longer rides across Ukrainian fields, which are unimaginable until experienced on a bus. Spoiled by the geographic diversity of my little Alpine part of Europe, I was constantly surprised by the vast, and I mean *vast* Ukrainian plains: the country could fit one state of California and a half (all together 233,000 sq mi). Dozens of miles driven through flat, beautifully cultivated fields on Europe's most fertile land, the Ukrainian black soil known as *chernozem*, transformed into hundreds: wheat, wheat, wheat, and then corn, corn, corn; and, on the other side of the road, fields of oilseed rape with their bright yellow flowers and fields of sunflowers in calmer tones. Only there was I able to grasp the introductory verses to another classic poem, *My Testament* by their national bard, writer, and painter, *batko* (father) Taras Shevchenko.[4]

> When I am dead, bury me
> In my beloved Ukraine,
> My tomb upon a grave mound high
> Amid the spreading plain,
> So that the fields, the boundless steppes,
> The Dnieper's plunging shore
> My eyes could see, my ears could hear
> The mighty river roar. [5]

Whenever we reached the summit of a barely noticeable hill, I often wondered what was on the other side — but it was the same landscape that spread until the next horizon. I found the plain not only spatially limitless, but also timeless, meditative: on the road, I kept feeling that time and space are passing by very, very slowly. That in this land, as Kocbek wrote on Gogol's stories, "[t]he reality and fantasy of life move ever in parallel."[6] Even Pannonia tires of its steppes and ends with the Carpathians. Well, in Ukraine, this mountain range is only the beginning.

Especially on my way to Odesa I could see almost no village, a rare building here and there, a gas station. Roads traversing the immense plains between towns were mostly empty, almost dead: populated by lonely cars, buses, a couple more trucks, occasionally, a rusty falling apart car or a van, more dangerous for its passengers than to us who passed it. Road rules on highways were often interpreted in unique ways: cars were making U-turns and joining the opposite lane, I could see horse-drawn carriages, agricultural machinery and tractors on the shoulders, but was most surprised by cyclists, bikers, hitchhikers and even pedestrians ("Where did they come from? There's not a soul to be seen on the long-stretching fields!") — I once saw a lonesome monk. Used to such scenes, my co-passengers paid no attention — until they burst into a loud laughter when they saw a car being towed by another car with a piece of strap (something I hadn't seen anywhere in Europe for about twenty years). Then they explained: the electric Tesla is not a car for Ukrainian steppes — there are no charging sockets.

I never saw any soldiers being transported to and from the battlefields; these transports probably run much more discreetly than at the start of the war. Reading the testimonies of soldiers and volunteers in various publications, I learned that in the early days units were dispatched in every which way, even with school buses or taxies — like they wanted to repeat the popular story about Parisian taxi drivers facilitating the French victory in the Battle of the Marne in September 1914 by driving soldiers there. I did, however, see a few military convoys, new tanks and howitzers on trucks. From the west, from Poland, ten to twelve of them thundered in an escorted line on the *march route* to the east, to the front, from where they returned empty. These couldn't be hidden away. Such demonic toys! I still hold the memories of the Yugoslav tank with Soviet provenance, called the T-72. The ones I encountered on the road were new, obviously made in the west, and designed like transformers from that popular Hollywood franchise, attracting the looks and the expectations of robots emerging from them at any moment. So much knowledge, skill, hard work, and material they require, and how much money was spent on them instead of something more sensible, I thought with amazement every time I caught them out of the corner of my eye. Every so often, I was reminded of the fact that the sky shares war with the earth when I heard the rumble of low-flying formations of military helicopters — which, in turn, reminded me of *the Ride of the Valkyries* and a scene from *Apocalypse Now* (1979) by Francis Ford Coppola.

Despite the graveness of the war atmosphere, my voyage was also full of unusual events. Imagine my surprise in Uzhhorod when I, a Gorizia-native, happened upon a lovely, Italian café called *Goriziana Caffè* that served tiny doses of strong *espresso* in small yet solid white cups — just

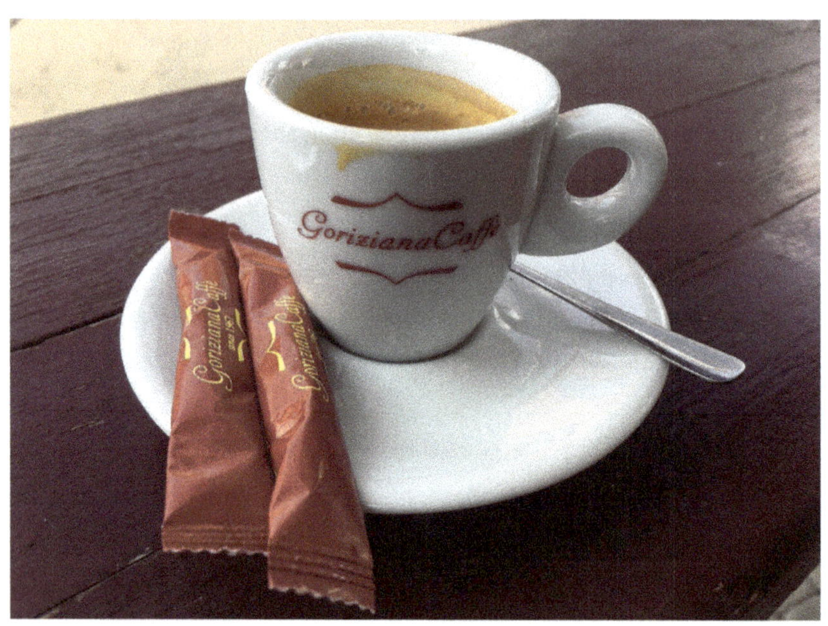

Uzhhorod, August 2023.

like I was on a Corso Giuseppe Verdi in Gorizia. The *Since 1967* on their front is a tad misleading as it stands for when the brand first appeared in Italy, not in Ukraine; the latter never knew private bars or shops until the end of socialism. The more I run from Gorizia, the more it returns to me, I thought while I was sipping the hot brew. The second surreal anecdote is, funnily enough, also connected to coffee. My Kyiv host and I met at a coffee shop one morning and she ordered *caffè macchiato*: two words with a noticeably emphasized double *f* and a prolonged, almost triple *k* were enough to give away her knowledge of Italian. When she was very young, Italian humanitarian organizations took in her and her Chernobyl peers and set them up with South Italian families; I was too surprised to remember exactly where. For years, even as an adult, she returned there, made friends — and even now, Italian, together with Russian, is her first foreign language. In English-laden Italian, we lamented not practicing it enough, neither her *a Kiev* (Kyiv in Italian) nor me *a Lubiana* (Ljubljana in Italian) — but ever since, our emails have only been written in this *lingua*.

While we're on this note, sport bars here are like those anywhere else: in one of them, with a great-sounding name of *Cantona Bar*, I fail to remember the town in which it found me, I saw a bunch of guys watching the evening soccer game — every single one of them really looking like legendary French soccer player Eric Cantona. In one of the small hotels I stayed at, I opened the drawer to find a beautifully packed set of — hey, hey! — condoms. No, not *that* sort of hotel, rented by the hour, but a perfectly ordinary one. Well, that's progress, I grinned when I remembered the one and only book from the entire treasure trove of world literature that I have always been finding in the hotels and hostels from the United States to Western Europe: the Bible. (This, hmmm, unimaginable scandal was *ideologically balanced*, to quote a cliché from the transition, in the very next hostel, which hid one of these in a drawer.) Ukraine, too, was in the grips of *Eurosis*, which is a term I invented years ago for the obsession with the new ideology of *Euro-Atlantic integrations*, with the new Eurocentrism: the suffix euro- can be found at every step — in the names of institutions, products, services, and even in graffiti. Harvard historian of Ukraine Serhii Plokhy even calls this uncritical pro-European fascination "new national religion."[7] If there is anything that puts all these towns up there with the rest of the *new Eastern Europe*, as imagined by ethnic chauvinists from the Baltic to the Balkans, it's the fact that they are completely white, whitewashed. In all my time there, I only encountered a few Indians and Pakistanis, a couple of East Asians, and three African people (and even one of these, if my ears informed me correctly, was local). Not that different to Ljubljana, actually, if you don't count a handful of foreign tourists and Erasmus students coming from the Western multicultural lands.

I travelled to and through places that had five, six, seven names, used in various periods, some quite recently. After every war, a new ethnic majority formed; a new official language was introduced; and a new largest religious group began dominating. I was most taken by the pulse of

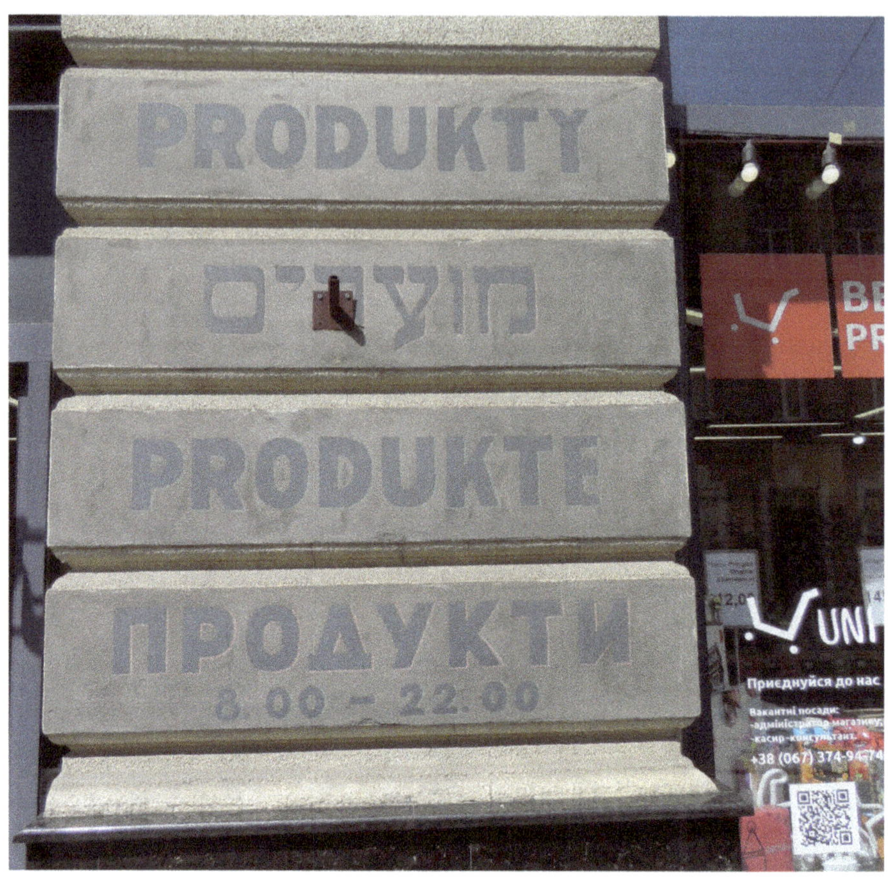

Lviv, May 2023.

the four larger cities, trapped between war and peace, with traces of their incredibly diverse past and the sinister future, which I visited a little longer. The devastation along the western artery told me I was nearing Kyiv: a collapsed and hastily rebuilt bridge, buildings and other infrastructure torn into pieces, newly constructed watch houses and containers to house soldiers, barricades waiting to be used. There are clear signs that tell you where, at the beginning of the war, the about fifty miles long convoy of Russian armored vehicles came from and where they had to turn back defeated. From there, the direct signs of the war diminish. The city itself is a true metropole with its over three million inhabitants, as many as for

   Ukrainian Vignettes: Essays on a Culture at War

example in Toronto: it is lively, features an entire specter of lifestyles, offers everything from exhibitions and performances to tourist trips. Just like everywhere else, there are hipsters and there are moneybags who, just like everywhere else, have no taste. Motörhead describes those perfectly: "You can buy up half of the nation, but you can't buy class." Just like elsewhere in Southern and Eastern Europe, elderly men sit in parks and on benches to play chess and loudly comment on each other's moves, while skater boys whiz past them — nobody more skillful than them apart from food delivery scooters, bicycles, or mopeds. Beggars, mostly Roma, here as well, mainly stop soldiers, greeting them with *Glory to Ukraine*! to try and persuade them to drop a coin. The major boulevards and squares are full of various shows: hip-hoppers and breakdancers here, singer-songwriters there, choirs singing folk songs in parks. After hearing it a few times in different versions, my ear grabbed hold of *Oy na Ivana ta y na Kupala*[8] — a love song, of course, as my hosts explained.

After a few days spent in Ukraine's capital, I, for the lack of a better word, befriended an Uzbek of a cheerful disposition and a hoarse voice, who was selling the best kebab ever, right in the middle of my street. We tried to converse, we laughed, he launched his Russian (as far as I could tell); I launched mine (i.e. all seven words that I collected either from songs by Vladimir Vysocky and by IC3PEAK, from the cartoon *Cheburashka*, and from the weeks spent while teaching in summer schools in St. Petersburg), we made extensive use of pantomime and onomatopoeia. After learning that I was a professor on a brief visit to Kyiv, it took him a few more kebabs to ask how come Ukrainian students were able to study in *Europe*, while the Uzbeks couldn't. I had no proper answer to offer him, but to myself I thought of *fortress Europe* building higher and higher walls to surround itself with. The affection I felt for him must have been mutual: he saw it in the substantial tips, I did in the free *ayran*, savory yogurt-based drink, popular in Central Asia and parts of the Balkans.

On the one hand, the towns were breathing in a completely normal urban pulse: people rushing to work, school, meetings, dates. The towns

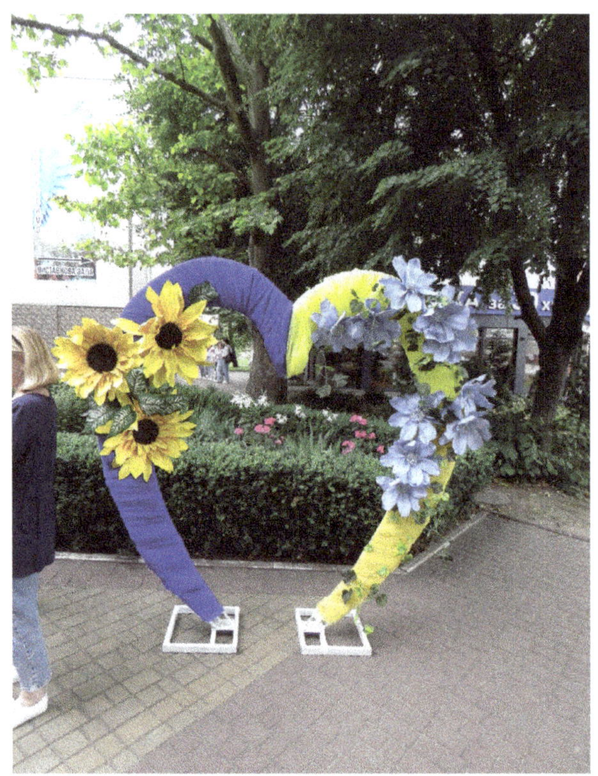

Chornomorsk, June 2024.

are noisy, tiring, full speed, just like the one (in reality, those) in *Man with A Movie Camera* by Dziga Vertov from 1929. Neglected infrastructure testified to the fact that the society has been in recession for decades: holes in the roads and especially in the cracked pavements, scant illumination in the remote neighborhoods (but not in tourist centers or next to new palaces of crystal and steel!), unmaintained apartment buildings, rusty fences, badly maintained public buildings such as schools, post offices, the remote public transport stops, etc. No construction knowledge was necessary to see that things were built or last renewed somewhere in the 1970s or 1980s. Typical post-socialism, akin to where it bared its teeth most, like in the Balkans.

On the other hand, there was the omnipresence of war. Streets were patrolled by uniformed soldiers, police officers, special forces — I was unable to tell them apart. Those more used to the war opened my perception to also see the ununiformed ones, the ones in civilian clothes that my untrained eye had missed completely as they seemingly causally lounged about the town — vigilantly surveilling key points — those with high *security risk*, to employ the now security Orwell-speak, where large numbers of people congregate. Black fanny packs stuffed full suggest hidden guns. In the first weeks of the war, these undercover agents hunting for saboteurs and diversionists were joined by civilians with arms, probably hastily composed militia. Some militias were included in the regular and reserve units, others remained independent — in front of their offices, you can see somber young men in uniforms, some wearing controversial inscriptions on their chest and tattoos on their forearms.

Yet it is the collapsed buildings and craters that point most prominently to the fact that the war is determined by the reach of rockets or drones. The Kyiv seat of Samsung is one such unique *monument* to the city under attack: the skyscraper with large blue mirror glass windows — many of them missing because the building was hit in October 2022. The accuracy of *precision-guided munitions* varies, I was explained. It can be by as much as 70 yards off; this is why there are so many civilian victims. They land everywhere, here and there, even in residential neighborhoods: for example, on a nursery (luckily empty at the time), and the yard of the largest university in the city, the Taras Shevchenko National University, a really impressive crimson building. By chance or on purpose is the dilemma that usually remains unanswered. Many windows in the city bear thick sellotape Xs; first-floor and basement windows are protected with sand sacks (even far away from the battlefields, for example in the safe Zakarpattia). I even saw a correct U-shape setup of these sacks at the foyer door of the main administrative building in one of Ukraine's *oblasts* or regions, surrounded by half a dozen guards. A colleague of mine who knew their commanding officers used her connection to get me in. The sand-filled sacks also guard the monuments and the statues around the city and in the parks; it took me a while to figure out that these high stalagmites of sacks have a solid middle, a marble or metal statue — the artwork that they are protecting. As, unfortunately, the war has been going on for so long, some of them have already peaked out, like the one of Dante in the middle of Kyiv, as if this was his way of forcing an analogy between the *Divine Comedy* and the situation he found himself in.

The capital of Ukraine is a regular target of air raids, but it soon developed a fairly efficient defense. And just like any city, it turned it into a series of urban myths. One of the most popular ones is the *Ghost of Kyiv*, the Ukraine Air Force MiG-29, which is said to take out six Russian planes in the first days of the war. When the former Ukraine president Poroshenko sent the photograph of an unknown aviator into the Twittersphere, it became viral, was memorialized in a mural in the center of Kyiv, and experienced pop-cultural fame and commercial success. Putin's army pays no attention to these myths, *celebrating* the city day (for Kyiv, the last Sunday in May) in their own way: sending the largest group of drones and missiles to date. This resulted in two deaths, several injuries and damage to property. Yet such devastation of civil infrastructure only encourages the bold plans for urban renewal made by Mayor Klitschko, who has been in office for nine years now. Change is obvious: parks maintained, old buildings revamped,

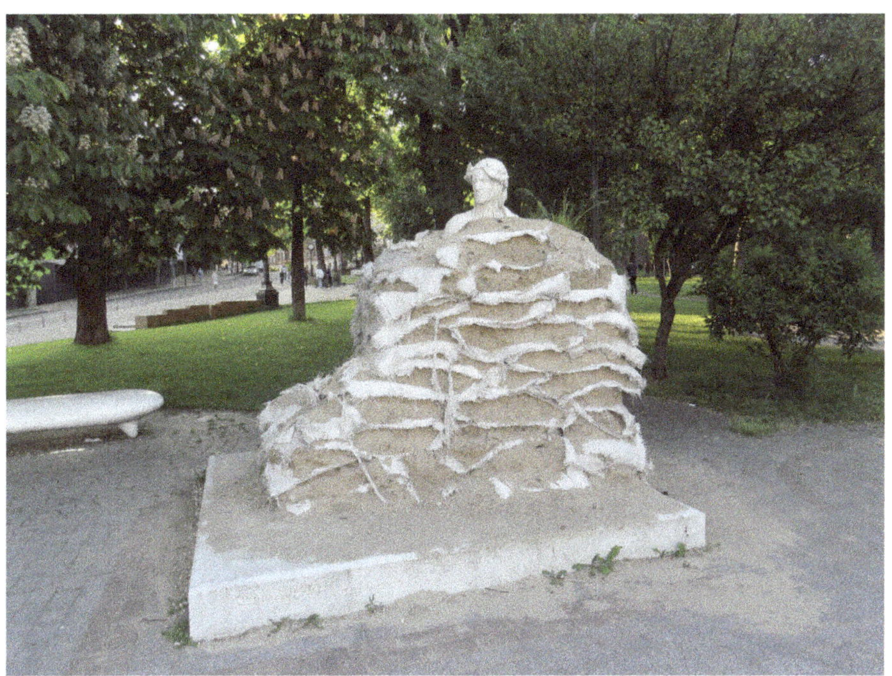

Statue of Dante, Kyiv, May 2023.

collapsed buildings rebuilt, roads reconstructed. An observation bridge for pedestrians and cyclists was opened, soon earning the name Klitschko Glass Bridge. "He is doing all of this out of spite," my host tells me. "While they demolish, he builds."

The atmosphere in Odesa, "the Marseille of Ukraine," was at my first visit different, harder — its inhabitants are in graver danger than in Kyiv; not just from air and land but also from sea. Much more than elsewhere, the people of Odesa observed me with a suspicion that they didn't bother to conceal, when I was taking photos in my naïve curiosity. Maybe they thought I was a saboteur or an informant gathering data. Unexpectedly, this city on the Black Sea relates to my home region: a direct shipping connection was once established between Odesa and Trieste. I was reminded of this just before my departure by the verses written by the contemporary intimist Greek poet Stamatis Polenakis: "Olga, if I die today, / I hope that you forget me tomorrow. / But remember the ship from Odesa / Going to Trieste one summer day ...”9 Until 1918, this main Austrian port on the Adriatic was also the starting point for the sandstone, from which the famous Potemkin Stairs were made of. Of course, I wanted to see them as soon as I arrived, but that entire part of the coast is closed and heavily guarded: military police were scaring away the few curious souls that tried to get closer. Apparently, a landing operation was still possible; the authorities therefore installed weapons in the vicinity, while the sea surrounding the port was full of mines. I kept searching for the names of the streets and the venues from *Odessa Stories* by Isaac Babel (1931): in this past century, they have certainly been changing their names, but the adventures of Benya Krik remained as inspiring. Empty restaurants and bars told me that, until recently, Odesa was a cosmopolitan tourist destination; some have persevered, and so did a few souvenir shops that still sell beautiful and inventive gifts, from statuettes and postcards with vintage photos to cans with true *Odesa air*.

On my second visit there, thirteen months later, this tension had eased: its port was unfolded to prying eyes, the Potemkin Stairs and nearby restaurants and bars were open to the public, attracting locals and even few tourists to enjoy sun and company, teenagers were gathered on improvised gigs with bands playing remakes of pop songs from Ukraine and from global MTV-culture like Radiohead or Nirvana, fresh graffiti, flashing neon signs and intense traffic showed that life returned to the city. Neighboring Chornomorsk with its big port, mainly for the export of grain and agricultural products, was also repeatedly hit, especially its port infrastructure. Just few hundred yards away from the devastation, it shows a completely other face: that of a typical holiday resort with the spectacular sand beaches and another impressive staircase, as if its architects wanted to imply that going to the sea is something sublime. However, on that June Saturday that I visited it, action was elsewhere: a cultural event with a strong patriotic note and accompanying decorations in front of the town library, which was part of the wider book-festival of the Odesa region.

   Ukrainian Vignettes: Essays on a Culture at War

The destruction of war was even more present in another Black Sea port, Mykolaiv, which was on my way from Odesa through Kherson to Kyiv. Its wide streets seemed to me ominously empty as they would remind me of the fierce battle for the city at the beginning of the invasion. Today it is firmly in Ukrainian hands, but with a frontline dangerously exposed. In the few still visibly damaged buildings where I've been — the department of humanities where I delivered a lecture, main university building and library where I donated some books — in some corners, they are saving parts of Russian projectiles (rocket wings, rocket casing etc.) as dark souvenirs and sad warnings that it is still not over. Danish companies help to reconstruct the port and shipbuilding capacities — locals told me that with a mixture of pride and satisfaction, as a proof that life is finally coming back to their city.

Uzhhorod, safely hidden behind the Carpathians, reminded me of Slovenia, also hidden somewhere under the Alps — fortunately or unfortunately enough, they share the same anonymity. Stretching along a river, this city is one of the rare ones on the map of Europe that is bravely McDonald's-free; it is peaceful and tidy. "Our country is being bombed, yet we have free Wi-Fi in the city," my host said, giving me a weary smile when we first met. I found Uzhhorod fascinating due to its almost textbook cohabitation of various architecture styles: Hungarian baroque, Austro-Hungarian art nouveau, interwar Czechoslovakian modernism (picturesquely presented in a 2018 brochure by local researchers Lina Degtyaryova and Oleg Olashyn), socialist functionalism in all its socialist realism and high modernism variants, the later postmodernism and post-socialist turbo-architectural *kitsch*. And in the middle of this, a perfect stylistically eclectic synagogue, now turned concert venue.

In the last year and a half, Uzhhorod, just like other western towns, became a harbor for thousands of people running from battle zones — entire families and institutions. It is difficult to estimate the number of these *internally displaced*, as goes the new bureaucratic newspeak. I read, and a few local people confirmed, that this affects the life in the region, the prices of rent and the prices of apartments. Otherwise, one can hardly feel that there is a war — apart from a few sirens sounding across the entire Ukraine when the air defense has not identified the exact targets. Until you literally stumble upon war. Like on a plate decorated in Ukrainian colors. Or the moment when I exited Corso, an old hotel on the promenade bearing the same name Corso, and almost bumped into a young mother walking her boy — she was dressed in full uniform: T-shirt, battle belt, and tactical boots. I was actually finishing this book of essays on its top floor, overlooking a bar that kept playing the same playlist of contemporary American R&B day in and day out. After day three, I knew the artists' order by heart: Alicia Keys, Stevie Wonder, Tina Turner, Anita Baker, Barry White etc., in an hour-long loop. It slowly became irritating, and I remembered the torture of Giancarlo Giannini from Fassbender's *Lili Marleen* (1981): in his cell, he was forced to listen to the title song playing on the gramophone, the record skipping in the same place over and over again.

Even more peaceful than Uzhhorod seemed to me the other cozy little town in the same relatively safe region, Berehove, where Hungarians — a recognized ethnic minority in Ukraine — make up half of the population. For them, it kept the old name, Beregszász. However, war symbolically reached it as well, with a giant monument erected in its center with plaques dedicated to the fallen soldiers, and a nearby wall of remembrance of the victims of the Maidan Revolution, with the firm promise: *Heroes Don't Die*. Closer to Lviv lies the town of Drohobych, whose urbanscape, impressive historical buildings and especially their façades cannot hide Ukrainian, Polish, Jewish and also German/Austrian heritage. Different from the cities and towns in east and central Ukraine, lots of buildings are decorated not only with Ukrainian national flags, but also with Chervona-Chornyi, the red and black flag of the Ukrainian Insurgent Army and Organization of Ukrainian Nationalists from pre-WWII and WWII. Another little town among some others I forgot their names (shame on me!) is Lityn in Vinnytsia province: all of them have in common monuments to Ukrainian victims of the bloody 20th century condensed on their main roads or on main squares

   Ukrainian Vignettes: Essays on a Culture at War

(war for independence after WWI, *Holodomor*, WWII, events in 2014 and from 2022 on). Maybe I was paying more attention to Lityn because it is close to the birthplace of the folk hero from the early 19th century, Ustym Karmaliuk (1787–1835), the *Ukrainian Robin Hood.*

Lviv, the center of Galicia, is about seven times larger than Uzhhorod and probably about that much more vibrant. "You'll see, this is the most Central-European of all Central-European towns around," I listened to a friend on his cigarette break before I left — himself being one of the most Central-European people I know. With its beautiful, yet tired buildings and even more

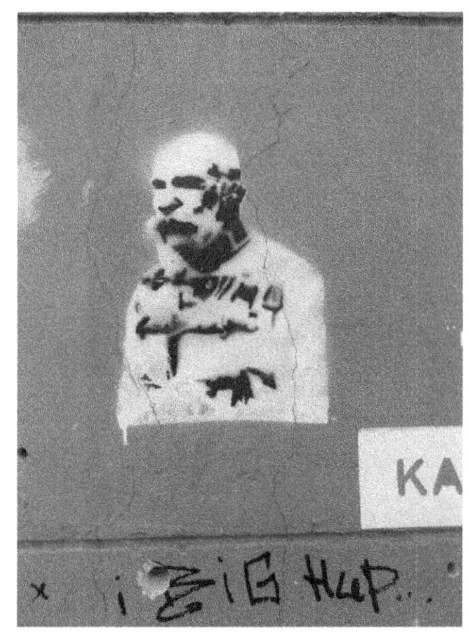

Lviv, May 2023.

tired façades, proud in their rusticity, Lviv reminded me of Krakow twenty or twenty-five years ago — Krakow, where, after two semesters of teaching, I felt quite at home at. Now, it must be different, all made up into another European trap for foreign tourists. The aging elegance of Lviv is strewn with the remnants of an apparently *golden* late Austro-Hungarian period; it radiates Austrostalgia, nostalgia for the Habsburg Empire, which I also encountered in Lesser Poland, Friuli, Trieste, and, of course, Austria and Hungary. The images of Emperor Franz Joseph I of Austria have become a veritable tourist trademark; they can be found on souvenirs, paintings, coffee packaging and famous chocolate bars, even on a stencil on a wall. I never saw a spray-painted image of *His Imperial Majesty* anywhere else in the lands of former *Kakania*, which is Austrian writer Robert Musil's name for the Dual Monarchy. Not even in its capital, Vienna. The central square and its surroundings smell of coffee; in this part of the world, Lviv is the coffee capital — just like Trieste was at the opposite end of the former empire. Many cafés are also bookstores, which gives the town an additional Central European *schmeck* — and every time I wander into one of them, I am surprised at how Ljubljana doesn't have that.

Ukraine's west is supposed to be less endangered than its east; it is livelier, there are even more tourists. And yet, returning from Lviv, I was surprised by my last air raid alert when I was getting into a taxi behind a fairly remote bus station. As if it wanted to remind me of a bitter tradition this town has in the history of two successive generations of men from my family. As an Austrian infantryman in the first summer of WWI, my grandfather fought "man to man with the Russians in Galicia, behind the Carpathians," as he liked to emphasize, until a shrapnel sent him to a Prague hospital in September 1914. It took them half a year to finally save his leg, which made him walk with a slight limp for the rest of his life. His was the fate of other inhabitants of Trento, Trieste, Gorizia, Istria, and Dalmatia, i.e. Italians, Slovenians, Croats, and Friulians, members of *Siebenundneunzig*, the 97th Regiment of the Austro-Hungarian Army, called *sibuniaizi*, who failed to contain the advances of the Southwestern Front of Russian Imperial armies. On my way through Galicia, I often remembered Rumiz' historical travelogue following the footsteps of his ancestors — and mine as well; they must have been *Kameraden*. Those less fortunate ended up in the Lychakiv Military Cemetery in Lviv: a memorial to the fallen Slovenian soldiers was also erected there in 2018.

Through this city, perhaps even through this particular busy station, twenty-eight years later, in the summer of 1942, the Italian Army in Russia (*ARMIR, Armata Italiana in Russia*) was being sent to the southern part of the eastern front. A member of the 4th Mountain Infantry Division (*Alpini* in Italian), called *Cuneense* after the town of Cuneo, was also his son, my uncle. Educated as a baker in Ajdovščina, he became part of the military baker squad, the Squadra Panetieri, as I read in one of the rare documents left behind him. In the letters he sent home he was amazed at how the "Russian women" (they were probably Ukrainian) were speaking a language similar "to ours"; when his mother wanted to send him woolen socks, he stopped her — the Russian women were knitting for them. "Don't worry, us commissaries are always seven kilometers behind the front," he wrote to calm down his family — until the moment the Soviets captured him at the flank of the Battle of Stalingrad in late January 1943. Skilled at mountain combat, his division followed the ingenious orders of fascist military strategists, ended up in a clearing, in a plain steppe environment, and was demolished; panicked escape only saved less than a tenth of the division.

Historical studies claim that Soviets, who captured the Italian soldiers with their mules, tiny tanks (called *tankette*), and WWI cannons, laughed cynically — *these* are the weapons and the equipment you thought was enough to fight us? My uncle, the young baker who wished to train as a pastry chef in Gorizia after his return, died of exhaustion just before/ just after the war ended, in May 1945 in a prisoner camp in Tashkent, Uzbekistan. The surviving sisters received an official note of his death — containing the Italianized name *Luigi* — from the Italian Ministry of Defense in the mid-1990s, after Russian military archives opened. Until then, military evidence had him marked down as *disperso*, missing. For decades, my grandmother kept hoping that he would return, a handful did. "He was a good boy, he never wanted to hurt anybody," she always said. Her last hope, with which she died, was inspired by the moving film *Sunflower* by Vittorio de Sica (1970): years after the war, the main character (played by Sophia Loren) goes to Russia only to find her missing husband (Marcello Mastroianni, who else) miraculously surviving the calvary of retreat and creating a new family in the foreign land.

The time it takes between the sounding of the alarm in the media or in numerous apps and the attack itself (by drones, rockets, planes, etc.) depends on the closeness of the front: in Odesa, it is significantly shorter than in Kyiv, where people have more time to find an appropriate shelter. If rockets of unidentified reach fly over Ukraine from Russia or its occupied territories, sirens are sounded across the country, even in the West. And yet, however it pains me to write it, life goes on more or less normally despite the blaring of sirens: people remain calm, mothers continue walking their children to school, groups of students meander by, cars rush no more than usual. It seems that, during the war, people grow to not only be patient and calm but also to accept their fate — if we blow up, we blow up. Or are just simply too tired to run to shelters. My caring hosts advised me that, once an alarm sounds, it is nevertheless wise to find a remote, more protected room in the apartment that has no windows or no outer walls (usually a bathroom or a corridor), if not a shelter or a cellar. Double walls should protect against indirect hits; there's no escaping the direct ones. They shared with me the anxious feeling that writer and photographer from Kyiv Yevgenia Belorusets noticed among her fellow citizens: "Caution and fear remain in the air. People discuss the safest spots in their apartments — where to sleep and where, under any circumstances, not to sleep."[10] Anyway, I was surprised to see shops and other public places close during alarms, with the customers or visitors being simply thrown out. *Isn't it more dangerous outside than in?* I wondered. Like many war things, I couldn't grasp this concept either.

The point of these non-selective night raids on civilian targets far away from the front lies in intimidation, scaremongering, tiring people out — so much that they may give up and think *Let them have that effing Donetsk, Luhansk, Crimea, we just want peace!* Constant danger not only wakes you up from your sleep, but also from your dreams. The percentage of Ukrainians who agree that the war should be fought until final victory dropped from 70 percent in the first fall of the war to 60 percent in the second fall. After expecting a quick win, their enthusiasm has been significantly grounded after the first year, as many told me. People are over it; the war is more tiring for the Ukrainians than it is for the Russians. The Ukrainian army is having trouble recruiting new soldiers. The BBC reported that, in the first year and a half of the war, 20,000 young Ukrainians illegally fled across the western borders to avoid being recruited — about the same number has been captured. Newer reports — the ones from December

2024 — show that more that hundred thousand Ukrainian soldiers were accused of desertion, and that military police is continuing to carry out roundups to find those who are avoiding conscription and deserters. My Uzhhorod hosts told me in horror that some of them simply want to swim over river Tisza to Hungary to avoid the draft: bodies of ten of them were found drowned just in May 2023 by Hungarian authorities. One morning I myself witnessed a military police roundup at one of the three-road junctions in Odesa: they were stopping all cars and checking documents for men aged 18 to 60. Those without proper ones, proving that they are unfit for military service, were then escorted to the armored bus, parked nearby. My fellow passengers explained to me that most probably they are sent to military training and later to the frontline. My assumptions were confirmed by Kurkov in his interview for *The Guardian* a few weeks after the war started: "The main thing is that you are tired all the time. Everyone is sleeping badly. Sirens are going off five times a night. [...] But you wake up and fall asleep constantly and try to decide whether you should leave the house ..." With his typical black humor, he describes the situation as "Russian roulette."

NOTES

1 Kiva, Iya. *Ilya*, translated by Katherine E. Young, 2022.

2 Duda, Tamara. *Daughter*, 2021. 227.

3 Pushkin, Alexander Sergeyevich. *Poltava*, translated by Ivan Eubanks.

4 Shevchenko, Taras, (1814–1861).

5 Shevchenko, Taras. *My Testament*, translated by John Weir.

6 Kocbek, Edvard. *Tovarišija*, (1972). 591.

7 Plokhy, Serhii. *The Gates of Europe: A History of Ukraine*, 2021. 365.

8 This can be found on YouTube: https://youtube.com/watch?v=ag-nM33WgXC8, 29 July 2024.

9 Polenakis, Stamatis. *Τα σκαλοπάτια της Οδησσού, Odessa's Stairs*, 2012, *Viola d'Amore*, my translation from Slovenian.

10 Belorusets, Yevgenia. *War Diary*, 2023. 83.

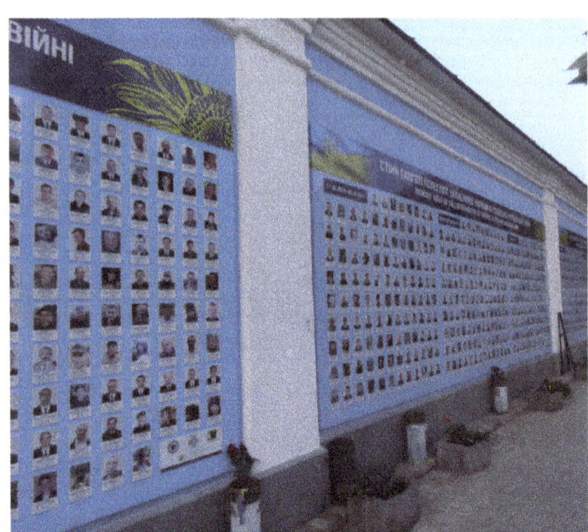

ЙНІ

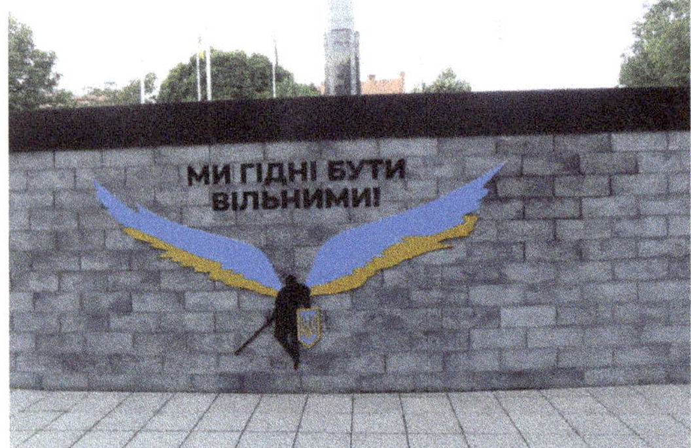

МИ ГІДНІ БУТИ
ВІЛЬНИМИ!

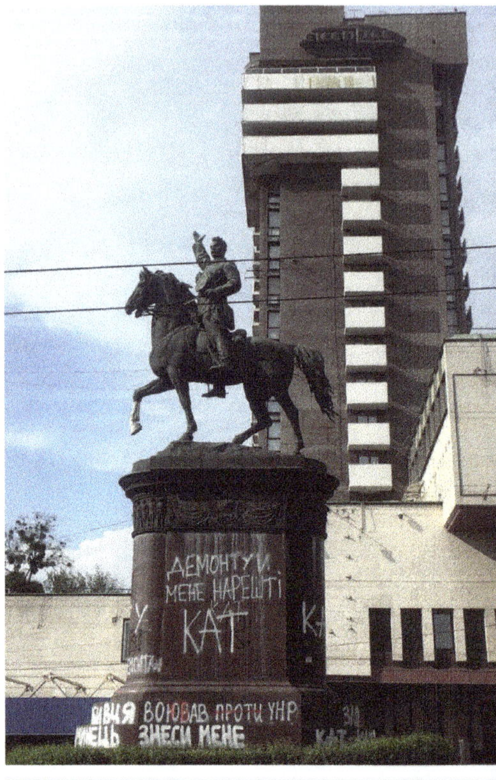

ДЕМОНТУЙ
МЕНЕ НАРЕШТІ
КАТ
ВОЮВАВ ПРОТИ УНР
ЗНЕСИ МЕНЕ
КАТ

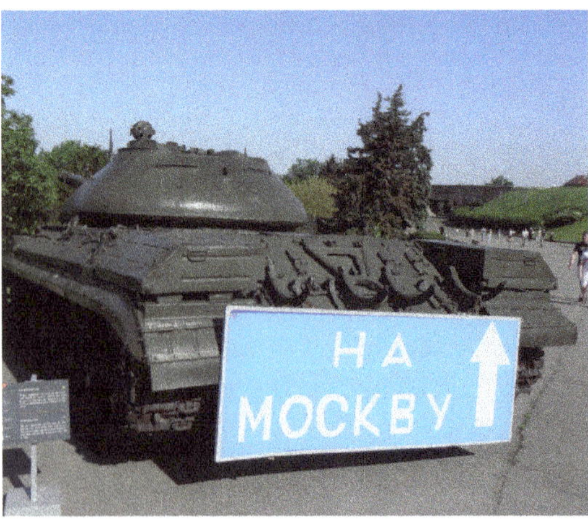

НА
МОСКВУ

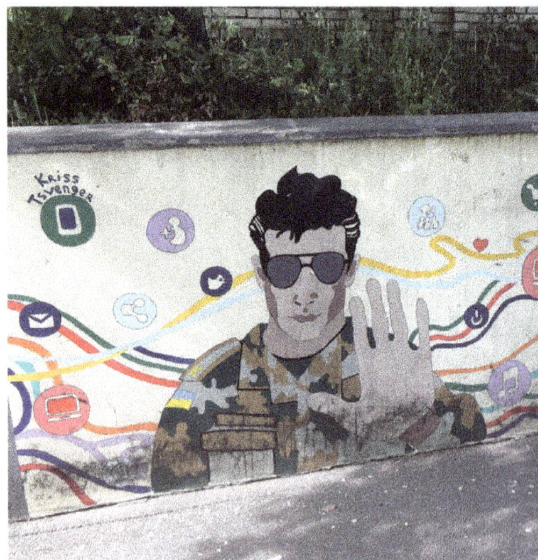

Kriss
Tsvenger

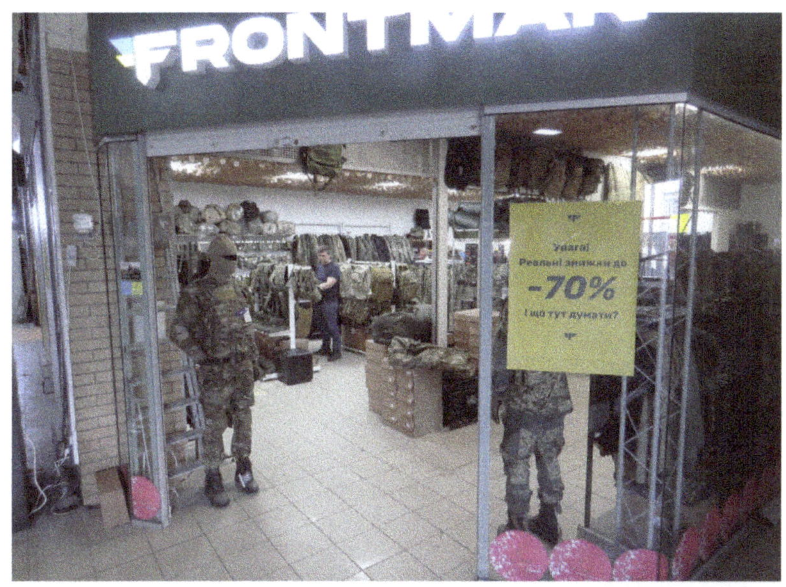

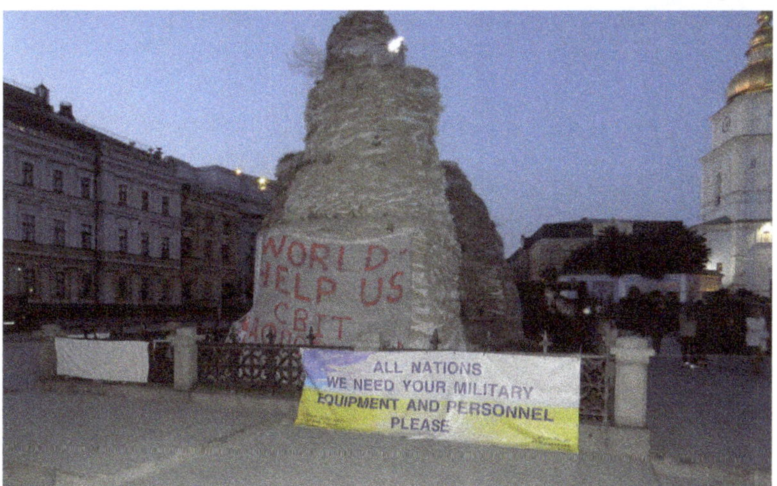

Opposite page:
Top to bottom, left: Kyiv, May 2023; Berehove, June 2024; "To Moscow,"
Kyiv, May 2023. Top to bottom, right: Monument of the Ukrainian
Soviet military leader Mykola Shchors (1895–1919), Kyiv, 2023, before
removal, photo by Zosia Kais. Graffiti: "Executioner," "dismantle me
already," "fought against Ukrainian People's Republic," "murderer,"
"offender," "tear me down," etc.; Kyiv, May 2023.

This page:
Top to bottom: Army Shop, Kyiv, May 2023; Kyiv, May 2023.

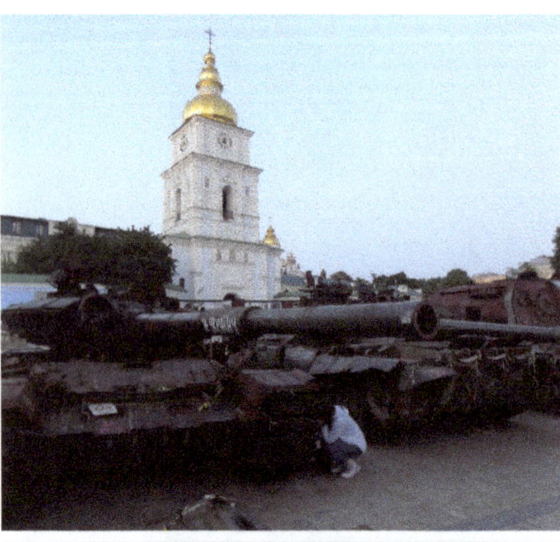

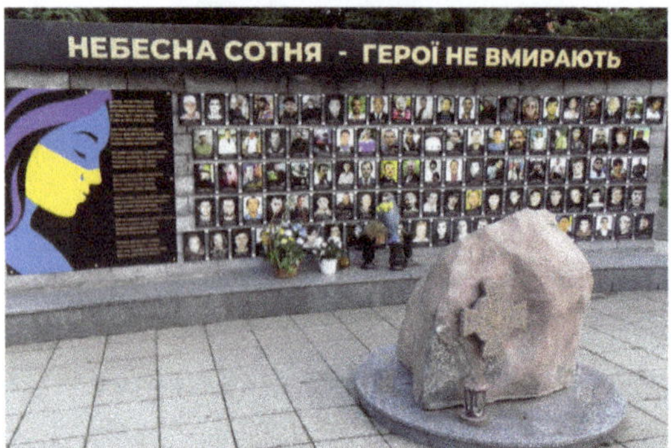

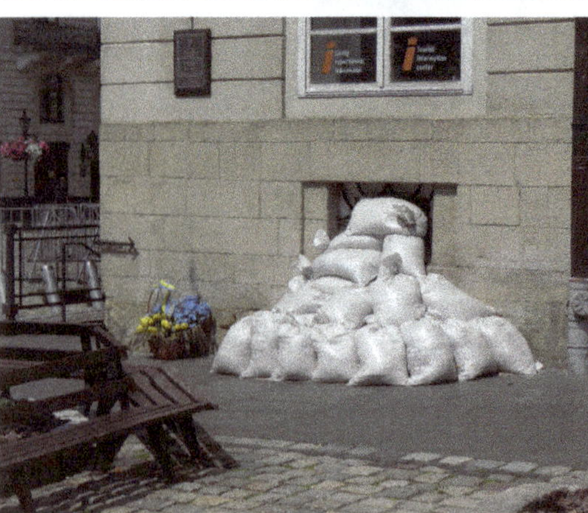

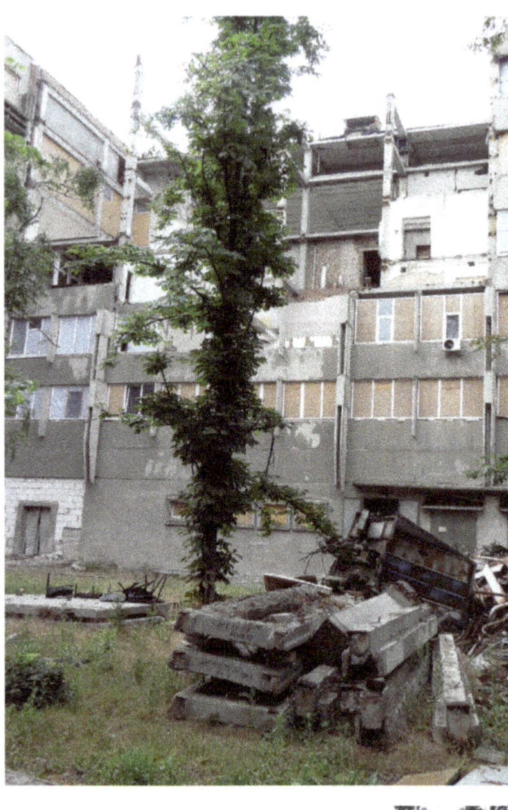

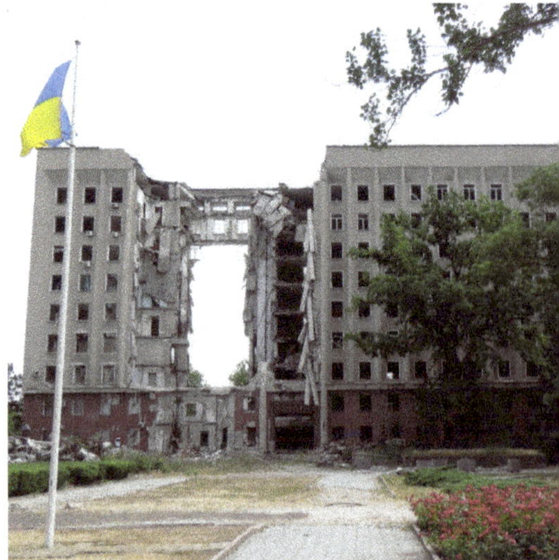

Top to bottom, left: Kyiv, May 2023; Berehove, June 2024; Kyiv, May 2023.
Top and bottom, right: Mykolaiv, June 2024.

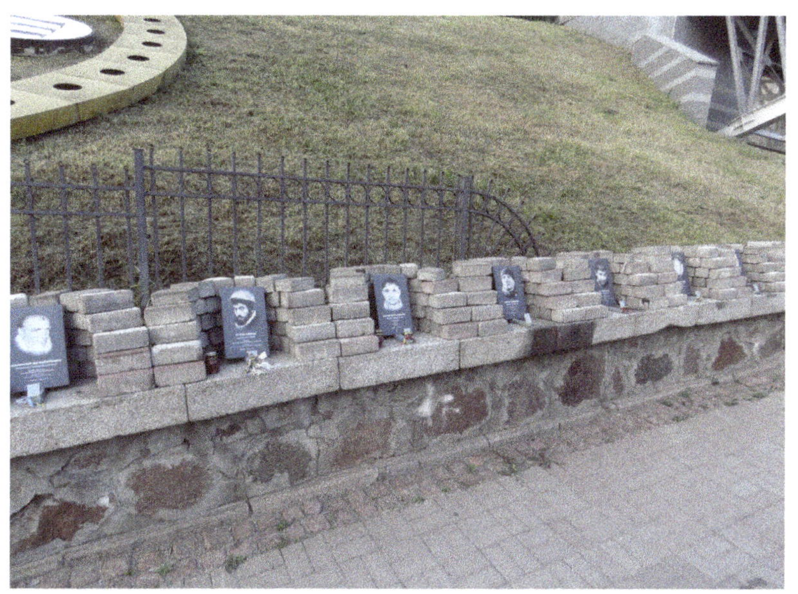

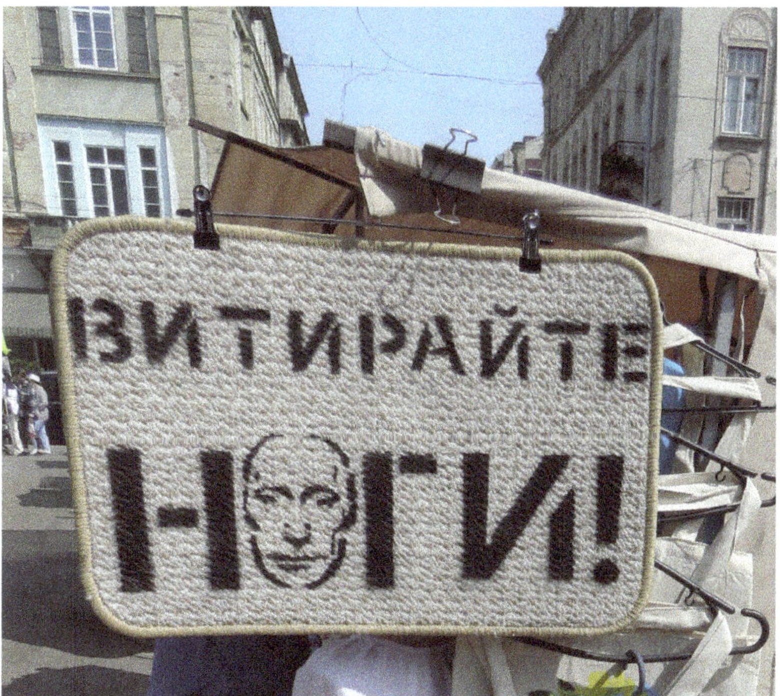

Top to bottom: Kyiv, May 2023; Putin doormat, Lviv, May 2023.

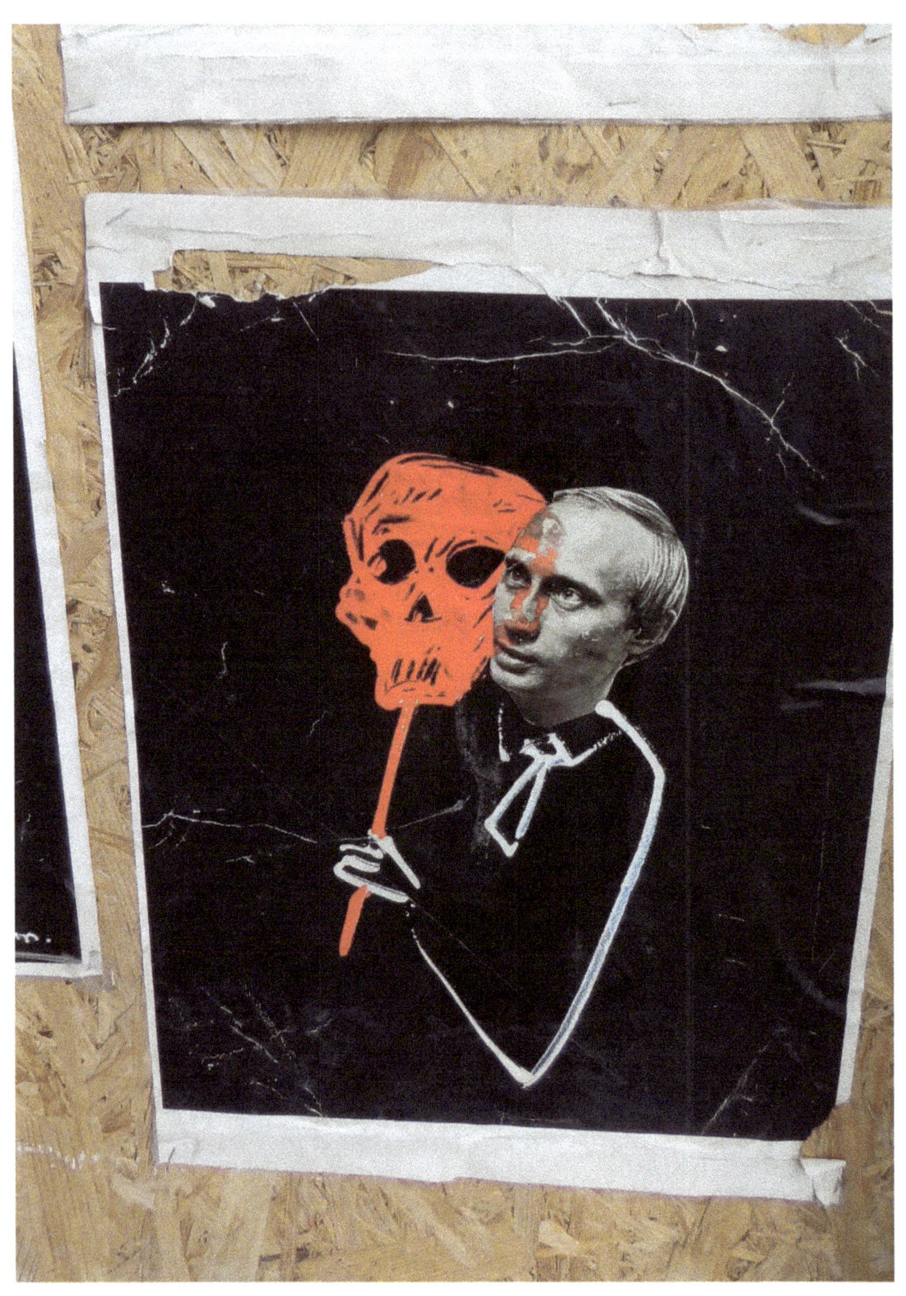

Odesa, May 2023.

III.

POLITICS OF WAR

> *"Where are you from?"*
> *"Slovenia, ex-Yugoslavia …"*
> *"Ah, yes, fall apart, wars, Serbians, Croats … Do you know why Yugoslavia fall apart?"*
> *"Uh, well …" I clear my throat, my head starts pounding with whens, hows, and whos, but he is faster …*
> *"I know why! Because you have no nuclear bomb. If you have nuclear bomb, you don't fall apart. Russia has nuclear bomb, nuclear bombs …"*
> *Talking to a St. Peterburg taxi driver in broken English, 2015.*

Either you have it, or you don't and then aren't. On that morning full of bright May sunlight, I had coffee with a Kyiv professor in a park, just next to the Golden Gate, the main gate to Kyiv since the 11th century. We spoke of the reasons for the war. In the 1990s, Russia guaranteed Ukraine's territorial sovereignty three times. The first time, the Soviet Union was still around when the Russian and the Ukrainian socialist republics signed an agreement in November 1990. The second time, in December 1994, the *Budapest Memorandum on Security Assurances* had Ukraine give up their nuclear weapons on their territory (until then, the third largest nuclear arsenal in the world!) in favor of Russia. The third time, in May 1997, the two countries signed the Russian-Ukrainian Friendship Treaty. Peace was obviously lost among the lines of these documents. In 2022, a few weeks before the first attack, both Sergey Lavrov and Alexander Lukashenko

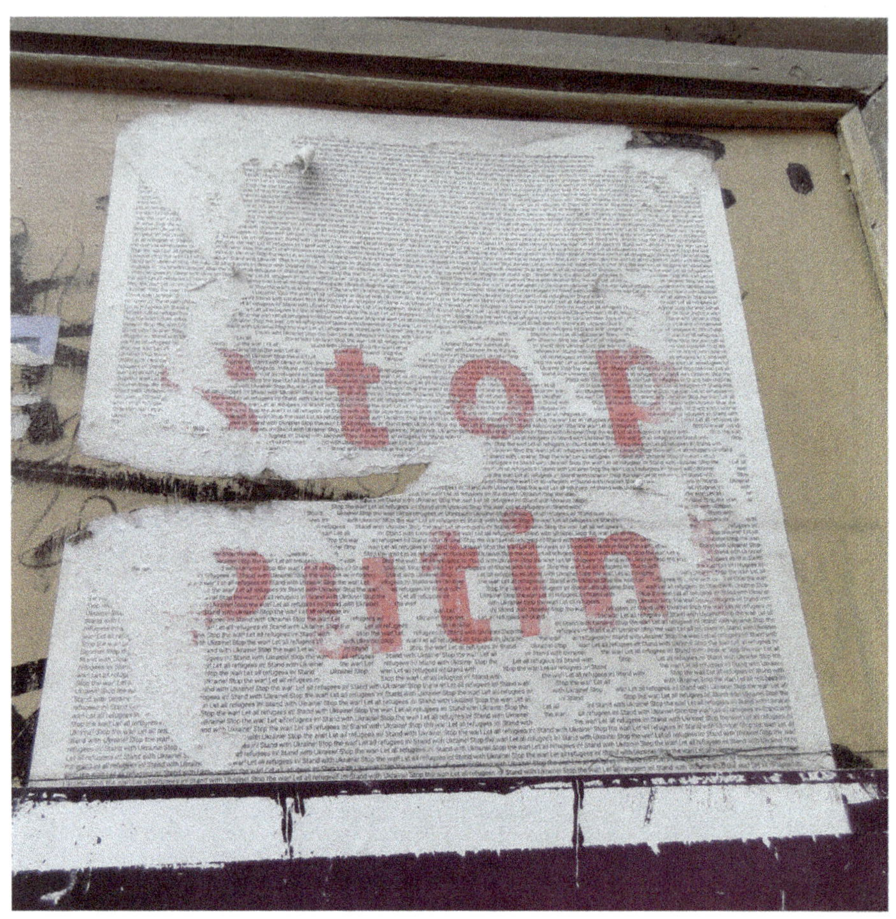

Lviv, May 2023.

loudly and publicly declared that there would be no war. When I wondered how Putin did not uphold this, the professor only lifted her eyebrows, looked at me, gave me time to realize how naïve I was (suspense is always the best message!), and calmy responded: "Do you really think that it stopped him for even a moment?"

I cannot treat my Ukrainian experiences outside the wider determinants of the situation there. I can offer only a general framework of the current war activities. Even though cultural studies are still often reproached for ignoring real factors in researching art and culture, that these are *soft sciences* (yes, these were the exact words I heard an arrogant older colleague once use) or *Mickey Mouse Studies* (a criticism I only read about), it is perfectly clear to me — and I begin all my courses and researches with this — that nothing is possible without the understanding of social structure, the asymmetry of power in a specific (geo-)political situation, without the knowledge of the cold hard facts. If you have no concept of class, gender, race, sexuality, ethnicity, age, and all other hierarchies, you will not understand the cultural dynamic — neither locally nor globally. Therefore, I cannot avoid these hierarchical social frameworks in this collection of essays as well. I distinguish three (intricately interconnected, of course): the first is global politics after the end of the Cold War, the second is Ukrainian domestic and foreign policy, and the third is Russian domestic and foreign policy. Opinions on who profits — *cui bono?* — from the war in these three frameworks are of course diametrically opposed. But their understanding will begin to shed some light on the war culture there.

The first wider framework of today's war is global politics. The *old* Cold War between the two global players of the era, the capitalist and the socialist bloc, transformed after the latter imploded. It became a *new* Cold War between another two mutually exclusive concepts. The unilateral West (as the self-proclaimed *global center*) is confronted by the plural world as imagined by new, pretender superpowers, the BRICS countries with a few regional powers to boot. To put it bluntly: in the architecture of the *new world disorder*, the West still holds global financial and cultural monopoly, but this is being contested by the growing power of these other global (and regional) players. These are leaving their peripheral and colonial position of providing cheap raw materials, energy sources, basic industrial products, and inexpensive labor force, and are more and more oriented towards high technology with all its profits (where they have a string of comparative advantages). The fundamental global political question today is whether the superpowers in this new reality accept one another as partners; try to control themselves as competition; oust each other as rivals; or try to subordinate each other as opponents. War hotspots around the world show that the latter is unfortunately predominant. In the new Cold War, conflicts are happening in the peripheries of superpowers, just like conflicts happened in the old wars: in the Balkans in the 1990s, in in the Middle East for all three decades, as well as in Africa and certain post-Soviet republics, and now in Ukraine.

The European Union and the United States support Ukraine wholeheartedly; well, almost wholeheartedly — until the radical change of the new Trump administration. But this was not always the case: American president George H. W. Bush in the summer of 1991, shortly before the attempted coup d'état in August 1991, visited Kyiv urging the Ukrainian authorities and parliament against independence, i.e. to stay in the Soviet Union, and — in the so-called *Chicken Kiev speech* — warning them against their *suicidal nationalism*. It is completely different now: war in Ukraine, as goes one of the frequent interpretations, supposedly benefits the politically and militarily powerful, economically declining — and geographically distant — United States. According to this theory, the politically divided European Union is paying a high economic price (as sanctions affect it more than Russia); it is submitting to American interests and becoming a mere appendix of the NATO pact ruled by the United States. Critics sharing this opinion insist that Europe is paying a very high price for the post-Cold War *Pax Americana*. For years, a renown Slovenian geo-political expert has been warning me that, in such a unilateral concept of world order, a weak, sold-out, and perhaps even collapsed Russia would benefit the United States the most. This is where the pressure for the Eastern European countries to join NATO (and the EU) comes from; it stopped with Ukraine, but it continues with Finland and Sweden. The main goal being the United States having access to the borders of the economically and politically increasingly confident China, the emerging industrial, high-tech, financial, military, and neo-colonial superpower, that is leaving the United States economically behind. Radical proponents of this thesis are determined that on the wretched soil of Ukraine, the United States are therefore waging an endless and profitable war against Russia aiming to

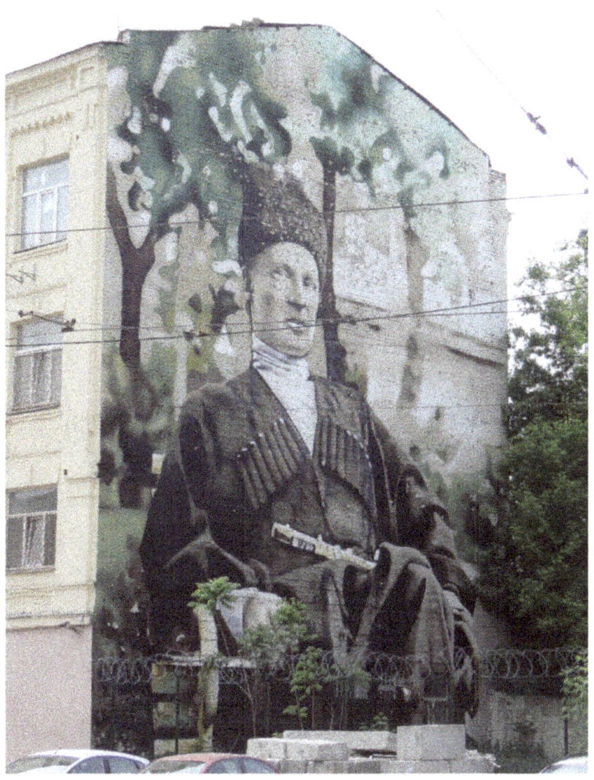

Mural honoring the last Hetman of Ukraine, Pavlo Skoropadskyi (1873–1945), Kyiv, May 2023.

exhaust and subjugate it — keeping their own global dominance. That's why they justify Putin's *special military operation* as self-defense.

The second wider framework of this situation is the Ukrainian transition. War is the most radical redistribution of power structures in a society — not just economic power, all power, as per Bourdieu. In terms of effectiveness, it is immediately followed by revolution, a fundamental political turn — in Eastern Europe, this is called *post-socialism*. As practical politics always needs a solid ideological background, today, this is provided by triumphant neoliberalism and ethnonationalism. They are constitutional for the *transition countries*, both their core of views and their practical consequence hidden behind the great words of *democratization, integration, freedom, protection of human rights*, etc. Neither knows what solidarity is: neoliberalism is dominated by obsessive individualism, ethnonationalism by tribal inwardness — but always and everywhere, they act solidly together, complementing each other. The are both governed by the principle of *homo homini lupus*, man to man is wolf, and that the only environment fit for a wolf is his own wolf pack. At the heart of both are the devastation of society and the condemnation of human and social solidarity as something bad. Neoliberal ideology justifies the systematic and legalized takeover of former common property by private entities, domestic or foreign, in short: it justifies *privatization* as the robbery of the (end of the) century. And contemporary nationalism is nothing more than a method of controlling the pauperized masses, poor because of neoliberalism. Neoliberalism creates class differences, nationalism levels them ethnically. In short, what neoliberalism impoverishes materially, ethnonationalism ideologically justifies.

In the last thirty years, many high-quality studies emerged from these environments that focused critically on the destructive, exclusivist, undemocratic, even genocidal processes and consequences of neoliberalism and ethnonationalism (while many were also apologetic). Two lucid researchers denote this period as a transition *from socialism to feudalism* (American anthropologist Katherine Verdery) or as a *re-feudalization* (Hungarian political philosopher Ágnes Heller). Neither nationalism, even in the extreme, nor new peripherization and poverty are a *faux pas*, a current painful regression, a weakness of post-socialism, an oopsie, an isolated incident that *Europe* intends to magically heal. No, they are the core of the neoliberal project. To paraphrase Max Horkheimer: Whoever is not willing to talk about ethnonationalism and neoliberalism, should also keep quiet about post-socialist transition.

A significant small example? A visibly shaken host in one of these towns told me the following story. Behind a giant patriotic billboard bearing the slogan *Building Ukraine Together*, there once stood a multipurpose hall, an excellent example of the interwar Central-European Crystal Expressionism in architecture. A few years ago, a local "gangster" (her words that she repeated several times), a former supporter of pro-Russian political parties and, which was obviously the determining factor, a friend of the mayor, bought it and calmly tore it down. In its stead, he plans to build an office building, of course. Nothing helped: not that the building was protected as a monument, no appeals of the Ministry of Culture, no responses of international organizations, no street protest, no street exhibition, no petition to the town council, none of the numerous newspaper articles. Hidden behind the yards of blue and yellow billboard was a construction site. Criminality disguised as patriotism; we know it well.

I better not even start the debate on the dangerous inflation of different European nationalisms or on Eurocentrism in general, this persistent ideology of European/Western superiority, as this book of essays would end as something completely different. We must always be conscious of the fundamental and therefore silenced double contradiction of the contemporary statehood. Firstly, as I've already mentioned: in its core, a state is a tool of the ruling group to control the society, nothing else. There is no social contract, just repression — an ideological one, in gloves, or a direct one, violent, ruling with an iron fist. And the second contradiction: by definition, *a national state* as we know it in Europe cannot be a state of the citizens but of a one, majoritarian, titular nation. "Democratic nationalism" as Plokhy[1] calls this, has more to do with the domination of one nation over others in the same country than to its civic power, meaning the equality of all its citizens. Parliamentary democracy is a misleading euphemism denoting actual national democracy. Consequently, civic identity in its core is nominal and secondary to nationality: the true name for *liberal democracy* is ethnocracy, the true name of *Europeization* is ethnic homogenization through assimilation or violence, which started with the emergence of modern countries in the west of Europe and is being finished in the east only in post-socialism. This is why the recent ethnic cleansing in Nagorno-Karabakh left no Armenian behind, which was the main news of world media for exactly one week. Poof and they were gone! This pessimistic scenario is shared by Palestinians in Gaza, Serbians in Croatia and

Kosovo, Serbians and Roma in Kosovo, and Bosniaks and other non-Serbs in the Republic Srpska, the Bosnian-Serbian part of Bosnia-Herzegovina. The Slovenian contribution this infamous list is the case of "The Erased," when about 25,000 inhabitants of Slovenia unconstitutionally were left without the legal status a few months after Slovenia declared independence, i.e., February 1992. Almost all of them were from other Yugoslav republics, so ethnically non-Slovenians. *But more about that next time*, an outro of a TV show would announce that they ran out of time.

Back to Ukraine, where the current war with Russians is hiding the domestic war of the rich against the poor. I believe all class hierarchy, racism, misogyny or patriarchy in general, ethnic chauvinism, colonialism in all its forms, homophobia, ageism, and all similar *fleurs du mal* are crimes, I consider them as much a war than the one fought with weapons. They are even worse, even deeper, and, most of all, never-ending; they are raging with no declaration of war. What good is it being united under the national flag if you are separated by a few zeroes on the right side of the monthly paycheck? This is why I claim that it is not just Putin who is leading war against Ukraine. For over three decades, the closed groups of oligarchs and tycoons, the *corruptionaires* as they are called there, are waging war against their own people. A Ukrainian colleague of mine told me that he feels as if he is coming from some parallel world when he attends political-sciences conferences in the West or reading studies from there, discussing ideological divisions between actual political parties — left-wing, right-wing, liberal, extreme-right, green, etc. parties. "In our country," he bitterly confessed to me, "that's totally irrelevant" (I omit his curse here): "the only thing that counts, the only thing that's really important is who financially benefits from what, from whom and for whom. Money trail, that's the only ideology."

Every single one of the people I spoke to emphasized that the main problem of their country is corruption. The deep dissatisfaction with the country being run in this fashion was the main motivation of the protesters in both revolutions — the Orange Revolution of 2004/2005 and Euromaidan or the Revolution of Dignity of 2013/2014, which began as self-organized civil movements. Sources and oral testimonies claim that they both united an extremely varied political spectrum on the same side of the barricades: from leftists to (far) rightists, from liberals to nationalists, all equally dissatisfied not only with the then-authorities but with the entire process of transition. However, in the studies I read, I found symptomatically little written on the post-Soviet pairings of authorities and capital, of legal and illegal crime; on social stratification; on new kleptocratic hierarchies and pauperized masses; on denying workers' rights; on the incompetence, cynicism and passivity of all successive authorities. Now, in the time of war, I see almost no mention of the extremely important class, economic, gender, and all other social injustices — neither in public discourse nor in culture, art, and the street. No, all attention is now focused on ethnic (Ukrainians, Russians, other minorities), political (pro-Western and pro-Russian parties and movements), and geo-strategic issues (talking about the future of the country). The rhetoric of war and patriotism successfully drowns out everything else and guarantees that internal hierarchies will remain unchanged even after the end of the conflict.

Sadly, Ukraine is an example of an unsuccessful transition, and a proof of the devastation caused by global neoliberalism amalgamated with local, post-Soviet specificities and ridden with patriotic demagogy. Nationalism is hiding poverty: the larger the poverty, the larger the national flags. In his bitter comedy *Carbide*, first published in Ukrainian in 2015, new wave Ukrainian novelist Andriy Lyubka claims that Ukraine is "a sublime and beautiful idea exploited by bastards hiding behind patriotic slogans";[2] for him, a "common theft" is how everything starts in the newly-independent Ukraine.[3] The essence of neoliberalism — endless richness and organized crime on the one hand and poverty on the other — is compensated and justified with the ethnonational excuse of *nation building*. This is why it comes as no surprise that the country is so focused on strengthening national identity, Ukrainization, and teaching Ukrainian and national culture rather than dealing with socially fair economic development that would benefit everyone, not just a handful of people. Nationalism does not question the origin of the wealth of some and the misery of others. The freedom that it claims to achieve is in fact tragic freedom.

Being a guest in Ukraine three times as a harmless, curious and trustworthy traveler who will leave soon, people spoke very honestly to me. (Countless times I remembered Austrian-American sociologist Alfred Schütz's essay *Stranger* I first read as a student back in the 1980s, and I identified with the benefits and limitations of now being one now in Ukraine.) I'll mention only two of many such cases. Two years ago, a young Ukrainian woman who had been living in Slovenia for a few years, brought her old and destitute, Russian-speaking grandmother from the combat zones in eastern Ukraine to her safe place in Slovenia. She was very upset about Ukrainian border guards' hostile treatment because of her poor Ukrainian. "Why aren't you speaking Ukrainian, but a language of the aggressor?" they asked both of them, to which the grand-daughter replied angrily, "The Ukrainian state gives her 120 euros of pension with which she can not cover even her medical expenses. I'm saving her life, and you are preaching us about what language she should speak!" Second case: not only disappointed, but very much frustrated because of the three decades of unfair transition with growing poverty and enrichment of the few, some of my interlocutors told me — again, discretely, in a hushed voice, not to be labeled as defeatists or even something worse — "Why would we fight for the country that was stolen from us? Not by foreigners, but by our own Ukrainian tycoons and other criminals?" As always and as everywhere, people's opinions are very often quite different from what we hear from the official media loudspeakers and from the political pulpits. You don't hear them unless you are there, ready to listen to them patiently and carefully.

Despite its natural resources, developed industry, and strategic position, Ukraine was already in ruins before the war. A renowned Slovenian expert on transitions claims that the transition in Ukraine is marked by the rule of home capital (which subjugates party politics and state policy in general); this capital is parasitic, unproductive (capitalists invest in foreign real estate, banking havens, in the world center, and not in home development); while the country remains a battle ground for capital fractions. In the introduction to her book, Shore draws clear analogies between the operations of "both American capitalism and post-Soviet oligarchy."[4] Plokhy claims that tycoon clans are groups of "young, ambitious, and ruthless businessmen," who got completely uncontrollably filthy rich during the collapse of the previous federation through criminal dealings and privatization, "which amounted to the sale of government assets at a fraction of their actual value." The methods of their money-making were innovation, opportunism, sycophancy, bribery, and even shooting.[5] This spread through the country as "crony capitalism at its worst," as historian Yekelchyk straightforwardly puts it: "The new rich usually owed their instant wealth to their government connections, if not for their own political appointments, but some of them came from gangster backgrounds."[6] Due to profitable insider information and insider business, these people finance the parties that, in turn, make political appointments to guarantee their immunity. With his typical sarcasm, Lyubka asserts that Ukraine is a country "with a legal system that encourages shady dealings, chicanery, and off-the-book transactions."[7]

Reading this I was reminded of a brutally honest song of Bosnian-Slovene punk-performer and artist Damir Avdić entitled "KK FU" (2018): he hit the essence of the post-social transition with the words *Nije sve u kapitalu / ima nešto i u kriminalu, It's not all about capital / there is also something about the crime.* The worst robbery is the legal robbery.

Slovenian comparatist and translator from Ukrainian Janja Vollmaier Lubej emphasizes that this results in "a huge gap between rich and poor, complacency and law-breaking on the one hand, and the erosion of freedom on the other."[8] The introduction to her article brims with frightening data on the collapse of the Ukrainian economy brought on by oligarchs — their quiet and unannounced total war against their compatriots. Especially their female compatriots; Vollmaier Lubej focuses on feminization of poverty. Everywhere, post-socialism brought on a drastic re-patriarchization

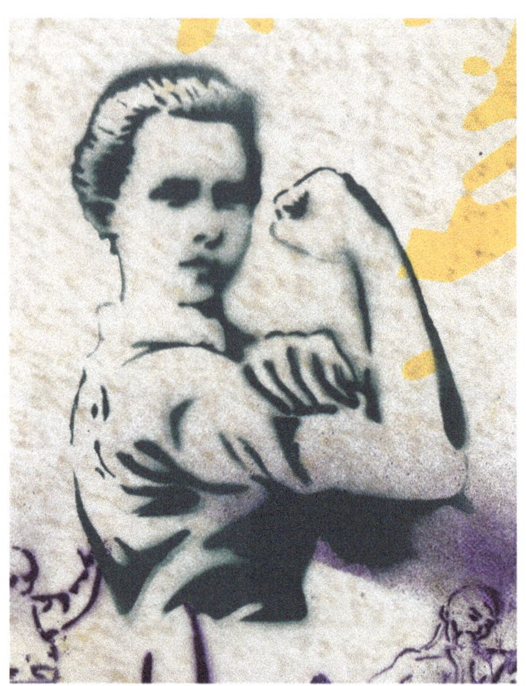

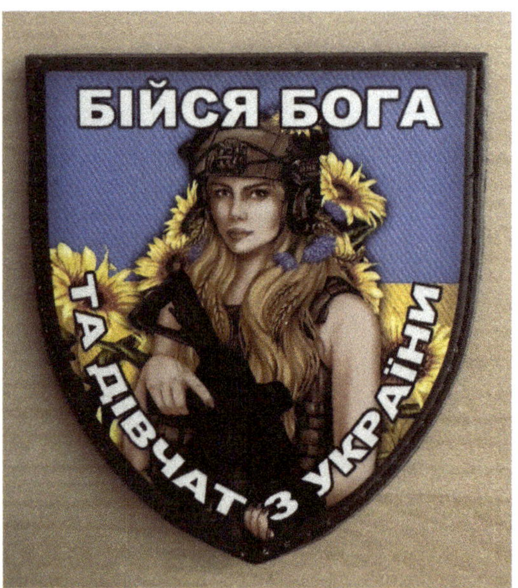

Top to bottom: street artist interpretation of Lesya Ukrainka (1871-1913), writer and feminist, Lviv, May 2023; Patch "Be Afraid of God and Ukrainian Women," Lityn, June 2024.

of the social status of women. Examples are quick to be found: I only had to look at Ukrainian banknotes. On nine different notes ranging from 1 to 1000 hryvnia, there is only one image of a woman. The number is the same as with the former Slovenian tolar and with many other currencies: in the set of five Polish and six American banknotes, there isn't a single woman. Or: in the splendidly designed book of one hundred most important Ukrainian artists *Names of Ukraine — 100 Artists* (2020), I counted exactly 11 women.

Already benefiting most from the transition, the *nouveau riche* profit from the war even more: nationalism, fully awoken by the war, enables them to keep their acquired property intact. War merely crystalizes the essence of neoliberalism. In a common fight against Putin's army, the "differences among Ukrainians are beginning to disappear," as writer and journalist Vitaly Portnikov enthusiastically writes in the anthology *State of War*.[9] Really? I heard, I read, I saw, I listened to how the colossal differences between the rich and the poor Ukrainians remain. In these difficult times, the corruption of the authorities has experienced a new boom, writes the seasoned Moscow correspondent and editor Miha Lampreht, mentioning senior government representatives and regional leaders. The complete domination of patriotic discourse in public space enables another type of leech to continue plundering: war profiteers. At the time of writing, one of the most influential oligarchs (and supporters of President Zelenskyy) was arrested and accused of fraud and money laundering by domestic and foreign law enforcement authorities. Even those who are seemingly pro-West had no difficulty trading and cooperating with the Russian regime before the attack (as pointed out by stencils with the portrait of Poroshenko and the word *Traitor*) or paying for Russian gas by exporting arms to Russia (again illustrated with stencils in Ukrainian cities). Today, more than high-level corruption, it is the everyday one that hurts more. From the hushed confessions of my Ukrainian interlocutors, I learned that everything can be *arranged* with different clerks; there are prices for, say, foreign travel permits for men or for avoiding military conscription. It happens that the *volunteers* in collection centers will sell foodstuffs and equipment that comes as aid and even donated military material and ammunition from abroad or from Ukraine itself. A recent scandal from their Ministry of Defense revealed how high officials and suppliers of food abused their position and appropriated millions of dollars intended for the needs of the military. They used it for dividends, to assist their own companies, transferred it to accounts abroad, and purchased hotels in Croatia.

Despite its natural resources and favorable geographical location, Ukraine was already marginalized in the Russian and then Soviet states. How will it fare not only because of the devastation of war and pervasive corruption, but also because of the nature of its economy (based on agricultural products, raw materials, and semi-manufactured goods) in the highly competitive and protected Western economy with new high-yield industries (finance, banking, high-tech)? Neoliberal capitalism mainly encourages the poor to fight each other: that is how the neighboring Poland, Romania, Slovakia, and Hungary, as well as Bulgaria immediately banned the import of cheaper Ukrainian grains. When profits enter the stage, all solidarity flies out the window, no matter how praised it is. End of romance. Anyway, can Ukraine only look forward to a change of its peripheral position, now in Europe? *Trovarsi un altro signore*, finding a new master, is a helpful, but ominous metaphor by Croatian writer Miroslav Krleža. I am also reminded of a title of an interview, a few years ago, with a renown Slovenian expert on transitions, who compared the European Union with Imperial Russia: if it only shifts from being the periphery of the latter to being the periphery of the former, Ukraine will continue to fare badly.

Ever since its independence, Ukraine has been among the bottom European countries in terms of gross social product per capita. Putin's *conquista* has caused an additional 35-percent drop and deepened the already drastic class differences in Ukrainian society, which are evident at every turn. In just over thirty years of post-socialist and post-Soviet transition, Ukraine has lost more than one quarter of its inhabitants: at the collapse

     Ukrainian Vignettes: Essays on a Culture at War

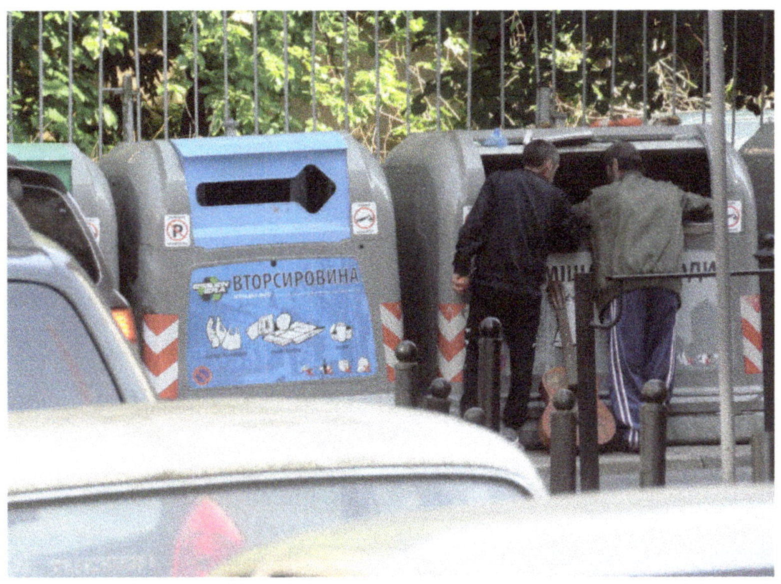

Lviv, May 2023.

of the Soviet Union, there were around 51 million people living in Ukraine; 45 million in 2014; 42 million in 2021; the number is estimated to around 37 million now. According to the latest data, a quarter of Ukrainians live below the poverty line, the average monthly pay is $500. Sadly, poverty is acute and on my Ukrainian travels — just like in every other place that is in the grips of neoliberalism — I saw beggars and homeless people, and the elderly poor of both genders. Yet the poverty I saw there seemed to be less creepy comparing to the one I experienced in the richest parts of the world — in my year living in Philadelphia, in its northern parts; for example, in the area of Kensington Avenue. Or on v in Los Angeles, where thousands scrape by living in a cluster — right next to the spiffy financial and business quarter, literally towering above them! The Ukrainian poor were dumpster-diving behind large commercial centers adorned with all the world-famous brands or scavenging for any food at vegetable markets since the morning. Mincing their feet, they every so often glanced up as if they wanted to see if anyone was watching their shame — even though the only people who should be ashamed are those who are causing this poverty. They were glad of every hryvnia I left them.

Others are unphased by war shortages. Sitting at the window of an obviously prestigious hotel that I passed on one of my morning walks, a shapely blonde in a plush tracksuit could not be overlooked. She was eating breakfast in full make up (*When I wake up in my make up*, I was reminded of slightly cynical lyrics of *Celebrity Skin* by Courtney Love) with her protector, who was probably three times her age and not even dapper, neither in his appearance nor in his behavior, just vulgar. His plate was full of eggs, sausages, cheese, and more sausages; she was sipping on a freshly squeezed carrot smoothie. Everybody plays their own game.

And everybody drives their own car. Similar discrepancies are extremely easy to observe also in their assortment of vehicles: a large percentage of cars, dare I say a third, is still the beaten-up Soviet Lada. The one I remember clonking and growling down Yugoslav roads in the 1980s (the classic ones were the Riva, the others Samara, either hatchback or sedan; we didn't know which were uglier) or even in the 1970s (which we called Zhiguli). But every once in a while, the city center could admire a really luxurious car slowly drive through for everyone to admire. (Would the kind reader excuse my lack of knowledge on cars; it is as non-existent as my knowledge on tanks. At home, I have been driving small Peugeots out of practical reasons: a car service around the corner. I have no clue, it could be a Lamborghini or a Bentley or a cabrio of another royal brand with another — what a cliché! — 50-year-old behind the wheel and another blonde bombshell next to him, perhaps the sister of the one above ... they all look rather the same.) For them, neither war nor transition exist — they have obviously already won them both.

Many rich people scurried away while there was still time, before the war — there's a class factor in this, as well. How many times in the past ten years, and especially in the last two, since the beginning of the total war, have I heard various people back home, when a rad SUV, a BMW or a Volvo with Ukrainian number plates passed us, utter a typically jealous

Slovenian comment (equating wealth with the size of one's car): "Look at the cars these Ukrainians can afford!" or "They must not do too bad if they drive this!" The rich fugitives can do so because they have stored their funds safely and in time. And, in contrast to their compatriots in the East, they are also safe themselves. Can the essence of post-socialist transition be any clearer?

Back to the third general framework of today's war: the new Russian geopolitical position. Let me begin with a literary idea from the last paragraph of Gogol's *Dead Souls* (1997): "And you, Russia of mine—are not you also speeding like a troika which nought can overtake? Is not the road smoking beneath your wheels, and are the bridges not thundering as you cross them, and everything being left in the rear [...] Whither, then, are you speeding, O Russia of mine? Whither? Answer me! But no answer comes."[10] In her book *Russia — Lost in Transition* (2007) American Kremlinology expert Lilia Shevtsova answers this more-than-180-year-old question by claiming that Russia is a combination of centralized and personalized politics, of nuclear superpower and of oligarch capitalism on the one side and bureaucratic capitalism on the other. In an interview (2023), Schulmann asserts: "We are an autocracy based on the depoliticization of people." In his comprehensive book *Third Rome* (1999), former Moscow correspondent and diplomat Anton Rupnik, a lucid expert on Russian history and present times, characterized Russia with "nomenclature democracy," the attachment of politics to an absolutist leader, the radicalism of political actors, the unresolved issue of national minorities, and the weakness of civil society institutions. In short, it's a new version of the old imperialist politics summarized in a formula by its proponent Sergey Uvarov from early 19th century: *Orthodoxy/Autocracy/Nationality* with added imperialism.

First, I would like to refute the incredibly prevalent and convenient explanation of the march to Ukraine, proposed also by various military experts, saying that this is *Putin's madness*, his *irrational move*, a *headless launch*, i.e. that he has *completely lost it*, as I recently read in a Slovenian journal. Other historical blood mongers, Hitler, Mussolini, Stalin,

Milošević, have been explained in a similar way. What persistent, almost pub-like lightness reduces these complex and dizzying social phenomena such as wars to personal — actually, psychiatric — diagnoses of their protagonists! More than anything else, this points to the incompetence in the rational thinking of these so-called experts.

On the one hand, I believe that Putin made four grave errors in his thinking and his double or even triple games. Firstly, when he overestimated Russia's military power and believed that Ukraine will fall at the first signs of aggression; that his tanks will dance through it and that he will be able to accumulate territory as easily as he did in the prelude to today's war, in 2014. They were supposed to parade down Khreshchatyk, the main street of Kyiv; in these months, that is what I heard and read countless times. Secondly, when he underestimated the power of Ukrainian army,

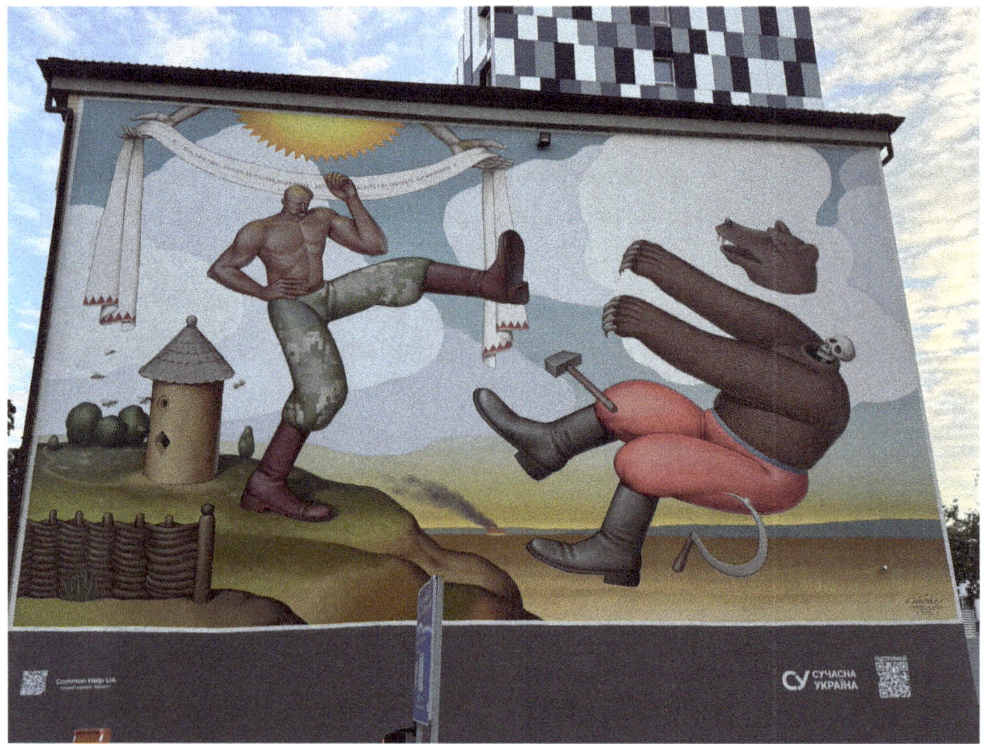

Kyiv, June 2024.

   Ukrainian Vignettes: Essays on a Culture at War

which has more than recovered from the lesson it received unprepared eight years earlier. It did not kneel but obviously found the true *fire, flames, and power* from the end of the famous novella *Taras Bulba* by Gogol (1917): "But can any fire, flames or power be found on earth capable of overpowering Russian strength?"[11]

Thirdly, I believe that Putin in his arrogance combined with the post-Soviet stiffness never expected the European Union and the NATO alliance to help Ukraine so generously this time. After the annexation of Crimea and the *spontaneous uprisings* in parts of Donetsk and Luhansk, the West did practically nothing. 2014 reminded me of 1938, like the Munich *appeasement* with new *Chamberlains* in the lead roles and with the sacrificing of a new Czechoslovakia, just to keep the peace. Since the winter/spring of 2014, things were almost normal between Russia and the West: the political and economic interests were too strong, especially in energy. Slovenia officially acted like everybody else did: like nothing had happened, the 2015 ceremony at the Russian Chapel at Vršič Pass (built by Russian prisoners of war in early 1916; it now serves as a symbol of friendship between Slovenia and Russia) was attended by Prime Minister Dmitry Medvedev; the next year, to mark its 100th anniversary, it was visited by Putin himself.

Ever since the attack in 2022, Ukraine has been gaining the sympathies of the European public; it does not seem forgotten. The 2023 summer Eurobarometer shows high support for the country: mostly regarding political, humanitarian, economic, and financial aid, a little less support is seen for military aid. Popular culture is doing much to contribute to this fact — I can think of numerous examples. On an August night in 2023, for example, I watched one of many similar events — a high-profile charity football match and concert at Chelsea's stadium in London — Game4Ukraine. During Eurovision, Liverpool hosted the Kyiv Pride Parade to support Ukraine, freedom and the LGBTQ+ community of the country. Even though such display of European solidarity is of course not decisive in the resistance against Putin's aggression, it plays a part.

The other side doesn't have this — although I have been surprised hearing words of support from some prominent public figures such as the former Pink Floyd member Roger Waters and the star of action movies Steven Seagal. Former notorious CEO of Formula One Bernie Ecclestone declared that he would *take a bullet* for Putin. American publicist Benjamin Abelow attributed the responsibility, if not blame, for the war in Ukraine to the United States, the NATO alliance, and the European Union as they provoked Russia. In 2023, the Scientific Institute of the Slovenian Academy of Sciences and Arts published a translation of his pamphlet *How the West Brought War to Ukraine* and I am right in worrying which is the next such work to be expected — perhaps one by Putin's ideologue Alexandr Dugin, whose views are practically the same to Abelow's. I am even more surprised by the fanboying of people from which I would never have expected it: from director Oliver Stone, whose films have always critically addressed the misuse of political power. From iconic anti-fascist Italian ska punk band Banda Bassotti, which performed in Donbas in 2014 and has since unconditionally and completely followed Putin's song and dance about the *Nazis of Ukraine*. From the guitarist and singer in the Belgrade band Repetitor, which is dear to my heart. And, last but not least, from Goran Bregović, who also had no qualms entertaining the Sevastopol audience in 2015.

But I am entirely astonished at the firm support Putin's politics are receiving by certain circles and individuals from the left on the political spectrum, also in Slovenia. A justifiable critique of neoliberal capitalism, ethnonationalism, western imperialism, and media monopoly — with which I wholeheartedly agree — drives them straight into defending great-Russian imperialism, chauvinism, neocolonialism, and their own media monopoly. Many of them simultaneously defend the invasion of Ukraine and repeat after Putin that its purpose is *denazification* — all the while condemning the Israeli invasion of Gaza after Hamas' attack. Allow me to clarify something first: at least since the end of the Cold War, global and local political situations are difficult to grasp with the vocabulary that we've had since the French Revolution. At least since then, the notions of political left and political right need to be redefined, explaining every time we use them: Do we mean political systems? Parliamentary parties? Movements? A multitude of various *ad hoc* initiatives? Today, China is a neoliberal and neocolonialist dictatorship, but it is run by the leading caste called the *Chinese Communist Party*. Nothing can be less communist than that. Is the American Democratic Party really more liberal than the Republican Party? Are British laborists or European social democrats really leaning to the left if they join their voices to unconditionally support and develop a neoliberal ethnonationalist progress? How left is the Slovakian *social democrat* Robert Fico or the Montenegrin *boss*, another *socialist* Milo Đukanović? Milošević, too, was peddling his Greater Serbia as a *socialist*, his wife as a *leftist*. The nominally *leftist* Putin supporters found enough argument in anti-Westernism to seek refuge in the bosom of Kremlin propaganda — and I highly doubt that any one of them ever stepped onto Ukrainian soil to observe the entire entangled situation then and now from up close. The narrowmindedness of blind, uncritical anti-Westernism has logically led them back to blind pro-Putinism. One of the main challenges of the left on every level is how to preserve a reflective and at the same time engaged position in face of every destructive imperialist, great-national, and neoliberal politics — eastern, western, any other — and not fall for the basic trick of defending one against the other.

And fourthly, the Russian president probably expected Poland to close its border for Ukrainian refugees, just like it selectively closes it for the refugees from the Middle East, who have been coming from Belarus after it liberalized their visas in the summer and fall of 2021. The measure was then also adopted by Lithuania and Latvia. There is a lot of bad blood between the Polish and Ukrainian people: during the last century, they both claimed the border regions of Eastern Galicia and Volhynia. The fight began right after the end of WWI and in 1943 and 1944, Ukrainian nationalists systematically killed between 60,000 and 100,000 Polish civilians there — something that they described as *liquidating the Polish element.*

During this time, the Polish people killed between 10,000 and 30,000 Ukrainians. But now, Poland has greeted Ukrainian refugees with an open heart: it took more than 1.5 million in and more than a few times that have crossed through it on their way to the West. Soon after the war started, a colleague from Lublin reported how the Polish people on the Ukrainian border, also in his town, take initiative, go to train- and bus stations and adopt a refugee family, offering to have the family live in their apartment. This solidarity, however, has its dark side: the country openly sticks to discriminatory or, to put it bluntly, racist criteria of accepting those who need help. The door is wide open to the Ukrainian white people and closed shut for non-European, African, and Near East/Muslim refugees. It is not irrelevant that the first are exclusively women and children, while the second are mainly (younger) men, prevalent in the refugee currents of the third world. Such duplicity has been pointed out by many humanitarian organizations and individuals, even Pope Francis back in April 2022.

Only time will tell whether the thesis about Putin's miscalculations is right or whether we should begin thinking in a completely different direction. On the other hand, I am convinced that such authoritarian leaders decide to go to war when they feel confident enough; when they presume to be at the zenith of their power; when they have achieved all that could be achieved in the situation. Afraid to decline and gradually fail, they want to preemptively consolidate and prolong their rule by preventively embarking on something big, epochal — like an expansion.

Putin is achieving the exact opposite of what he declares to stand for: a *demilitarized* and *de-Nazified* Ukraine and the deterring of Western threats. As in every self-fulfilling prophecy, the consequence is presented as the cause. Today, Ukraine is much more *militarized* than it was two years ago, NATO has a much greater presence there; because of the attack, there is a larger number of radical nationalists; another Russian neighbor, the traditionally neutral Finland has entered NATO —followed by Sweden just in March 2024; Poland is building the strongest army in Europe; NATO forces have also grown in the other member states in Eastern Europe. The West has imposed several packages of economic and financial sanctions against Russia (and Belarus), freezing or even confiscating the assets of Putin's supporters. These are all the anticipated consequences, which leads me to assume that the main goal of *liberating Ukraine* is in fact a reinforcement of Putin's absolutist reign at home. Schulmann, too, sees the reasons for war especially in the internal activities in Russia, in strengthening Putin's power from within. As creepy as it sounds, following this line of thought, Ukraine is merely a side victim, the *collateral damage* of Putin's ambition for a total power at home. With the argument of an external threat, of *American imperialists* and *Ukrainian neo-Nazis*, he can unify his citizens as a populist and deal with the last remnants of the opposition, while the dissidents have already been dying in peculiar circumstance as it is. The more the West intervenes, the more there are *Nazis* in Ukraine, the better for him at home! In an interview with Eviane Leidig (2022), Canadian investigative journalist Michael Colborne, the author of the study on the Azov movement and Regiment, is convinced that, as ironic as it sounds, "The one person in the world most interested in seeing Azov grow because of the war is Vladimir Putin himself." He can afford to isolate himself from the West as he immediately compensates it with new allies and friends. Just like the old revolutionary maxim goes: *the Worse* (for all), *the Better* (for us).

It seems that the resolute answer from the West does not lessen Putin's power but, on the contrary, benefits his illimited power. I am astonished to read polling data that around seventy percent of Russian citizens support the war (although I take these numbers with a kilogram of salt: in a state with such a level of repression, it is difficult to measure *the voice of the people*). With its power of absorption — the resources, connections, allies, army —, Russia is no small Milošević's Serbia, no brittle Sadam's Iraq, no weak Gaddafi's Libya, no puppet Assad's Syria, which sanctions or external pressures could break. The more enemies his regime creates externally, the closer they are, the stronger he is internally. The tragic paradox of contemporary Russia lies in the fact that Putin's loudest critic was the leader

of until recently its most striking military formation, Yevgeny Prigozhin
— literally one of his *masters of war*, not of peace. In an interview (2023),
Schulmann warns that the coming "great national disappointment" can
make the following Russian leader even more radical than the current one,
i.e. that "our Hitler may yet be coming into power." And on the side of the
pacifists, I follow news of parents being questioned if their child writes
pacifist essays, of deserters being court-martialed, of anti-war journalists
being let go or even arrested. Political graffiti artists and protesters critical
of the Kremlin are in for nothing good if they are caught by the police, as
one of them told us via zoom at the Ljubljana Street Art Festival in 2021.

Nevertheless, the list of Russian critics of Putin is impressive despite
the unimaginable repression. Peace demonstrations were held in all major
Russian cities immediately at the outbreak of the war, and those against
general mobilization at its announcement in early autumn 2022 (including
the open letter from the mothers of the Russian Federation) — in all of
these cases, hundreds of people were arrested. According to some data,
around a million people, especially the younger ones, the educated ones,
but also the rich ones, have escaped Russia in a year and a half. I heard
many Russian-speaking people wherever I traveled and wherever I stayed
during this time — from tourist sites and capitals to playgrounds around
my home, from parks to stores. Nothing but *traitors of the people* and *fifth
columnists* if Putin and Medvedev are to be believed. Just before the war,
three thousand public figures signed a petition calling for peace; another
180 members of academia wrote a protest note; even certain priests of the
Russian Orthodox Church, loyal to the regime, have expressed an aversion
to war. People declaring themselves opposed to Putin's regime include
oligarch Mikhail Khodorovsky, political activist Vladimir Kara-Murza,
chess grandmaster and activist Garry Kasparov, authors Vladimir Sorokin
and Lyudmila Ulitskaya, editor of the discontinued *Novaya Gazeta* Dmitry
Muratov (who sold the 2021 Nobel Peace Prize medal a few months after he
was awarded it and donated the money to Ukrainian refugees), journalist
Marina Ovsyannikova, and the human rights NGO Memorial (which won

the Nobel Peace Prize a year later). From the world of culture and sports, they include pop icon Alla Pugacheva, prima donna Anna Netrebko, rocker and cofounder of the cult band Aquarium Boris Grebenshikov, his contemporary Andrey Makarevich from the band Mashina Vremeni, tennis master Darja Kasatkina, her Belarus colleague Aryna Sabalenka, and many others. And practically every Russian I know and am in contact with. But apparently their words do not reach Putin nor move him even a tiny bit.

Although it may look like Putin's regime is digging its own grave by occupying Ukraine, it is far from being isolated, forced into autarchy, as the West would want to believe. Russia today is diplomatically, politically, economically, and militarily not alone. There is no doubt that a large part of the world is furious at the indulgent unilateralism of the West after the end of the Cold War, still following the compromised principle of *West and the Rest.* The terrible politics in the Near East; unauthorized interventions in the Middle East; chaos in the north of Africa; in the case of the United States, interferences in the internal affairs of Central and South American countries, i.e. in their *own backyard*; the support for oppressive regimes and gross violators of human rights and international law, etc.; not to mention the ruthless exploitation of the "Third World," i.e. extreme neocolonialism — all of this has earned the West strong criticism and fierce opponents.

Additionally, no matter how ideologically and politically different if not opposite the countries are — with China, Iran, North Korea, and India standing out the most —, they are united by common resentments and common interests against Western domination. It is an old maxim (also) in foreign policy that the enemy of my enemy is my friend. I feel that the estimations of international politics all too often forget the smoldering anti-Westernism or at least the suspicions harbored against the West. By force, through support or with a combination of both, Russia and China are creating new alliances throughout developing countries, especially in Africa, which is turning away from the old colonial metropoles. After decades of persistent grave errors, the self-proclaimed *Free World* is left with practically no moral right to judge other superpowers, which are doing nothing different that the West itself. No need to add that I personally condemn such hypocrisy, and even more so the actual violence of any of today's *global players* — be it the West, those of the colorful gang of the aforementioned BRICS countries, or the regional *sheriffs*.

Another thing that must not be forgotten are the clear sympathies between Putin and European authoritarians and their supporters, their voters, as well as the strong pro-Russian movements (e.g. in Serbia). In the past, Viktor Orbán, Silvio Berlusconi, Matteo Salvini, Marine Le Pen, Robert Fico, new Serbian *vožd* (leader) Aleksander Vučić and Milorad Dodik, or the Slovenian Zmago Jelinčič stood much more publicly on the side of the Russian dictator with a seemingly illimited expiration date than they do now. But they still share his ideas and practices of authoritarianism, populism, militarism, machismo, chauvinism, islamophobia, homophobia, and similar evil. Other Western politicians used to support him (or still quietly support him), too, such as the former German Chancellor Gerhard Schröder or former French President Nicolas Sarkozy. But the one pathetic compliment that I cannot seem to forget is the one uttered by American President George Bush Jr. when they first met in Brdo pri Kranju, Slovenia, in June 2001: "I looked the man in the eye. I found him to be very straightforward. I was able to get a sense of his soul."

Pragmatic contradictions with cynical solutions go on, at the expense of Ukraine, of course. Prolonging the war is also useful for the NATO hardliners: this alliance can play a more active role again, military budgets fill with no major opposition, membership is increasing, old stocks of arms and equipment are being depleted and new ones are being field-tested. War is an excellent *business opportunity* in the three most profitable industries — think about the Western interventions in Iraq: weapons, construction, and energy industries. *Good money.* In such circumstances, profits soar and just like in any war, the question is who will profit the most — on every involved side. Poor as it is, Ukraine is currently the world's third-largest arms importer, after India and Qatar, and ahead of problematic countries such as Saudi Arabia, Kuwait, and Pakistan.

On one of those May mornings, I was still drowsy after a sleepless night full of drone attacks, when I read that after ten months of constant battle, Bakhmut fell. Bakhmut, the site of fierce battle with strong symbolic meaning, the *Ukrainian Stalingrad* or the *Ukrainian Vukovar*, as media called it. In the afternoon of that same day, the news was denied, then confirmed again, and a couple of days later the *victory/defeat* was no longer mentioned, only that there was *fierce fighting*. This furthered my belief that the battling sides there, as much as on other fronts, are in a stalemate, that the war has turned into trench warfare, a war of attrition. It seems that neither side can pull a quick win, regardless of their military and political efforts; they have reinforced their positions and can try to make minuscule advancements without breaking the front. Two key factors will influence further development: on the one side, Russian nuclear weapons or the threat that it would be used, and the West's so-far-convincing commitment to help Ukraine, on the other. And lastly, none of the leaders can concede; they cannot afford to lose, not even to retreat. Vladimir and Volodymyr — two versions of the same name of two presidents that will face the same destiny if they fail to persist: political death. The stakes are simply too high. If for no other reason than their own political survival, they are betting everything on the military card for the time being.

This card can be either active or passive, offensive or defensive — and I believe the latter will prevail. Putin has gained a lot, realistically the most he could have: in 2014, he occupied around 7 percent of Ukrainian territory; in the spring of 2022, the total was over a quarter. After losing a few percent in the following months, he is now occupying around 18 percent of Ukrainian territory. His focus can now shift from further advancements to integrating the occupied territories into the framework of Russian Federation. For now, the north of Ukraine seems safe. I am no military expert, but it looks like the introductory attack on Kyiv was merely the tried and tested Soviet military tactic of *maskirovka*, a deception. In the meantime, the two main goals, the east and the south of Ukraine, were (almost) reached. On the other hand, local experts explained that the forces advancing towards the capital were receiving misinformation, expecting an easier route — but who can really tell. Be that as it may, the entire maneuver reminded me of Milošević's political poker from mid-1990s: he calmly played the Croatian Serbs' parastate to get the statelet of Bosnian Serbs, Republika Srpska.

I believe Putin follows one of the main tenets of Yeltsin's foreign minister Yevgeny Primakov's foreign policy doctrine of the 1990s, that of the necessity of Russian domination over the post-Soviet states, i.e. a kind of continuation of Brezhnev's policy of *limited sovereignty* of the states in his bloc. In what he sees as a post-Soviet *backyard sphere*, which he still understands as his, i.e. *Russian World*, Putin is leading politics in three ways. Firstly, he is pragmatically renouncing the influence on Baltic states. After the turbulent 1990s, these have gone too far and too deep into *Euro-Atlantic* integration and are in any case a fish too small to be worth the risk. Secondly, he accepts, supports, and holds on a short leash those who are slowly transforming into docile governorates with inclined leaders and an economy dependent on them (Belarus, Kazakhstan, occasionally other Central-Asian post-Soviet countries, and Armenia and Azerbaijan). This also makes them potential allies in the common resistance against various opponents (and an always convenient place for refuge following a hypothetical fall).

If the carrot doesn't do the trick, the stick will. The third version is to follow the Ukrainian, Moldavian, or Georgian script: punish the naughty and disobedient children by engaging in the frozen conflict between local separatists, supported by their protector across the border, and the central government. Neither war nor peace but something between cold war and hot peace. A Tbilisi colleague used similar words to describe the situation in her country: "If Ukraine is confronted with the destructiveness of the Russian war, Georgia is confronted with the destructiveness of the Russian peace, which doesn't look very dramatic from the outside, but is nevertheless deeply destroying Georgian society." As they are literally in the same mess as Ukraine, their support comes as no surprise: from armed volunteers to street interventions both in Ukraine and in Georgia (e.g. graffiti emphasizing their alliance in resisting a common enemy, the flags of the two countries flying together).

The current Chief of the General Staff of the Russian Armed Forces Valery Gerasimov is playing this exact card: he is a proponent of a constant smoldering conflict of low intensity that erases the line between war and peace, combining direct military action with non-military (diplomatic, financial, economic) pressures. This immobilizes the disobedient state, which can consequently be controlled and kept in check, while any of its different ambitions, especially the pro-Western political and institutional ambitions, are crippled. If a country has no full sovereignty on its territory or worse, if it is at war, it cannot join the European Union or NATO, not to mention other reservations if it wants to enter wider economic and political processes. A permanent state of war rather than a short-term victory; a middle- and long-term stalemate — perhaps this is the real goal of Putin's aggression. Since the collapse of Soviet Union, Russia has developed an integrationist politics towards Ukraine, meddled in its internal politics, and pressured it with the Gazprom *gas war* since 2005. Then came the surprising result of the complicated presidential election in 2004, where the pro-Western candidate supported by the protesters of the *Orange Revolution*, beat the pro-Russian candidate and, as a result, Putin developed a much harsher politics towards Ukraine. Ever since, the state has slowly but surely started to lean towards the West more than it did towards Russia — despite fluctuations and setbacks. The very next year, Putin declared that "the collapse of the Soviet Union was the greatest geopolitical catastrophe of the century" with dramatic consequences for the Russians as tens of millions were left outside the Russian borders. My Uzhhorod contact told me that the final incentive for a total war was Zelenskyy's being elected as President of the country in March 2019 — running his candidature by promising to solve the burning conflict with Russia and the issue of the occupied territories in the East and South.

It is impossible to foretell what will happen in the following months and years of this "apocalypse," as Lampreht calls the Ukrainian war. I can only repeat the words of one of two protagonists of the war novel *Toreadors* by Chkvanava, uttered in the lull between the fighting: "No one knows anything in advance"[12] At the moment, I find a sort of permanent ceasefire, but not a permanent peace to be the most probable. An exhausting Korean script of unfinished war, a fragile balance at the tip of the knife. War in Ukraine has been slowly losing the attention of the world's political public and news media, reports from its fronts are no longer on the front pages, supporters and patrons are losing their vigor, compassion is fading into tiredness and fatigue, "transforming it from tragedy to statistics," as Zabuzhko bitterly writes in her sketch story for the anthology *State of War* (2023).[13]

So far, diplomacy has remained silent; regarding the front, there will probably be more fighting talk than actual movement towards either side. A *usual* state of war can gradually calm down and be compensated with *peacetime terrorism. Special operations* (again, I remember the expression and the concept from my own military service) may be reinforced: terrorist actions on civilian targets — be it organized and systematic or planned by the *desperados* who have lost everything in the war and wish to execute a personal revenge. Such massacres have been accompanying every silent war/loud peace: the Troubles (starring IRA with all its fractions, the oppositional loyalist militia, and Great Britain), the Palestinian, Basque, and Kurdish situation, etc., the list is too long to go on. Russia has been facing Chechnyan (or Caucasian Islamists) terrorism since the first war against the secessionists in mid 1990s: remember the massacres at Moscow's Dubrovka Theatre in October 2002, in Beslan in September 2004, or on the Moscow metro in March 2010, which together claimed hundreds of victims. And, ultimately, remember the post-Soviet guerilla fighters after WWII: nicknamed *Forest Brothers, Cursed Soldiers*, etc., who fought up to the Baltic republics and Poland in the North and down to Ukraine in the South until mid-1950s. War is never over once weapons can no longer be heard. It is not only continued by those who cannot accept defeat but especially by those who continue profiting from it.

NOTES

1 Plokhy, Serhii. *The Gates of Europe: A History of Ukraine*, 2021. 316.

2 Ljubka, Andrij. *Karbid*, 2019, translated by Janja Vollmaier Lubej and Primož Lubej. 7.

3 Lyubka, Andriy. *Carbide*, 2023, translated by Reilly Costigan-Humes and Isaac Stackhouse Wheeler. 59.

4 Shore, Marci. *The Ukrainian Night*, 2018. xvi.

5 Plokhy, 2021. 330.

6 Yekelchik, Serhiy. *Ukraine: What Everyone Needs to Know*, 2020. 69.

7 Lyubka, Andriy. Carbide, 2023. 29.

8 Vollmaier Lubej, Janja. *Ukrajinske družbene spremembe v romanu Dvanajst krogov Jurija Andruhoviča*, 2018. 140.

9 Portnikov, Vitaly. *State of War*, 2023. 159.

10 Gogol, Nikolai. *Dead Souls*, 1997, translated by D. J. Hogarth. 236–237.

11 Gogol, Nikolai. *Taras Bulba*, 1917, translated by Isabel F. Hapgood. 284.

12 Chkvanava, Gela. *Toreadors*, 2013. 126.

13 Zabuzhko, Oksana. *State of War*, 2023. 219.

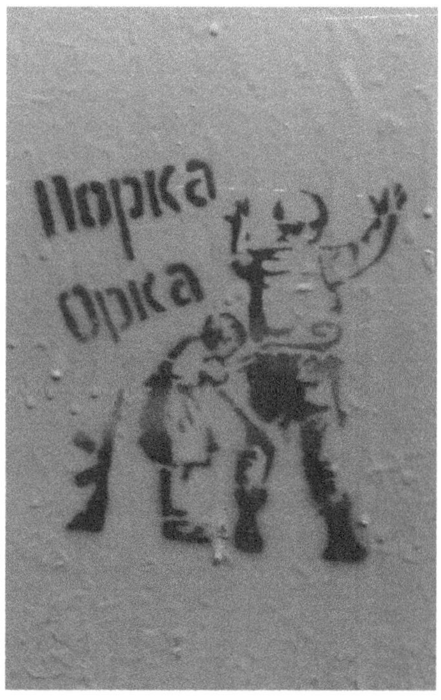

"Frisk the Orc," Lviv, May 2023.

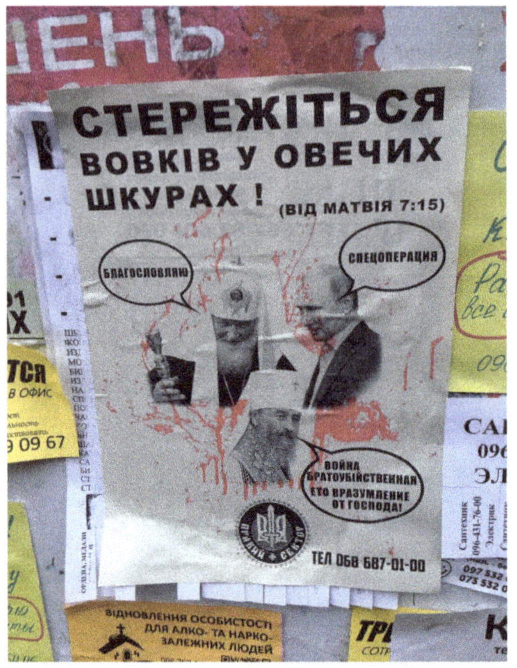

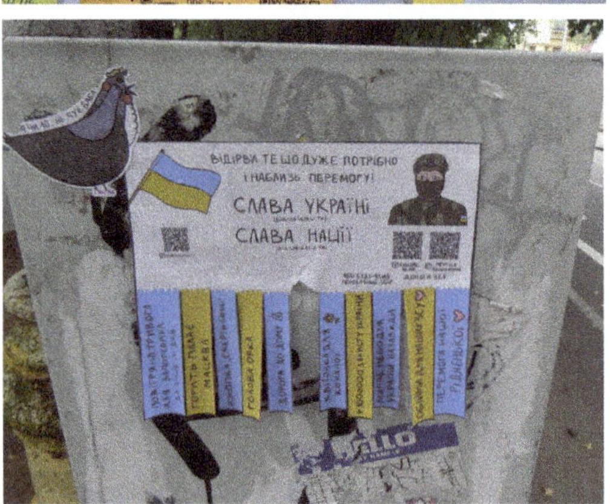

Top: *"Beware of wolves in sheeps' clothing! (Matthew 7:15)," a poster by Right Sector, a coalition of right-wing and nationalist organizations, warning against the anti-Ukrainian alliance of Russian secular and religious powers, featuring Putin and Patriarch Kiril, Kyiv, May 2023.*

Bottom: *"Rip off something you really need to make victory closer! Glory to Ukraine! Glory to the nation!" with QR code for donations and tabs for things like a "death button" for your enemies or "flower for your lover," and other comments on the war, Uzhhorod, August 2023.*

IV

IDEOLOGIES OF WAR

> *"Ukraine is a game to you!?"*
> *an angry Ukrainian to Newman and Kramer on a*
> *New York subway, where the two are playing "Risk" and*
> *Kramer speaks disparagingly of his country.*
> Seinfeld, "The Label Maker," 1995.

As always and everywhere, nationalistic radicalization of Ukrainian society is a consequence of *Realpolitik* — a politics of practical interests — and not its cause. The ideological trick of nationalism is to *a posteriori* reinterpret political conflicts as ethnic (and/or religious) — from the end of the Cold War, in line with the famous Huntington thesis of *the clash of civilizations*. The seductive simplicity of nationalism replaces cause with effect. Wars are fought by countries that are always and only exclusively in the hands of the ruling elites and that monopolize violence while pursuing their own goals. But to do so, they need slowly ethnified masses: the real victory of any fighting side is not a victory against the other side but can be seen when the power holders persuade and mobilize people in the conflict for their own interests and through their transmission apparatuses. When they achieve, to use a Gramscian term, ideological dominance over them.

To accept the explanation that *the Russians are fighting against the Ukrainians*, would mean to be irretrievably caught in the loop of the ruling interpretations of war. Following a tested method, these ethnify, culturalize, and historicize war, seek civilizational incompatibilities, historical grievances, and inherently conflicting *national characters* between nations — in the past months and years, we have seen, read, or listened to more than enough of this. But what they are forgetting is the essence: (geo)political factors. When interpreting this war, too, a materialist turn must be made: ethnopolitics is the consequence and not the cause of the pragmatic *Realpolitik*. Contemporary wars are largely fought by mercenaries, soldiers of fortune, militias, private soldiers, *security companies* — not just states and much less *nations*, as some tendentiously insist. The same situation applies on the fronts of Ukraine, where the Russian regular army fights side by side with the infamous private military companies of Wagner, Redut, and Patriot, as well as the Sparta, Somalia, and Rusich militia (the latter with distinctly Great-Russian, as well as neo-Nazi ideology and symbolism), or the Chechnya units (*Kadyrovites*), which are sponsored or at least supported by Russia. I can also include the Night Wolves Motorcycle Club, supporters of Putin, the Great Russian ideology, and Orthodoxy, who get up to anything from organizing concerts and managing clubs to engaging in the conflict with Ukraine (how significant it is that they ride America's most prestigious Harley-Davidson motorcycles!). *Volunteers* from virtually all over the world are fighting on both sides. The Ukrainian side is helped by battalions of Chechens, Belarusians, Georgians, and even anti-Putin Russians (in the Freedom of Russia Legion and in the Russian Insurgent Army). Military engagement of *contractors* is therefore similar to those in other crisis hotspots all over the world, which make the covers of the magazines or are featured as top news only if the footage contains enough images of devastation, dead bodies, and thick black smoke rising above them. Similarities with the activities of groups and companies such as Triple Canopy or Blackwater/Academi, which were involved in shady activities and dealings in post-war Iraq and Afghanistan, are self-evident.

I will repeat: this is an aggression led by Putin's regime, the regular army of the Russian Federation, and the mercenaries against the neighboring sovereign state of Ukraine although the two states have repeatedly assured each other of the respect and inviolability of post-Soviet borders.

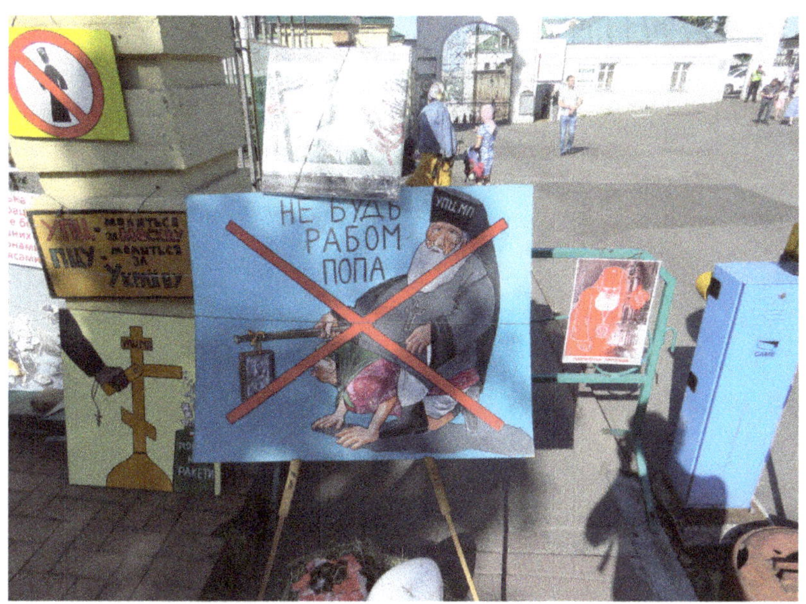

Entrance to the Kyiv-Pechersk Lavra monastic complex, Kyiv, May 2023.

Despite the complexities of the more distant history, and despite the far from simple, far from black-and-white recent history, the fact remains that the former attack and the latter defend, not vice versa: the end, full stop, *ende, fin.* There is no excuse for a full military attack — not even the new geostrategic orientation of the sovereign state of Ukraine or the provocations of Ukrainian nationalists, as hurtful as they may be. Russian invasion has its own political and military leadership — Putin's impermeable circle — and its military ideology justified by Great Russian imperialism. Declaring the West-supported *Ukrainian nationalism* or its extreme form, *Ukrainian neo-Nazism* as a convenient excuse, Putin justified his actions as *protecting the Russian people* and *demilitarizing and de-Nazifying Ukraine.* Let's ground these high-sounding words: there are two main and almost attained goals of this attack, and they are both very "practical" and useful. The first is the geo-strategically important Crimean Peninsula with its military bases on the Black Sea coasts; the second is the so-called Novorossiya (gradually conquered by imperial Russia in the 18th century) with Donetsk, Luhansk, and the southern parts of Kherson and Zaporizhia, rich in grain, mines, heavy industry, and ports.

Today, Ukraine is the stage for an ideological, not only a military or political fight. Internally, there are two fighting nationalisms, as the countries' official ideologies both insist on ethnic homogenization — the Russification of Russia on the one hand and the Ukrainization of Ukraine on the other. No nationalist in any place or time would disagree that *our country is for our people only.* The main difference between these two nationalisms lies elsewhere: in self-perception and in foreign policy ambitions. Shevtsova asserts that the "Ukrainian public does not lay claim to great-power status" and "the great majority of Ukrainians are prepared to join the West"; while in Russia "the political class continues to foster popular phobias and complexes, insisting that Russia is fated to glory and a special destiny."[1] At the moment, Ukrainian nationalism is largely pro-Western, while Russian nationalism is largely anti-Western.

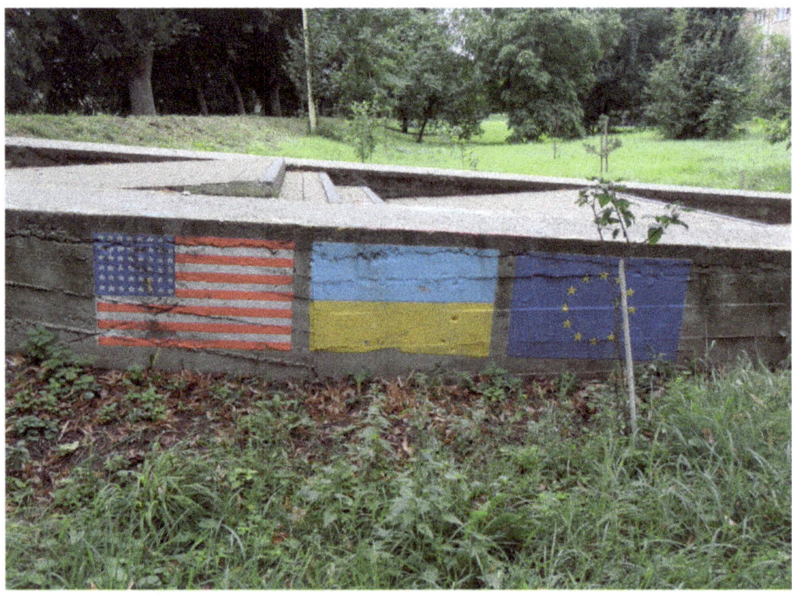

Uzhhorod, August 2023.

   Ukrainian Vignettes: Essays on a Culture at War

The idea of Russia's chosenness, messianism and, consequently, imperialism — be it in their tzarist and Russian Orthodox version or their Bolshevik version (written on extensively by different writers such as Anton Rupnik, Zagreb sociologist Nikola Dugandžija, or the exiled Georgian social democrat Noe Zhordania almost a century ago) — brings the extreme nationalist, conservative, traditionalist right wing together with the right wing that is only proclaiming to be left wing based on its anti-Westernism, illiberalism, and the resistance to global capitalism. Together, they form a brown-red coalition in principle and in practice. Its political specter includes everyone from Eurasian-nationalist philosopher (such as Aleksandr Dugin) to artists (such as Aleksey Beliayev Guintovt); from extreme right-wing national-Bolshevik politicians (such as Vladimir Zhirinovsky, who died from Covid only a few weeks after the attack) to new old communists (such as Gennady Zyuganov); from soccer hooligans to military volunteers, who have been recruited for crisis areas since 2014. Many credible first-hand information on the topic can be found in an excellent book on nationalism and protest in post-Soviet Russia (2020) by Fabrizio Fenghi, researcher of contemporary Russian art and politics.

All of these mentioned groups have two things in common. Firstly, they strongly support Putin's Great-Russian foreign policy, especially the one aimed at *Ukrainian junta*, the *neo-Nazis*, *Banderites*, etc. Just like elsewhere in the world, a large part in this was played by the national minority that had been set against them. Fifteen years before the first battles, Rupnik had the amazing insight to predict that this is what could endanger Ukraine's territorial integrity, especially in the densely populated East and South. Ukrainian nationalists saw it as an extended arm of imperialist policy, which is not entirely true. Data shows that more than a half of Ukrainian Russians voted "for" Ukrainian independence at the referendum on 1 December 1991 (which was won easily, with 92.3 percent and with the majority of the voters supporting the Act of Independence in every oblast, in the Crimean autonomous republic, and in the special municipalities of Sevastopol and Kyiv).

The second thing they have in common is the continuation of the possessive, condescending and insulting or, in short, de-nationing Great-Russian attitude towards Ukrainians. Since Imperial Russia and the later, asymmetric Soviet federation, Ukrainians have been considered *Little Russians*, *khokhols*, *rednecks*, and *little brothers*, whatever name they used to denote their provinciality, while their ethnic and linguistic differences were contested along with their political tradition. There were also many Russians with whom I have talked about the relationship between the two nations, who pointed out the paternalistic, sometimes openly humiliating relations towards Ukrainians, their language and basically anything Ukrainian in daily life. In the best-case scenario, nationalists saw Ukrainians — along with Belarus — as a part of the whole, triune, all-Russian nation. To quote American literary historian Edyta M. Bojanowska, ethnic kinship represented "an argument for imperial rule and a license to punish political insubordination" or "an argument for compulsion and entrapment."[2] Putin is convinced that Russian and Ukrainians are one people: he spoke publicly about this before the occupation of Crimea and after it. Until this day, there are fierce discussions and appropriations of history among Russian and Ukrainian autochthonists — historians, journalists, politicians, artists — on issues from who inherits the Kievan Rus' to the heritage of the Soviet Union. These "battles for history" reveal another paradox of contemporary historiography and social sciences in general: it is difficult to analyze the old times as they are too distant and as we don't have enough facts, evidence, and testimonies — while it is equally difficult to draw conclusions about current events as they are too close and as there is an abundance of different facts, evidence, and testimonies.

Despite the concerns about the usefulness of analogies in analytical thinking, similar happenings in the Balkans provide an easy ground for comparisons. On the one hand, the expansive, offensive, great-national ideologies and their concrete political (and military) campaigns, i.e. the Serbian, Greek, Croatian, and Albanian versions of the *great-national idea*, the *Megali Idea*. On the other hand, the more introverted Bosniak or

Slovenian nationalism, which does not want to expand externally, but follows the goal of an internal ethnic homogenization, by choice or by force. In the case of recent Slovenian history, this reached its sad peak in the previously mentioned unpunished crime called the Erasure.

Ukrainian (counter-)nationalism follows this latter, defensive model — but just like the offensive one, this one also follows the wider repressive ethnonationalist logic of contemporary nation-state creation and organization. In the last ten, and especially in the last two years, two diametrically opposite sides have been blowing it out of proportion. The Russian and pro-Russian side is potentiating it exponentially: Ukrainian nationalism is *neo-Nazism* with *genocidal* tendencies towards the Russians (just like the last Balkans war labelled the Croatians as a *genocidal nation* and all Serbians as the followers of the *Great-Serbian* idea, etc.). The other side, the Ukrainian and the pro-Ukrainian one is minimizing the current Ukrainian nationalism, almost making it a taboo — it is as if it did not exist; at the same time understood as something positive, defensive, as *patriotism*. This side has the same alibi than the Bosniak nationalists in Bosnia-Herzegovina or the Albanians in Kosovo had: both were the attacked sides. But like I've been saying since the beginning: being inclined towards something does not include being uncritical, blindly apologetic, and understanding when it comes to the (armed) extremists on the side you find closer or is even your own. No serious research of the situation in Ukraine and no serious author, no matter how strongly they feel for the *Ukrainian cause*, is uncritical to the history and the present of Ukrainian extreme nationalism that features anti-Russian, anti-Polish, antisemitic, and other anti-elements. The same goes for my home environment and the critic of Slovenian nationalism, which was first anti-German and anti-Italian, then strongly anti-Balkans, and now anti-refugee.

So, yes, of course, just like most contemporary countries, Ukraine is constitutively ethno-political, too. In a typical and, again, universal — it can be found practically everywhere — patriotic *pathos*, its supporters see it as *soft power*, its resistance as a *just war*, its fighters engaged in a new

Battle of Thermopylae, differentiating from its enemies because of their *mutual connection of love and tenderness*. They see a *civilizational chasm* between them and the Russians, they tie their homeland to the words such as *pride, freedom, self-determination*, they describe their nation as *heroic* and as a giver of new life to Western civilization, etc. Essentialist exaggerations on the integrality of Ukrainian identity are present even in art projects, where a higher degree of criticism is to be expected; let me only mention two, DNA UA (cinema) and Ukrainian DNA (a project at the 2023 Venice architecture biennale).

But in times of crisis, ethno-politics can easily blow into extreme nationalism. Whenever Russian or Ukrainian or any other nationalism is condemned, we must realize our own nationalism and condemn it as one of two main ideologies and political practices of today. The more there are pressures of Great-Russian nationalism and imperialism (some openly call it *Russian fascism* or merge the two words to form *Ruscism* or *Rashism*), the more the other side responds with extremes (neo-Nazism, white supremacism, new alt-right versions of fascism, etc.). Sadly, these are numerous, too, and span everything from individual and spontaneous to organized and even structural varieties.

This is why I believe every country, especially when it is at war, should not use problematic symbols and burdening references from the recent past. Certain circles, also the official ones aside from the *usual suspects* such as football fans and right-wing hooligans, celebrate the Ukrainian 14th Waffen Grenadier Division of the SS. The division was also charged with serious war crimes. (Which makes the reception and the standing ovation given to its surviving member in Canadian parliament in September 2023 even more conspicuous: he was praised as a *Ukrainian and Canadian hero*. A few days later, the ensuing international scandal cost Canada's House speaker his position and is merely another typical example of how colossally uneducated the ruling political caste is.) The salute *Glory to Ukraine! To the heroes — glory!* has been widely accepted and can be heard literally everywhere from the President's speeches, army, media, and schools, to foreign statespeople and political leaders (from former American president Bill Clinton to President of the European Commission Ursula von der Leyen). It originates in the Ukrainian War of Independence of 1917 and was later adopted by the League of Ukrainian Nationalists and the Ukrainian Insurgent Army. The latter fought against the Soviet, but also against the Nazi army, while it also collaborated with it in the joint resistance against the Red Army. This fact and the systematic antisemitic and anti-Polish views and campaigns makes the salute compromised for many at home and abroad. Although many protesters have distanced themselves from it during both Maidan revolutions, claims Shore (2017)[3] among others, the salute remains popular.

The same goes for historical personalities, especially for Stepan Bandera (1909–1959) and Roman Shukhevych (1907–1950). Their images appear on stamps, in the names of the streets, in restaurant decorations, on commemorative coins and souvenirs, and, of course, on memorials (*daddy* Bandera, to use the expression from Ukrainian rural tradition, himself has over 40 monuments!). They are the subjects of odes and museums, they are found in textbooks and among patriotic paraphernalia. Anti-Soviet resistance is a great excuse for their proven collaboration with the enemy, antisemitism, extreme nationalism, and persecution of Poles and anti-fascists — something they did along with many other *patriots* and *freedom fighters*. Posthumously awarded the title of *Hero of Ukraine* (which was immediately contested), they became a hotbed of internal political struggles in today's Ukraine   between the liberal intelligentsia, the left wing, the pro-Western and the pro-Russian politicians — as well as in the concerned international public (provoking harsh responses from Poland, Russia, European Union, and various Jewish and anti-Nazi organizations). Among those who strongly criticized Bandera's rehabilitation was famous American historian and expert on Eastern Europe Timothy Snyder in a *New York Review* article with the telling title of "A Fascist Hero in Democratic Kiev." Sceptics will argue that there are countless controversial *fathers of a nation* and wonder if there is any non-contaminated historical persona

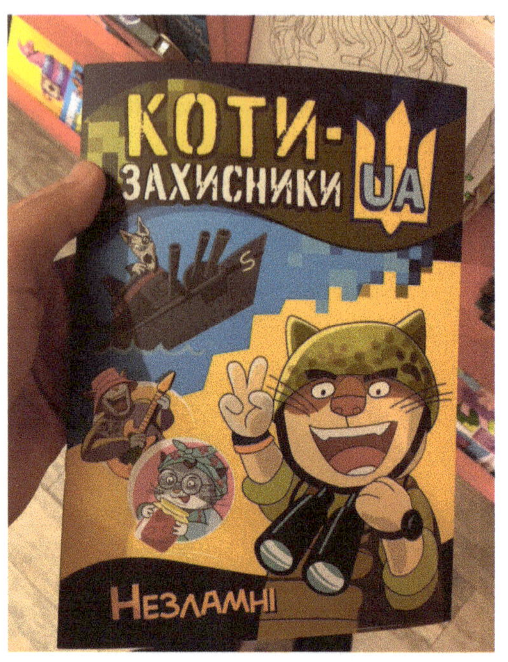

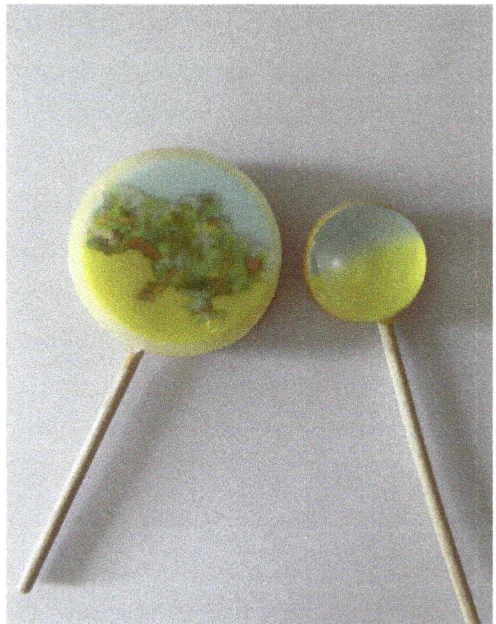

Top to bottom: Comic book, Lviv, May 2023;
Lollipops, Mykolaiv, June 2024.

or event at all. Surely not, as the fact of being historical personae is what makes them painfully fatal for both sides — but it also doesn't mean that they should be non-critically accepted or even emphatically praised.

If the official propaganda of one side praises Putin (and Stalin), it cannot be more wrong than to praise controversial historical and present personas on the other side. Pro-Ukrainian authors try to lessen or relativize such compromising: Yekelchik (2020) claims that "in present-day Ukrainian mass culture, Bandera functions more as a recognizable symbol of anti-Russian resistance, a vague protest statement not unlike the image of Che Guevara on a t-shirt," that "the image of Bandera acquired new meaning as a symbol of resistance to the corrupt, Russian-sponsored regime, quite apart from the historical Bandera's role as a purveyor of exclusivist ethno-nationalism." He also states that the mentioned "nationalist greeting from the 1940s, 'Slava Ukraini!' (Glory to Ukraine!)" referred "to a hoped-for democratic and pro-Western Ukraine and regarded as heroes those who had fallen in service to their cause."[4]

Social and political tensions, especially in combination with external threats, are causing the rise of extreme nationalism everywhere in the world and Ukraine is no exception. In the recent decade, they gave wings to movements such as the Right Sector (and the Patriot of Ukraine before it) and the National Corps party, both of which are practically irrelevant on the party map. On the last two elections, in 2014 and 2019, the extreme right wing did not make it to the parliament. More popular — and loud — are the Azov movement and paramilitary entity and the Sich Battalion with their openly extremist agenda: they are extreme right wing, chauvinist, neo-Nazi, homophobe, and antisemitic. Lately, there have been attempts at taking that ideological edge off their character, but experts are divided whether this is true or not. As such, they are mirror image of the aforementioned paramilitary units on the Russian side, starting with Wagner. How symptomatic it is that both share neo-Nazi ideology and symbolism. This includes the sad classics of swastika and *valknut*, the *Black Sun* or the *sunwheel*, and the *kolovrat spoked wheel*, a double swastika, which is the

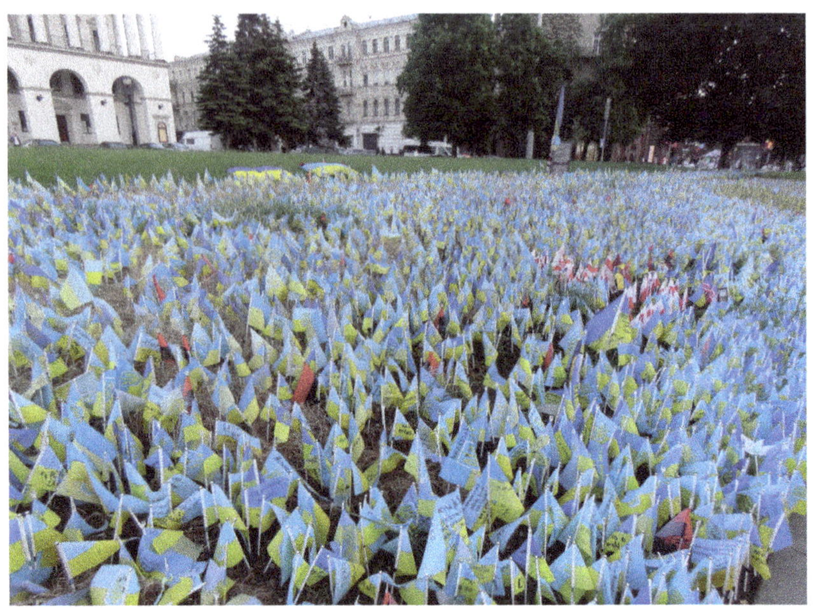

Maidan, Kyiv, May 2023.

symbol of extreme-right ideology, a pan-Slavism and white supremacism. I was on my second trip to Ukraine when a commander of the Russian neo-Nazi militia Rusich, Yan Petrovsky, was detained in Finland on charges of war crimes and Ukraine immediately requested extradition.

The unsanctioned existence of the extremist military unit itself, along with the public support they are receiving from the nationalist part of the society, and even the state's blind eye, as Colborne writes in his book (2022), definitely keep the anti-nationalists at home and abroad from sympathizing with the attacked country. Colborne ends with stating that "the Azov movement's continued presence on Ukraine's social and political scene, even as it remains forever the preserve of a small minority, poses a threat to liberal democracy in Ukraine."[5] I heard this deep dilemma from many people I spoke with: although these units are putting up a strong resistance against Putin's attack, they simply cannot accept them as their own. They don't have anything in common with these units, and they don't want to have anything in common with them as it is crystal clear

    Ukrainian Vignettes: Essays on a Culture at War

that, once the war is finished, they can be their next target, as they do not conform to their political ideology. They cannot agree with the logic that these extremists, no matter how small their numbers are in comparison with the entirety of the Ukrainian army, defend them from the attacking extremists: they are averse to both their *own* and the *foreign* ones. And most fatal of all, the existence of these paramilitary units serves Putin as a convenient propaganda argument: the entire country is like this, *genocidal* and *Russophobe*, led by *neo-Nazis* and *drug addicts*! Several people I contacted complained that one of the most frequent questions about the war if not the most frequent one involves the Azov Brigade and other extremists — not everybody else who is defending Ukraine. "It's really annoying," I heard from two colleagues discussing how they receive the most coverage, both at home and abroad, in a good and in a bad way.

Looking at the phenomenon of neo-Nazism from a wider perspective, I can describe it by turning the phrase *same, same, but different* the other way around: *different, different, but the same*. Neo-Nazism, white supremacism, extreme nationalism, etc., are far from being local features. I am sad to say that they can be found on ideological levels as well as in concrete political practices, and even in the form of armed militants all over the world — including the self-proclaimed *cradles of democracy* such as Europe and the United States. Russian and Ukrainian extremists bearing swastikas on their sleeves and hearts are only more open in displaying something that is ignored in other places until it explodes (like it did in Norway during the Utøya and Oslo attacks, in New Zealand during the Christchurch shootings, during the Capitol attack in Washington, or during attacks on refugees, to name but a few tragic examples).

One of the foundations of Ukrainian nationalism — starting with their anthem, which begins with *Ukraine has not yet perished*, akin to the Polish anthem — is self-victimization. In *To My Fellow-Countrymen, in Ukraine and not in Ukraine, Living, Dead and as Yet Unborn My Friendly Epistle*, Shevchenko addresses Ukraine with these words:

Come, my brothers, and embrace
Each your humblest brother,
Make our mother smile again,
Our poor, tear-stained mother![6]

We are therefore seeing a continued a unilateral history of aggression and discrimination of the Ukrainian people by neighboring nations and imperial countries, especially of course Russia and the Soviet Union. An important point in this history is the Ukrainian Famine (*Holodomor*), which took the lives of between three and four million Ukrainian people in 1932–1933 and which more than 30 countries all over the world consider a genocide. Although the famine hit other parts of the federation, as well, Plokhy (2021) claims that "only in Ukraine did it result from policies with clear ethnonational coloration."[7] It coincided with Stalin's reversal of the 1920s policy of *Ukrainization*, the campaign of *dekulakization,* and the pogrom against the local leadership and artists. Namely, the purpose of early Soviet Ukrainization, encouraged in the wider process of *korenizatsiia*, i.e. the support for the development of local identities which ended in mid 1930s, was to bring the Soviet Federation closer to the Ukrainian people.

Because of the history of Great-Russian cultural and linguistic domination and its assimilation politics, a loud or silent *Russification* of mainly urban populations, today's process of Ukrainization of public life — a sort of cultural and linguistic decolonialization — can be understood. I read that even twelve years ago a larger part of printed newspapers, magazines and books, music played on radio stations, and TV programs in Ukraine was in Russian. "Let's drop the Little Russian identity" appeals Zhadan in his war diary.[8] Defined as "gentle Ukrainization" by its proponents in the 1990s, after the invasions in 2014 and 2022 required and enforced as "conscious Ukrainization" by more determined advocates, it was criticized from the beginning as "forced Ukrainization" by its opponents.

The position of victim can justify revenge and radical, i.e. just as painful, retaliatory measures, while the *righting of wrongs*, if it is not well thought out and delicately executed, can lead to new injustices: the pendulum effect, which was also happening in the Balkans. Although mostly defensive, Ukrainian nationalism "was always full of anti-Russian sentiment," claims Rupnik,[9] and was no less offensive towards other ethnic and religious groups, such as the Poles, the Jews, also the Tatars. I repeat my previous thought: if chauvinists on one side hate the Ukrainian nation, language, and culture, if they recognize none of these, the worst thing to do for the other side is to do the same, to only mirror their violence. I do not believe (counter-)nationalism to be the answer to nationalism. In these situations, I often remembered how Friedrich Nietzsche warned in *Beyond Good and Evil*: "He who fights with monsters should be careful lest he thereby become a monster."

In my academic and artistic *bubble* of hosts and elsewhere, in random chats, I personally felt no anti-Russian sentiment — in contrast to much anti-Great-Russian resentment, which is now bearing the face of Putin. On the other hand, I did feel reticence and discomfort toward anything connected to Russia, Russian culture, language, or music. Until the relations between the two countries became more tense, the native tongue of many was Russian even though they ethnically defined themselves as Ukrainian and that they are only learning Ukrainian as adults. No affection, not

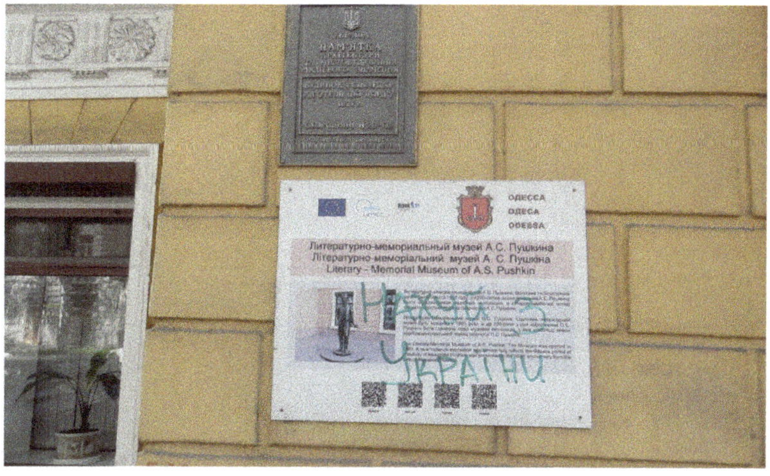

"Get away from Ukraine" graffiti, Pushkin Museum, Odesa, May 2023.

even similar to the position of Adam Michnik, who defines himself as an *anti-Soviet Rusofile*; I met no *anti-Putin Rusofile* — at least none that would admit it to me.

In the wider public, however, this is wide-spread: too easily, Russians and Russia are equated with Putin; Great-Russian imperialism and chauvinism with Russian culture and art in general. A few years ago, especially Western Ukraine began to temporarily prohibit the performance of any artistic, cultural, or educational works not only by Russian artists but in the Russian language. Kyiv followed this in July 2023 with an explanation that this is *the language of the aggressor*. The country prohibited the import and the distribution of Russian books and the broadcasting of Russian music (apart from those musicians who have explicitly declared to be against Russian occupation) — even music performed by street musicians. Since 2017, a law has been in force guaranteeing a 75% quota of Ukrainian-language programming on all their TV channels. PEN Ukraine, the Ukrainian Book Institute, and a string of other cultural institutions have appealed to the world public to non-selectively boycott Russian publishing houses and books in general that they believe to be "affected by Russian propaganda)"; their PEN is also refusing any contact with Russian writers and participation in joint events abroad until war and the occupation end, which is why I was not surprised to see a sticker with a seal dressed in Odessa Brigade uniform saying:" Everyone who appeared on 'Russia Today' as an expert, a guest of the studio or otherwise, should be stigmatized, including the damned Slavoj Žižek."

Such moves are supported by many other prominent individuals and civil society movements. Among the more vocal ones are *Vidsich* (best translated as *Rebuff*), which call for a boycott of everything Russian on Ukrainian soil (from language, movies, music, or culture in general, to Russian goods and fuels). Political street art joins the movement — an Azov poster urges: *Join the de-Russification of Ukraine*; I found a billboard that said *Speak Ukrainian — because the enemy doesn't know how to*; helped by Google Translate, I read a sticker in the colors of the Ukrainian flag: *I don't understand Russian — In a year, everything will be in Ukrainian*. And there it is again — a flashback to similar language cleaning campaigns after every transition. (While leafing through old books, another weird hobby of mine, I discover something similar. This was written in a special sub-chapter of *Slovenian language practice books for year 4 of primary school*, approved by the Ministry of Education of the People's Republic of Slovenia in Ljubljana in 1947, titled *Cleanse our language of foreign expressions!* "Foreign expressions are corrupting our language. Foreign masters have imposed them on us through centuries of serfdom. But now the Slovenian people are their own master. Let us therefore **cleanse** our language of unnecessary foreign expressions. **Let the Slovenian language be pure!** Let us compete at home and at school for the eradication of all unnecessary foreign expressions from our mother tongue!" (original emphasis, author's note) These expressions specifically include German, Italian, and Hungarian words; after the next *liberation* at the beginning of the 1990s, the list of *eradicated* words also included Serbo-Croatian expressions.)

And lastly, to slowly bring the arc of ideological backgrounds of this unfortunate war to an end: just like the post-Yugoslav wars, this one is also strongly marked with a religious element, with the church, to be more precise. Integralist tendencies, i.e. equating religious and national identity, are appearing — and coming true on the Russian and on the Ukrainian side. Orthodox churches follow the ancient Byzantine tradition of *symphonia*, mutual collaboration and support between the state and the church — something that sociologist of religion Marjan Smrke wrote about extensively. Every leader is supposed to be *God's Messiah*, including Putin, who is purported to be *God's Miracle*. Here, like in other larger churches and religious communities in post-socialist countries, the prevalent currents are conservative, fundamentalistic, politicking, revanchist, and sometimes great-national; more liberal and ecumenical currents are in the minority. The Russian Orthodox Church has always supported the Great-Russian idea and regimes — even during Soviet repression of the churches, it achieved the repression of the Ukrainian Greek Catholic

Church, and it took over its property. The *Uniates* returned to the religious map only after independence; today, they are the second largest religious community in the country.

The first remains the Orthodox Church of Ukraine, formed in December 2018 and officially recognized by the Ecumenical Patriarch in January 2019 through the merger of two existing churches: the Ukrainian Orthodox Church of the Kyiv Patriarchate and the Ukrainian Autocephalous Orthodox Church, which are joined by hundreds of parishes and their bishops of a third organization, the Ukrainian Orthodox Church of the Moscow Patriarchate. To make matters even more complicated, in May 2022 the latter announced its independence from the mother Moscow Patriarchate and proclaimed itself an independent orthodox church in Ukraine (officially, the Ukrainian Orthodox Church). It has strained relations not only with the previously mentioned Orthodox Church of Ukraine, but also with the state, which it suspects of dual loyalties, if not fifth-column activities. The famous picturesque Kyiv monastery, the Kyiv-Pechersk Lavra, otherwise under the purview of the Orthodox Church of Ukraine, supposedly still houses many pro-Moscow oriented orthodox monks, the *puppets* of Patriarch Kirill of Moscow and Putin, as their opponents call them. Ukrainian authorities are chasing them out of the country, while militant and loud protesters are camped in front of the complex. Due to their numbers, various formats and techniques, and especially the force of their messages, their banners would deserve a longer analysis. Perhaps someday; I made numerous photographs just in case and keep them in a special folder.

While the Ecumenical Patriarch of Constantinople has recognized this new orthodox church, the leadership of the Russian Orthodox Church, the Russian political leadership and, explicitly, Putin, of course do not recognize the *secession*, nor do other orthodox churches (among the most prominent, besides the Russian one, the Romanian, and Serbian ones), which are in the best case reticent in this regard. The Russian Orthodox Church simply keeps annexing orthodox parishes of the occupied territories in

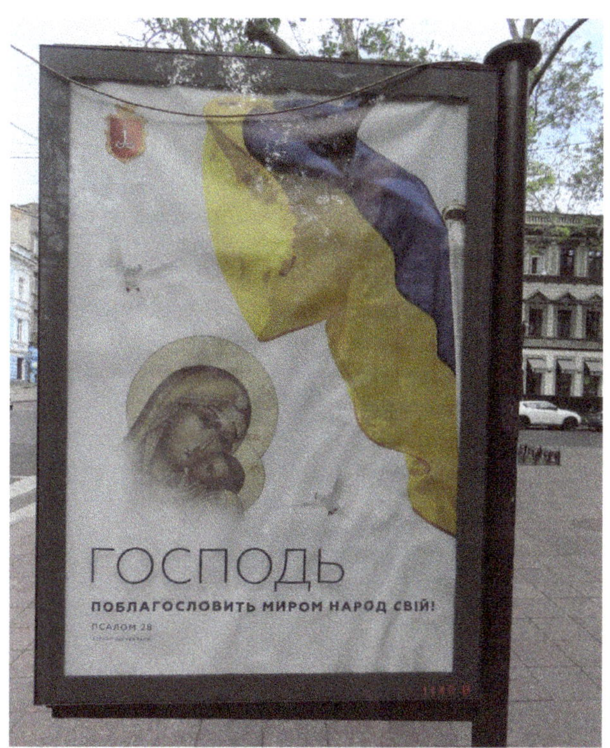

"Dear Lord, Bless your people with peace," Odesa, May 2023.

the East and South into its jurisdiction and organization. Its Patriarch, Kirill has repeatedly publicly and unconditionally defended Putin's war, repeating his arguments and syntaxes and, of course, blessing the troops. This is reflected in a Kyiv poster covered in red paint (i.e. blood) showing the two and warning: *Beware of wolves in sheep's clothing!*,[10] while their proponent Onufriy, bishop of the Ukrainian Orthodox Church, explains that the fratricidal war is an act of God. On the side of Ukraine, I noticed prayers for the protection of the homeland, as well as calls for prayers for peace, *Peace Relays*, and similar anti-war activities. We can see blatant political interference in the ecclesiastical sphere, too: President Zelenskyy has signed a law which, from 2023, moves Christmas from 7 January of the following year, as in the (Russian) Orthodox calendar, to 25 December of the year, as in the parts of the world with a Catholic cultural and religious basis. He explained this with the need to "renounce the Russian heritage."

Religious nationalism has the same structure, and extremely similar syntagms and maledictions everywhere. Russian separatists are repeating slogans such as *God is on our side* and *Russia is on our side*. On the side of Ukraine, I have found analog slogans of *God is with us; Christ is risen, Ukraine is Risen*; *Pray for Ukraine*; and, of course, *The Lord will bless his people with peace*, along with other various ways of expressing gratitude and supplication toward God. With the help of a translator, I read *We work for victory! God and Ukraine are with us!* on the wall of a factory. Street installations and posters often feature a cross or images of Jesus and Mary on one side, and armed Ukrainian soldiers, a map, or the national flag on the other. Roofs of many churches and chapels are covered with distinctive blue and golden/yellow roof tiles or roof plates, imitating Ukrainian national colors. The new national holiday, *Defenders Day*, coincides with the Orthodox holiday dedicated to the Virgin Mary, which falls on 14 October in the Julian calendar. Spraypainting stencils, signed by Banderivets all through Ukrainian towns, chose *God, Ukraine, Freedom!* as their slogan. Religious symbols are becoming landmarks of everyday life, as well: the cross is now the official emblem of the Armed Forces of Ukraine and an extremely popular pendant, especially for young girls. I took photos of graffiti of the Ukrainian coat-of-arms, with the cross rising from the middle arrow of the trident, implying ethnic and religious unity. On a Christmas postcard, the carolers wearing national costumes are protected by an oversize soldier accompanied by an angel on either side. In one word: "Christo-Slavism," as the mix of Christian mythology with the different Slavic national ideologies was described by critical American sociologist of religion Michael A. Sells.

But let us take a step back: waving God around is not a rarity in the contemporary, supposedly enlightened political discourse of today. *God bless ...!* we hear, read, and see everywhere on the political map. Also in the West, which loves to boast of its *civilizational achievement* separating church and state. In the Balkans, the post-socialist transition and its most tragic dimension, war, drove the secularized masses back to churches and mosques. In this process, the opportunists are, of course, on the front lines — usually those with an exemplary party career in the previous system. In Slovenia, I find it tragically comical when I hear such elated words from the mouths of former promising youth.

Allow me to bring my musings on the ideological bases of war to a close with a famous saying by Churchill: "The first casualty in war is truth." The warring sides in Ukraine are calling each other *Nazis, fascists, terrorists*, accusing each other of *genocide*, drawing swastikas on the flag and Hitler's hairstyle and moustache on the caricatures of opposing leaders. As national ideologies of state, Russian nationalism is definitely expansive, Ukrainian nationalism defensive. In its core, every nationalism (or, to use a euphemism, *patriotism, love for the homeland*) is exclusive: patriarchal, conservative, primordial, anti-liberal, and — in various ways and degrees — potentially homo- and Islamophobic, antisemitic, racist, militantly anti-leftist. The usual. Even though it is developed by the attacked and wounded side, many still find it alien, and it can only serve to reinforce the position that I stated in the beginning: to stay critical despite feeling affection towards the ones I feel closer to. Or perhaps because of it.

NOTES

1 Shevtsova, Lilia. *Russia. Lost in Transition: The Yeltsin and Putin Legacies*, 2007, translated by Arch Tait. 297.

2 Bojanowska, Edyta M. "Pushkin's 'To the Slanderers of Russia': The Slavic Question, Imperial Anxieties, and Geopolitics," 2019. 25.

3 Shore, Marci. *The Ukrainian Night*, 2017. 54–55.

4 Yekelchyk, Serhiy. *Ukraine: What Everyone Needs to Know*, 2020. 50, 97.

5 Colborne, Michael. *From the Fires of War: Ukraine's Azov Movement and the Global Far Right*, 2022. 151.

6 Shevchenko, Taras. *To My Fellow-Countrymen, In Ukraine and Not In Ukraine, Living, Dead and as Yet Unborn My Friendly Epistle*, translated by Vera Rich.

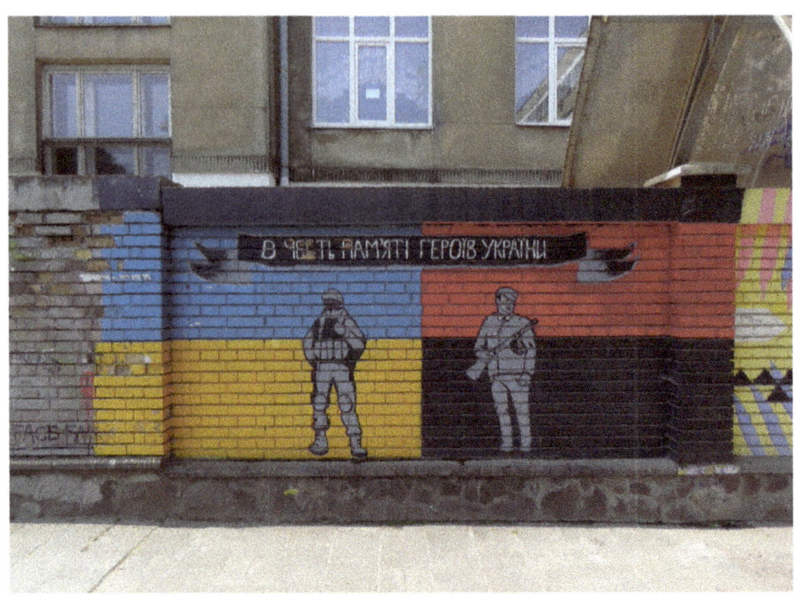

"In honor and memory of heroes of Ukraine!" Lviv, May 2023.

7 Plokhy, Serhii. *The Gates of Europe: A History of Ukraine*, 2021. 254. For meticulous collections of different materials, sources, documents and research about holodomor, see Klid and Motyl (2022) and Applebaum (2017).

8 Zhadan, Serhiy. *Sky Above Kharkiv: Dispatches from the Ukrainian Front.* 27.

9 Rupnik, Anton. *Tretji Rim.* 275.

10 Matthew 7:15.

V

EVERYDAY LIVES OF WAR

"To every time, its own 'normality'. The once terrible was now common-place, meaning that people accepted it as the norm and went on living..."
Andrey Kurkov, *Death and the Penguin*, 2003.[1]

"War is also life," resigns a protagonist of a novel by the aforementioned Chkvanava (2013).[2] From the wider political and deeper ideological framework of war, I am now stepping into the microlevel, crossing over to the other, concrete side, finding out how war has become something ordinary, normal, banal. Researching how the current political culture, its discourses, the *jargon of authenticity* to refer to Adorno, have been transposed to popular and consumer culture and what dimensions they have acquired there. How this shows in the ways of dressing, choices of color, decorating public surfaces, food, advertisement, media and consumer culture, and in the radically changed map of Ukraine's memorials. During my rides or whenever I had to wait, I did a little test: how long does it take before I see an image of war, militant iconography, emphatically *patriotic* vocabulary, or clips from the front, or hear a nation-awakening song. Usually, it did not take more than a few seconds.

The most obvious street theatre of the culture of war is clothing. Spring opened the season of T-shirts — appropriate for the situation, they were adorned with motifs of war and patriotism. Street stands were buckling under their weight, and I couldn't but wonder who was buying all this. Many did, and it was a display of various fashion imperatives. Men,

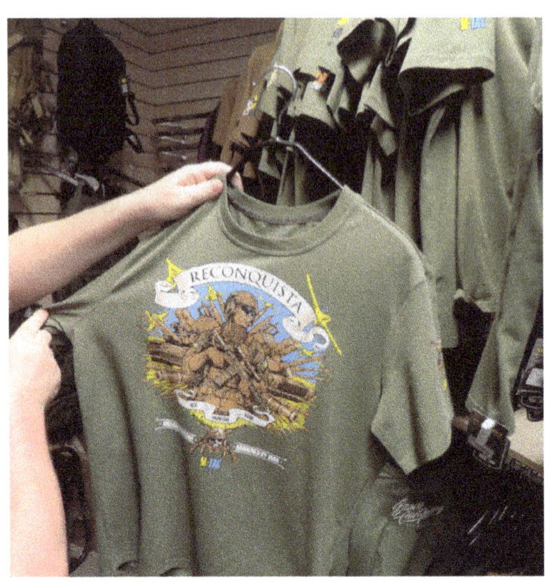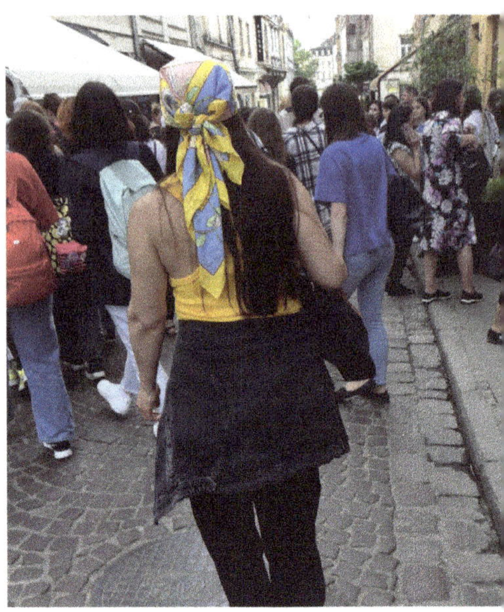

Left to right: Army shop, Kyiv, May 2023; Lviv, May 2023.

especially young men, wore black T-shirts with dramatic warrior motifs and strong suggestible slogans (like *Reconquista* or, what seemed popular and omnipresent since the beginning of the war, *All will be Ukraine*). A true hit were the ones with English slogans: *I'm Ukrainian, Fight Like Ukrainians, Crimea — We Will Be Back*, and *Ukraine — Feel the Freedom*. Some featured ancient Cossacks or knights, others contemporary hi-tech soldiers, others still, undefinable muscle men, *Ramboids*, or even bulldogs — all frowning. Among the specific personalities, I noticed Shevchenko or the controversial Bandera, and little David overcoming Goliath with his sling. The more neutral yet nevertheless orthodox enough were images of a (yellow) wheat field on the bottom with (blue) sky on top. Women, especially girls, wore more poetic, lyrical T-shirts: with hearts, flowers in the colors of Ukraine, or slogans such as *My heart is in Ukraine* (or so people translated that for me). A more daring young woman wore a tight tank top with two palm imprints on her chest — in Ukrainian colors, to be sure. Young lovers also express their affection by wearing T-shirts with the same patriotic motif. Blue and yellow were also motifs on children's

T-shirts, although I could also discern more fighting spirits on those for boys. Other people chose a more subtle way by wearing black T-shirts with only a discreet trident, a small Ukrainian bicolor flag, or a trimming in those two colors.

Like everywhere else in the *post-socialist desert*, as Igor Štiks and Srećko Horvat call the still nameless period in Eastern Europe from the early nineties on, Ukraine, too, shows a neo-traditional turn, i.e. a creation of cultural values and subjects of an invented past. I define neo-traditionalism as a "cultural logic of the post-socialist transition," also a title of a lecture I gave at Yale a few years ago. I deliberately use the prefix neo-, new, as this is no return to the past, no re-traditionalization of society, no simple travel back to the *good old days* after decades of *communist totalitarianism*, to use a phrase that has been worn thin through the past 35 years. This is no regression, but a forward-looking post-traditional phenomenon fabricated in the very place where neo-liberalism and ethno-nationalism disintegrate society and destroy solidarity. A pragmatic invention of an imaginary past, rather than its revival, which can serve new political goals. In post-socialism, examples of this are found on every step. Historian Plokhy claims that Ukraine was united by a "fascination" with a historical narrative — that of the Cossack past — even before the Soviet Union disintegrated.[3]

A perspective of neo-traditional turn is *folk* ornamentality in popular and consumer culture and fashion. In Ukraine, too, men and women of different ages and financial status expressed their belonging with embroidered folklore elements. I know too little of their ornaments to judge how authentic this was: when I asked around, people explained that it finds more inspiration in the olden days than it really once was. Speaking generally, examples from other parts of the (post-socialist) world are more *fakelore* than *folklore*, more pastoral fantasies, more invented traditions in the most textbook Hobsbawm fashion. These ornaments are especially intricate on *vyshyvanka*, Ukrainian embroidered shirts, or as details on ordinary clothing, e.g. on cuffs, along the button-holes, shirt or blouse collars and on skirts and ties. Regardless of their (in)authenticity: they looked good on white canvas, often in blue with a yellow accent, less often in a red and white color combination. In their performances home and abroad, Ukrainian artists like to wear clothes with homely inspiration. During special ceremonies, President Zelenskyy is also wearing the *vyshivanka*, and on a round table on the perspectives for Ukraine, I also saw a famous pro-Ukrainian professor wearing it. Ah, I thought, we are going into the future wearing *national costumes*. One Saturday, I sat my tired frame in a café, coincidentally right across from a Greek Catholic church during a wedding ceremony, and I saw that the ratio of newlyweds and in-laws wearing folklorically inspired and decorated ceremonial garments to those in *civilian clothes* was about fifty-fifty.

Men of all ages, however, much rather wore camouflage-colored clothing, from hats and T-shirts to shoes and rucksacks. Some were actually military, others only fashionable, inspired by military symbolism, or a combination with civilian clothes. Veterans — or *veterans* — strode with recognizable pride through the streets wearing military clothes, many of them featuring a typical Cossack hairstyle (called *oseledets*). The eye of my camera even caught one died blue and yellow. Otherwise, the most popular color combination of clothes was, of course, blue and yellow, like the Ukrainian flag. But, as an average wardrobe contains more blue (jeans) pants than yellow T-shirts or shirts, the combination was turned on its head: blue bottom and yellow top. These are the dominating colors athletes wear in international competitions. In the west, this color combination is joined by red-and-black clothing, the Bandera combination. The accessories in this *patriotic fashion* trend are head scarfs, scarfs, and socks, which, if not yellow-and-blue, at least communicate sayings such as *Be Brave Like Ukraine!*

Especially popular were the one- or two-centimeter-wide ribbons in Ukrainian colors sold on stands; on the more frequented sites, really young women — teenagers — tried to tie them to my hand, sometimes even forcibly. People — also in the institutions that I visited — wore them proudly as bracelets or as small bows on their chest. I found them everywhere in

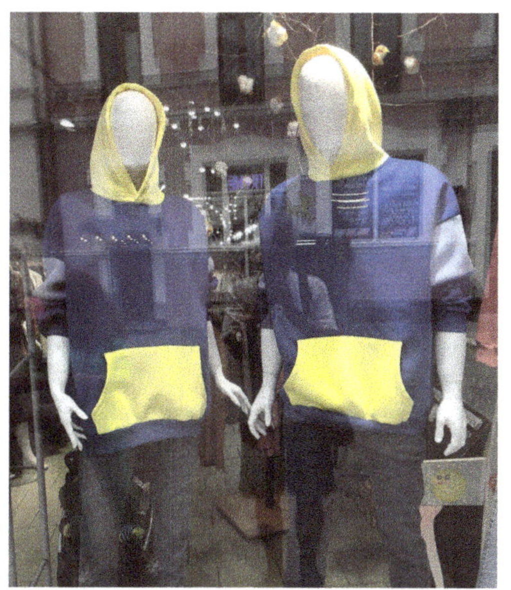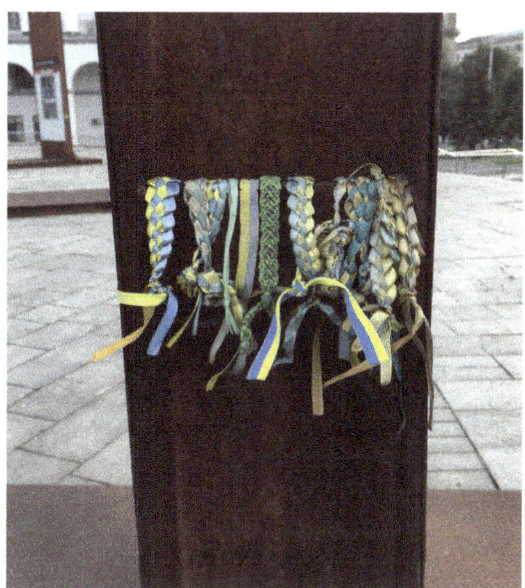

Left to right: Uzhhorod, September 2023; Lviv, May 2023.

the urban landscape: tied to fences, nets, poles, bikes, handles. The second type of expressing patriotism in this way were the rubber or silicone bracelets. Media reports from the (pro-)Russian side show that black and orange ribbons called the ribbons of Saint George, a popular Russian military symbol, were worn by self-proclaimed *Heroes of Novorossia*, often combining other Great-Russian, secessionist, tzarist, and far-right symbolism, and the most recognizable symbol of the attack, capital letter Z.

Among the various badges and patches on teenagers' bags, I could usually see a Ukrainian flag, coat of arms, or another national symbol. I saw girls wearing crowns, wreaths from fresh blue and yellow flowers, on their heads. It was also interesting to observe how proudly and with their heads held high women or girls strolled arm in arm with their uniformed men. With a different sort of pride, scouts — adolescents and almost-children of both genders — also strode through the towns in their uniforms. More than two decades ago, I discovered their peers in the Polish units; I must confess that I was shocked both times, then and now. Religious order combined with the military discipline — I am completely repelled by such a demonstration of allegiance to two totally hierarchical institutions, the church and the army, even more when they are united. Apparently, I will never understand these young people who see themselves in this (and I will forever be reminded of another *Seinfeld* scene where Elaine can get how her boyfriend is lazy and stupid, but not how he can be religious…).

The warm late spring uncovered many patriotic, fighting, and extremist tattoos. On the upper arms and forearms, even cleavage, shone tridents of various sizes, and again the apparently very popular *kolovrat spoked wheel*, sometimes in combination with a *folk* ornament. I could often see the old Nazi symbol of *Wolfsangel*, which can also be found in the symbolism used by the Azov group and the now-defunct Patriot of Ukraine organization. Its proponents understand it in their own way: the capital *N* with a capital *I* in the middle supposedly stands for the *Idea of the Nation*. When I was watching clips, I also saw a few uniforms with the patch of the spoked wheel.

Fashion nationalism may bother people; I can already hear the haughty comments by life-style gurus who swear by *freedom of choice, self-expression, exclusivity* in everything, including dressing. "Are we really so different?" I wrote in my road notebook. It is difficult to say, but in the Ukrainian towns that I visited, I didn't see as many elements of national costumes, as for example in the Sunday clothes worn in Carinthia in Austria, in Salzburg or Munich; I saw fewer of them on Ukrainian TV channels than on Slovenian national TV during weekend prime time slots. To go a step further: I saw less blue-and-yellow combo in Ukraine that first summer than I saw pink in the newest travesty of global pop culture of the year 2023, *Barbiecore* or Barbiemania. Less than T-shirts with Disney heroes. Less than fan jerseys in the colors of soccer or basketball clubs worn not only by children but also by adults. Not to mention the increasingly prevalent face painting in club or national colors done by fans, who also wear wigs, etc. And, speaking as generally as possible: in Ukraine, just like elsewhere in the world, the most popular are still pieces of clothing by Boss, Armani,

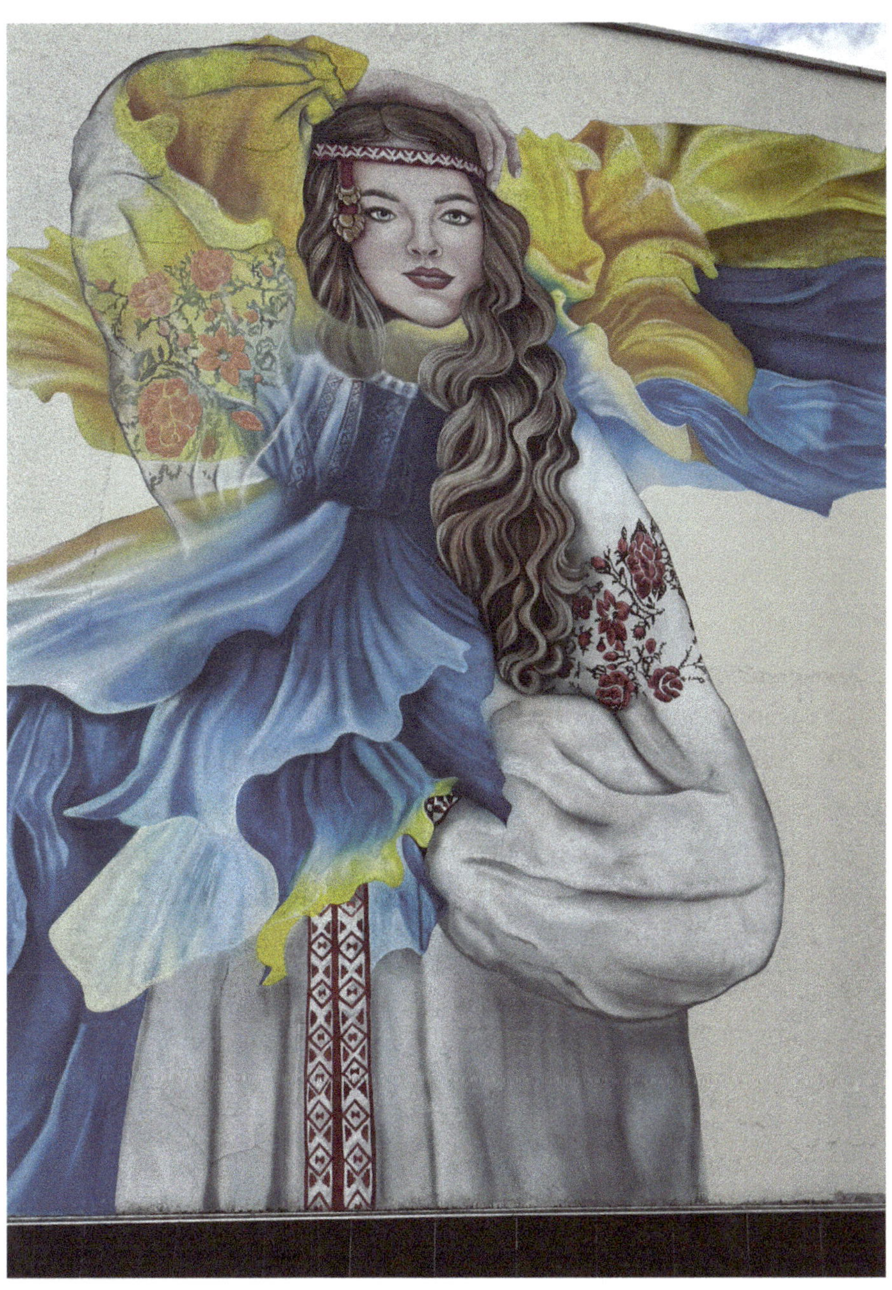

Uzhhorod, June 2024.

Jack&Jones, and Calvin Klein, as well as Nike, Adidas, Puma, and similar global street fashion. At its core, the imperative of popular culture is the same as the imperative of nationalism: cultural uniformity and ideological unification, here and there and everywhere, in war and in peace. These are the two most decisive contemporary collective ideologies and identities, once the old religious ones cease to matter. So much for the fashion culture of war being completely different from the fashion culture of peace ...

(This is why I begin my university lectures on methodology with a simple principle: before thinking about others, we must always think about our-selves; autocriticism, an analytical insight into oneself, must come before criticism. We must be aware of, see and explore our own *normality*, our own everyday sociocentrisms, our own cultural taken-for-grantedness, before tackling what we perceive as the *abnormality* of others.)

All of this made every other dress code stand out even more: the unique characters from the (big) cities use their clothing and appearance to state their exceptionalism. I was, for example, surprised by an occasional sea-punk hairdo with the corresponding colorful attire underneath. Then there was a guy with a brand-new T-shirt by the American death-metal band Autopsy (who also just released a brand-new album that I heard on Radio Študent, the oldest student radio station in Europe). Another two guys wore T-shirts featuring the classics of their genres — Motörhead and Bullet for My Valentine, while there were also T-shirts with the name and the iconography of the good old Sodom band. Quite a few people wore homages to Nirvana and Tupac Shakur — in the last few years, their T-shirts have been a hit all over the world. The rapper has become a retro icon, but I fail to understand why (and why not, say, Biggie, The Notorious B. I. G., his contemporary in life and tragic death). Once more, the honor of the punks was saved by Pennywise. Interestingly enough, however, I saw no T-shirt featuring local pop rock attractions such as The Hardkiss or Kalush Orchestra.

The attentive reader has realized that I couldn't shake my culturolog-ical professional deformation while wandering around these towns: I am

listing things because the more examples you have, the more you understand a phenomenon. This is why my notes also contain T-shirts with
cheap ironic slogans like *Fuck Me I'm Rich* or *Weekend Offender* or *You
Will Like My Cock* (with *Tail* in small print). My winners were *Unexpected
Success* worn by a cleaning lady at a bar and *Introverted but Willing to
Discuss Cats* by a teenager wandering the promenade. But patriotism also
reached this level of street culture: on one of my many walks, I met a young
guy wearing a black T-shirt with the AC/DC logo — in Ukrainian colors!
And I crossed paths with a young woman in full grunge plaid outfit and
a typical, slightly absent walk, as if she was on her way to a Skin Yard or
Mudhoney concert in Seattle in late 1980s — but with a shiny trident on a
short necklace around her neck.

For much longer, I have been fascinated by the *goth look* of Nordic and
Eastern Europeans — the women, to be more precise, as they are in the
majority as well as more consistent and bolder. Freshly died raven-black
hair, even darker clothing, red lipstick, and recognizable tattoos contrast
strongly with their — allow me this essentialist slip — lighter complex-
ion: their morbid look and attitude are textbook to this subculture. Or
the eclectic alternative fashion that you can see in squats and autonomous
cultural zones in European cities. I remember a young mother carrying her
baby in a wrap carrier on her chest, dressed in light high summer clothes,
hidden behind large glasses and hat, tattooed all over, a smart phone in
one hand, a small cake in a plastic box in the other. There you go, I said to
myself, one of those must have been the inspiration for the hit single by the
Belgrade group S. A. R. S. *Praktična* žena, practical woman.

The next indicator of how everyday war has become are flags: official
flags, country flags, yellow-and-blue flags, and, especially in the West,
the black-and red flags used by the WWII Ukrainian Insurgent Army and
Bandera followers (black is supposed to represent the Ukrainian black soil,
chernozem; red the life or blood given for Ukraine). "The further west you
travel, the more black-and-red flags you will see flying; the Ukrainian idea
is the most hard-core there," a fellow passenger informed me. Country flags

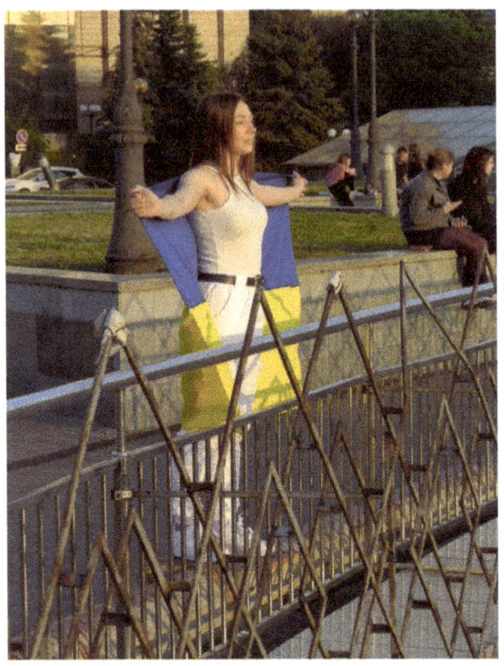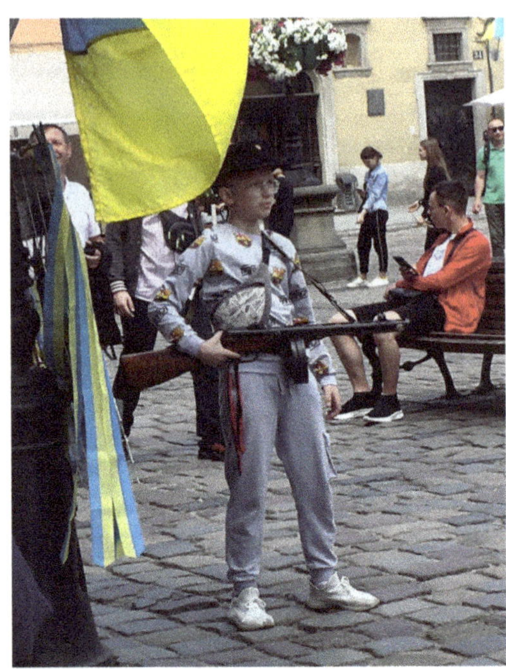

Left to right: Maidan, Kyiv, May 2023; Lviv, May 2023.

are flying practically everywhere: on institutions and homes, on balconies and stores, they are pasted on shop and bar windows, appear on huge billboards and graffiti, are almost mandatory inside cars, on the dashboard or behind the rear window. Whole bouquets of them stand, for example, in roundabouts or in parks or memorials, while the smaller ones hang from streetlamps. In Maidan, or Independence Square, there are thousands of these small blue-and-yellow ones with this or that inscription, dedication, or promise on them; strewn between them are the black-and-red ones, ones dedicated to Azov, and also Georgian ones. In the vicinity, I managed to photograph a young woman, first wrapped in the flag, then she lifted it up over her head. From a later chat, I found out that she was posing for the social media of her boyfriend, a local rapper doing DIY publicity.

It was in the Maidan's field of little flags where one of the most heartbreaking events of my three travels occurred to me. I was taking photos, from the discrete distance, of a kneeling middle-aged woman, accompanied

     Ukrainian Vignettes: Essays on a Culture at War

by a man of her age, both in military uniforms, crying in front of a photo of a young soldier among the flags. A few minutes later they approached me, explaining to me — again, combining three, four, five different languages — in tears, that it is about her younger brother, killed on the front. When I revealed I was from Slovenia, the man hugged me convulsively and then the woman started to kiss my hand, thanking me for Slovenia sending Ukraine *grenades* and *tanks*. This sad and touching scene lasted few dozens seconds that felt to me like hours: unprepared for the delirium of mourning, I couldn't pull myself together that day. I cannot even imagine how devastating it must have been for her.

To widen my perspective again, I am not sure if there are more flags flying in Ukraine than on posts in front of Danish homes (that's the tradition there), or in car dealerships or in random suburbs in the United States. In my book *Eurosis* (2005), I analyzed the almost complete visual single-mindedness of Slovenia entering the European Union: flags everywhere, everything was *Euro-* from leaflets to chewing gums, from company names to children's books. While writing these essays, I took a short trip to Bosnia-Herzegovina — during the festivities/commemorations of the *Operation Storm* (taking place in August 1995 which decisively put an end to the war in Croatia from 1991 to 1995), celebrated by Croats as a victory and considered by Serbs as a defeat. On the Croatian side of the Sava River, a disproportionate amount of disproportionately large Croatian flags flew on half-collapsed or provisionally rebuilt small houses of almost-empty villages. On the other side of that same river, in Republika Srpska, just as disproportionate an amount of disproportionately large Serbian flags flew as a sign of both mourning and commitment. War made poverty almost the same on both riverbanks, everybody is a loser; nothing can hide this but large flags.

Simultaneously, those who are leading the war are always the winners: for them, war is the best business. Crumbs of the war profits are also strewn among the *small entrepreneurs,* to use another unfortunate expression of transition newspeak. A solid hierarchy rules the *laws of the market*: wholesale and retail, wholesalers and retailers, war profiteers and *small* war profiteers. Just like in all other similar tragedies, the production and sale of various patriotic and warrior paraphernalia boom — they also did so in early 1990s in Yugoslavia. (A tip if you wish to compare this with the situation across the Atlantic: the turistification, kitschification, and commercialization of memorials to terrorist attacks in Oklahoma City and the New York Twin Towers were critically researched by the splendid American cultural critic Marita Sturken in her book *Tourists of History* (2007). (I highly recommend the read!) There are no limits to the imagination of the sellers: every (un)imaginable thing was sold in stores, on stands, in city markets, in info- and tourist points, and also on random corners where poor people struggled to get any hryvnia (Ukrainian currency) they could.

There was a sea of Ukrainian flags and the flags of Ukrainian war nationalists of all dimensions and with every imaginable trimming; badges; ribbons; pins; caps; patriotic books; biographies of notable Ukrainians and pamphlets; statuettes of President Zelenskyy; tarot cards; mousepads; tarot cards; pendants from cartridges; other pendants; cups with portraits of Zelenskyy, Bandera, and (now former) commander of the Ukrainian army Valerii Zaluzhny; fan scarves; magnets; everything and anything. Street vendors also sell dramatic images of war and loyalty to the homeland in oil paintings or reproductions. I am sad to say that here, just like a good twenty years ago in Krakow, Poland, I noticed reproductions of old paintings of Jews in extremely antisemitic tones: how they hide at home to count their coin, how they rub their hands together with evil grins; every one of them racially stereotyped as *Jewfaces*.

Restaurants and bars are given patriotic names or at least welcome greetings like *Glory to Ukraine*. There are also patches that contain everything from flags and emblems of various military units to slogans *Orcs must die*. All in a blue-and-yellow (or black-and-red) combination. The vendors are dressed accordingly; one was even wearing the Ukrainian flag. All these positive characters, motifs, and appeals also have their antagonist: Putin's

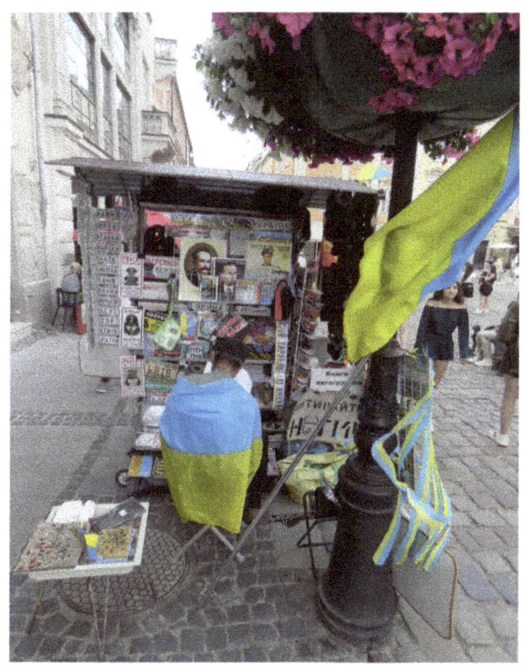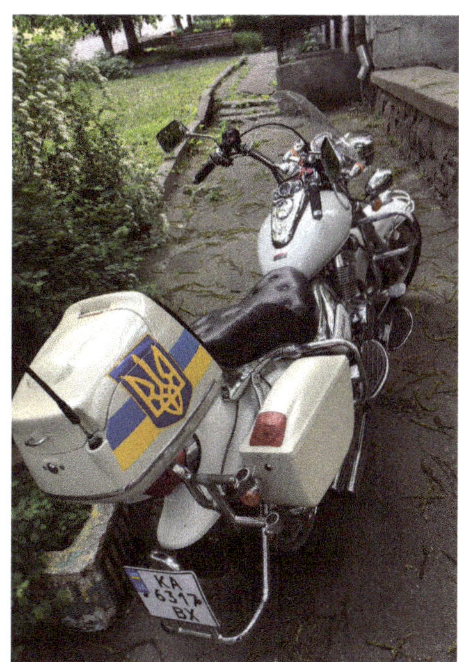

Left to right: Lviv, May 2023; Kyiv, May 2023.

face can be found on doormats (with the instruction *Wipe your feet*) and on toilet paper (no instruction needed); on targets for air rifles (shaped like Kalashnikov rifles) with an accompanying slogan of *Shoot the coward!* In the last two years, I encountered similar street stands with Ukrainian paraphernalia, T-shirts, key chains, ribbons, pins, postcards, and especially donation boxes for Ukraine or, more concrete ones, for the Azov Battalion, for example, also in the other two post-Soviet neighbors under the eerie appellation of *Big Sisters* Russia: Estonia and Georgia.

The support of war endeavors can be seen in the most unexpected places and in the most unexpected ways. Soon after the war began, symbolically on 8 March 2022, a young Ukrainian and a young Belarus woman launched the online platform Teronlyfans,[4] short for Territorial Defense OnlyFans. In exchange for a donation for the Ukrainian army and for the people who had to flee because of the war, they offer nude photos. The homepage tells the clients that "Every hryvnia you donate helps Ukraine win."

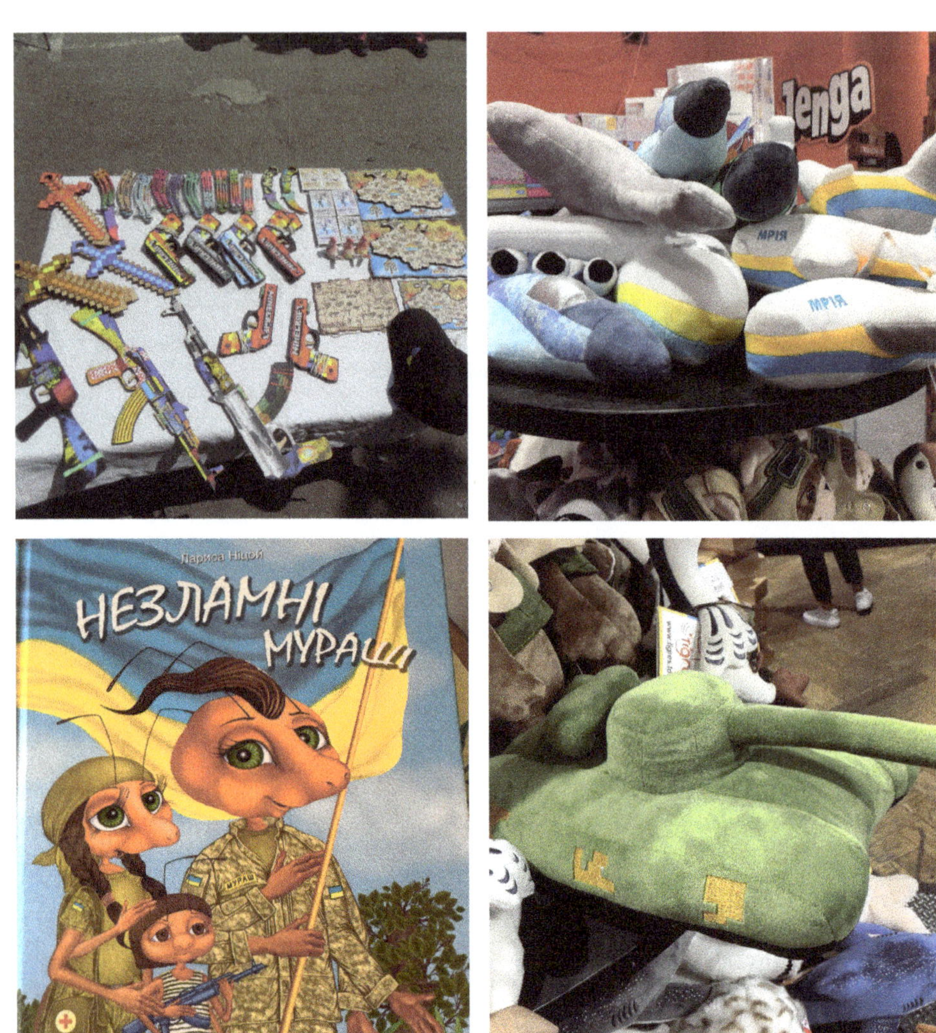

Top to bottom, left: Children's book, Lviv, May 2023; Kyiv, June 2024.
Top to bottom, right: Lviv, May 2023; Lviv, May 2023.

War culture is also seen in children's toys: on the cover of a cute picture book, a smiling *Protector Cat* in a military uniform and a Ukrainian ribbon tied to its paw is rejoicing at the sinking of a Russian warship — which alludes to the fate of the cruiser Moskva in April 2022. It is accompanied by caricatures of famous people of the era, e.g. the frontman of Kalush Orkestra, or the Kyiv grandma who took down a Russian drone with a jar of pickles. Another one featured a different popular motif: the Ukrainian tractor that proudly dragged the captured Russian Tor missile system, full name 9K330. The third one is of a family prepared to face the enemy on the battlefield: the father with the traditional Cossack haircut *oseledets*, mother as a medic, kid holding a Kalashnikov, all three in military uniforms, firmly holding Ukrainian flag. Toy store shelves are not only full of stuffed bears and cats, but also of stuffed tanks, stuffed pillows in Ukrainian colors and what has become a folk greeting from a verse in the song *Good evening, we're from Ukraine!*,[5] dating from the beginning of the war. And the stuffed Antonov An-225 *Mriya* transport aircraft, the Dream, destroyed by Russian troops in the first days of the war at Hostomel airfield. A detection dog by the name of *Patron* (*Cartridge*), a cute Jack Russell Terrier who helps Ukrainian bomb disposal technicians to neutralize unexploded grenades and landmines, gained immense popularity after a video of him was posted on the Facebook. Since then, he was incarnated in a number of different (plush) toys, illustrations and picture books for children, postcards etc. and received high-ranking foreign politicians who took photos with him. The obsession with guns that accompanies every war is evident on stands, too, with wooden and plastic rifles and pistols; knives; bats, or axes in Ukrainian colors and adorned with folk ornaments and patriotic inscriptions; puzzles with *our weapons*, etc. On the main square of one of these cities, children — boys, of course — could borrow a military cap, the likes of which was worn by WWII Insurgent Army fighters, and a typical Soviet machine gun from the era, the PPD-40: the local vendor allowed them to wear the accessories for the parents or friends to take pictures.

But are such fetishization of weapons and military culture in general even that very different to elsewhere in the world? Two examples from the time when I was finishing these essays gave me the answer to what it is like here in Slovenia. In every main Slovenian media outlet, I could read, see, or listen to practically identical, almost child-like fascinations of Slovenian journalists reporting on, and I quote, *the biggest, most expensive, most modern, fastest, strongest* American aircraft carrier stopping in the port of Trieste. Especially disturbing was an almost orgasmic reporting of one guy whose unselfconscious militarism was awarded with a plane ride. No reflection whatsoever of the fact that this is actually a killing machine! To become aware of the war culture with no war and no culture, you don't have to go far.

"Everyday nationalism," to borrow the excellent concept coined by the British social scientist Michael Billig, also has its culinary or gourmet dimension. Again, *same ol', same ol'*: I remember the absolute silliness of the American renaming of *French fries* into *freedom fries* when the French expressed their reservations about the 2003 American invasion of Iraq. Today, the fact that the famous *pizza Margherita* was made to honor the Italian queen by the same name has almost disappeared from memory; its ingredients symbolize the national tricolor scheme — tomato for red, *mozzarella* for white, and basil for green. In basically every country of the Balkans, the *cordon bleu* steak is known by its local name: the *Ljubljana*, *Zagreb*, *Karadjordje*, or *Skenderbeg* steak — the differences among them are either minimal or non-existent. The *Real American burgers* are often decorated with a small toothpick flag, while the British chocolate boxes never come without their *Union Jack*. The most recent bizarre case of such "politics of food" is Vučić's Pariser sausage breakfast in front of TV cameras as part of his populist project aiming to lower the prices of basic foodstuffs in Serbia.

Therefore, I was not at all surprised to see similar examples in Ukraine, such as the blue-and-yellow spread on a plate of a perfectly ordinary light dinner. Stores sell simple and delicious ice-cream in yellow Socialist-design like packaging with large blue lettering *Be Brave — Support Ukraine*, an explanation, and an infographic: *enjoy* (an image of ice-cream), *donate* (an image of 5 hryvnia) and *support* (an image of a flexed biceps). In his war diary from besieged Kharkiv (2023), Zhadan mentions the *Bandera salad* and the *victory borscht*. Without trying too much, I have also casually come across gingerbread, boxes of chocolates, and lollipops in these colors and with a map of the country on them.

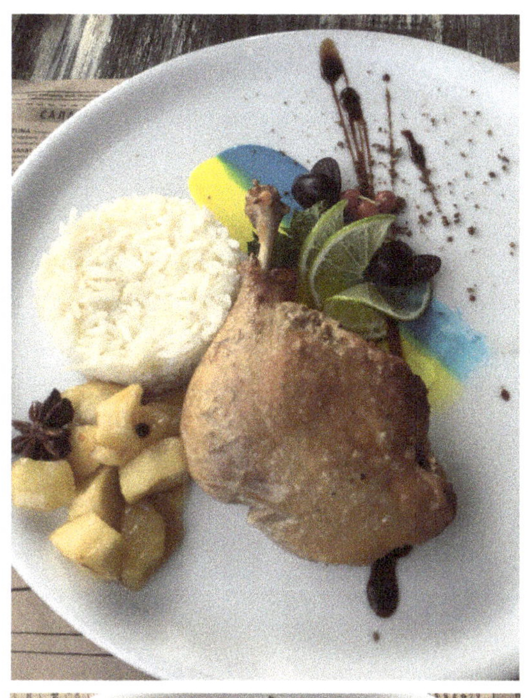

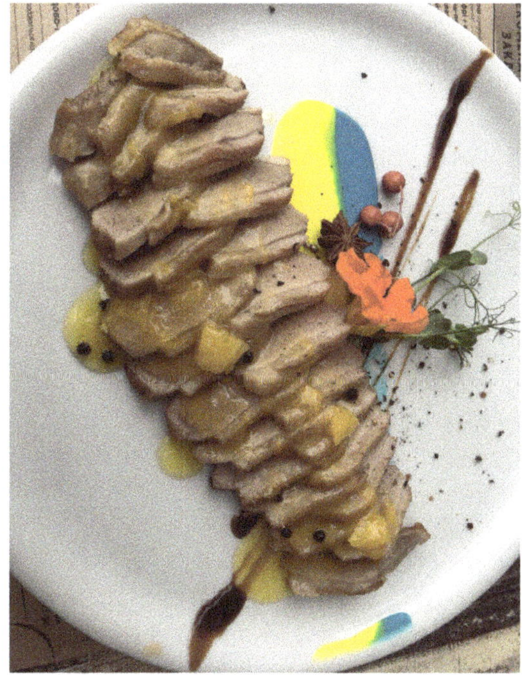

Top and bottom:
Uzhhorod, August, 2023.

A patriotic momentum is also conveyed in the blue-and-yellow combination of floral decorations in parks and flowerpots around towns and in front of bars. It is featured in store windows, on advertisements, and on bar chairs. It is a frequent choice for fences, metal doors, benches, e-scooters, playgrounds; in an artistic action, artists painted anti-tank barriers and other signs of war with folk motifs — I've read about it and seen the photos. Stickers of flags or coat-of-arms are pasted on rear windows or bumpers of cars and motorcycles, ribbons are tied around car antennas. But the wittiest move of posting a sticker on a car was on a Lada: I saw a trident pasted right across the brand of this car. So, this originally Russian car became a Ukrainian car.

Spoils of war or *authentic* souvenirs from the battlefields also seem to be gaining *market interest*. In the major squares or on the promenades, hm, how to say — abundant — men in camouflage uniforms (they reminded me of the members of the Slovenian *varda* paramilitary unit I used to marvel at in TV clips a couple of years ago), who don't seem in the slightest like brave soldiers or anyone with war experience at all, are selling empty bullet casings, destroyed pieces of god-knows-what military equipment,

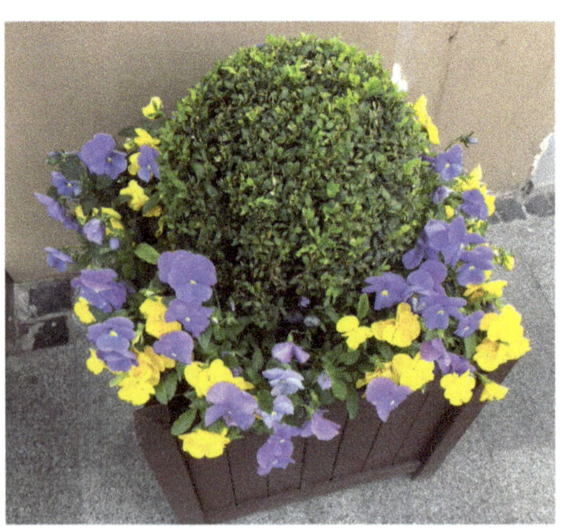
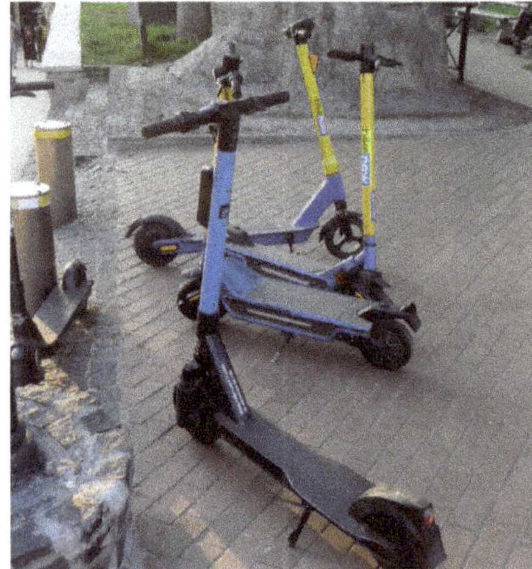

Left to right: Lviv, May 2023; Kyiv, May 2023.

   Ukrainian Vignettes: Essays on a Culture at War

or parts of bent green metal full of bullet holes and supposedly belonging to the destroyer Russian tanks and military equipment. Especially hard to forget were the suddenly multiplied *army shops*, now in large halls and no longer in obscure little stores like normally, and street stalls with army equipment. My hosts explained that the Ukrainian army was facing — is still facing, actually — a shortage of quality-grade military gear: uniforms, bags, bullet-proof vests, jackets, and trousers. Many volunteers and even recruits or their families buy all of this themselves (and sometimes but not always be refunded). In these veritable military markets — where a crossed-over flag of Russia on the door clearly states that they carry no equipment of the *aggressor country* — I met young boys surrounded by their near and dear ones. Girlfriends, mothers, wives, entire families, friends from basketball, etc. were walking around with them, trying on balaclavas, belts, boots, underwear, T-shirts with fighting motifs, bags, cartridge carriers. On the buyer's side of the till, you could feel a tense mix of love, worry, and pride; on the other side, the desire to do business mixed with a quasi military mistrust, as I was often sternly warned not to take photos.

During my trips, the supply was virtually uninterrupted in all the towns I visited: shops abounded with domestic and imported goods (literally anything you can think of, from Haribo gummy bears and Legos to L'Oréal shampoo), white goods, clothing and footwear — everything like there was no war. I was told that a year earlier, things were completely different. Shops were empty, people were stocking up, shelves were immediately emptied of basic necessities, flour, eggs, meat, even old, already spoiled sandwiches were for sale, one of my interlocutors complained. Power cuts caused fridges and chest freezers to melt, and the smell of spoiled food spread from abandoned flats. They lacked everything but imagination: my Kyiv host gave me a candle that can burn for up to 12 hours, all night long: it is made from an old food tin, into which a strip of thick cardboard is rolled, so that one piece sticks up in the middle: the whole thing is covered with reused wax — and *voilà*, your lighting problem is solved!

In general, some people faced the war well prepared, having stocked up their storerooms and shelters. I began chatting with the waitress in the bar I had coffee in a few days in a row. As soon as the first tensions appeared in 2014, a friend from a tourist agency, some Momo, Momir from *Belhrade* (Belgrade), advised her to buy basic food and supplies as soon as possible, because things were about to get real. He predicted that "there will soon be a war just like ours in the Balkans." (By the way, wherever in the world I chat with people, there will unmistakenly be someone who would smile and remember a *Milan* or a *Sheki — naše ljude,* or *our people* in the language of Yugo-emigration — and often add, with their smile now radiating, a — mispronounced — swear word that they sourced from that same guy.) Although she didn't believe him — this couldn't happen to them, could it? — she nevertheless heeded his advice. And, unfortunately, later realized how right he was. In an interview, a correspondent from Irpin, Yevheniia Podobna, explains how she prepared for the war: her bag was equipped with the basic essentials, she stocked up on food and water and made an improvised shelter in her basement. Her neighbors laughed it off, thinking that Russia is only bluffing, that these were false alarms.... The fact is that many, including experts on regional developments, simply refused to believe that Putin would really strike, and were not convinced of what was inevitable until the last moment. And politicians as well, including President Zelenskyy. I totally agree with the opinion of the American specialists in this field, Rajan Menon and Eugene Rumer, that "although few, if anyone, predicted the crisis, after its outbreak it appeared all but inevitable, fueled by various causes both at home and abroad."[6]

As in all ongoing wars at the moment, everything is instantly and copiously photographed, recorded, noted, documented, sent, broadcast — and disseminated to world publics at home and abroad in every way possible, in classic printed media, as well as in electronic and online outlets. Now, there's no more "we never knew." At every given moment, not only every day, we can *see* what is happening. The digital dimensions of war culture today are astounding: all kinds of information are best and most found on social media and the web in general, there is a lot of horizontal messaging (which is sometimes hard to distinguish from vertical messaging), there are (too) many pictures, opinions, statements, instructions, interviews, videos, all kinds of (un)possible things being (re)sent hither and tither. On their smart phones, the locals showed me sets of Telegram apps that warn against danger, show action on the frontline in real time, broadcast explicit scenes that are hard to watch, movements of *our soldiers* wearing bodycams, drones and rockets falling in the West, etc. One of these apps fervently follows the losses of the attackers: how many men, helicopters, tanks, and other weaponry and equipment was lost by the aggressor today (this data is also broadcast on TV news). Their phones keep beeping with messages, warnings of attacks here or somewhere else. On online platforms, everything is instantly commented and emphasized with emojis, as if people are following a soccer match or the elections. Abundant news and reports can also be found in blogs on the war (*warblogs* or *milblogs*), in YouTube clips and channels, and elsewhere online.

As far as I could understand and gather, TV programs focus almost exclusively on the war. The official newscast called *United News* are broadcast on every channel (many of the people I spoke with harshly criticized such journalistic singlemindedness). Media reports are accompanied by strong visuals, speaking in maxims, fascinating infographics, usually with either a flag or a map of the whole of Ukraine in the background, some of the footage from the battlefields is definitely purposefully explicit, bloody. Often you see the mansplaining combo, so typical for the war situation. This is no hyperbole; there are men with abundant facial hair explaining the situation to female reporters in the field or female presenters in studios, be it the first morning news or the main TV news of the day. Special morning shows on one of the channels teach you how to how to bandage a wounded limb, where to apply pressure to a major vein, how to stop bleeding, or what the much-anticipated F-16 can do. One afternoon, I caught an *interview* with Russian war prisoners ruefully confessing to their violent exploits in front of the cameras. The armed forces even have its own *Armiya (Army)* channel broadcasting reports from the front, clips

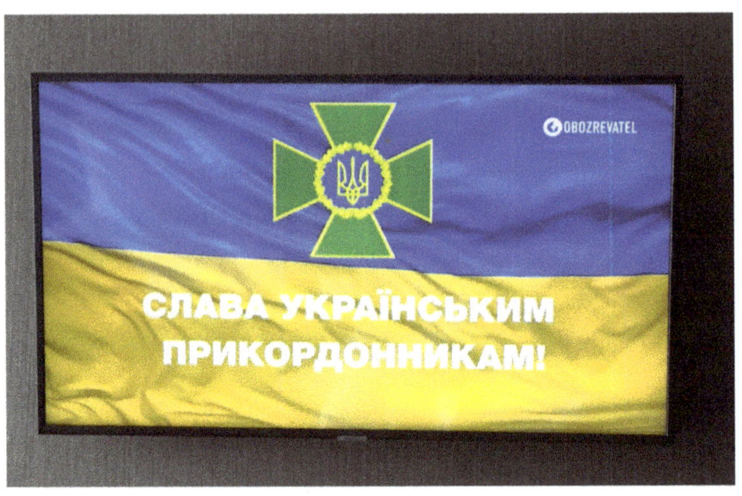

"Glory to the Ukrainian border guards!", TV program, Lviv, May 2023.

of weapon testing, the history of the Ukrainian army, the descriptions of heroic acts and sacrifices, etc.

Commercials and clips supporting war efforts, both on screens and on posters, are another story. One type features different branches of the military: e.g. *Glory to Ukrainian Border Guards* (who suffered greatly in Putin's *blitz*) on a flying flag, next come the tanks of the armored branch, ground warfare, engineers, etc. One especially stayed with me: clips of carefree young men and women in national costume shirts covered in folklore elements in an idyllic rural environment, as if they stepped out of one of Gogol's stories from *Evenings on a Farm Near Dikanka* (1957), when, suddenly, the fun is over and they put on their uniforms: military, first aid, firefighting, police, medical, civil protection. Although war imagery is always forward-looking, anticipating the coming victory, it is also always returning to traditional identities and cementing them. Another poster features a portrait of a girl, half of whose clothing is a military uniform, complete with helmet and goggles, the other half a rich national costume with exuberant flowers and traditional ornaments. A poster for a local theatre festival is similarly adorned with a portrait of a woman in a national costume and an aura around her head spelling out *Freedom* in Cyrillic and Latin alphabets. "People always find themselves somewhere in between," I thought, caught in the media crossfire of the two extremes that practically don't exist today: an invented past and an uncertain wartime future.

These advertisements present soldiers in an ambivalent way, as was already analyzed by the excellent Serbian ethnographer Ivan Čolović in *Politics of Symbols* (2000), using the example of the wars in Croatia and Bosnia-Herzegovina. On the one hand, they are superhumans, heroes, they recall virile alpha warriors like John Wayne or Jean-Claude …. On the other hand, they are presented as modest, reserved, still innocent boys, practically teenagers, but nevertheless with a strong sense of patriotism and commitment. On page 68 of his book, he writes that, in the discursive construction of a fighter, the gentle side suggests that his main role in the warrior mythology is the role of a victim, not the role of the victor: "as we know, gods demand the blood of an innocent victim as their sacrifice." The economy of sacrifice — the innocent, *holy* victim suffers for and instead of us, silently demanding retribution — is, as cultural theorist and historian René Girard taught us, at the core of every social order. Along Ukrainian roads and streets, jumbo posters are lined with portraits of fallen fighters, *victims*, and the dates and places of their births and deaths.

The storm of war is radically changing the towns on the home front, not just those on the frontline. Its omnipresence is largely evidenced also by their changed symbolic geography: monumental and topographical. The Russian side is de-ukrainifying, the Ukrainian side de-russifying. Another telling similarity with the post-Yugoslav post-socialist landscape, in which the spatial relics of the dead federation, its political system, and now defunct *others* are being erased, as well. Or a similarity with 1945 in our region: a Dalmatian friend never forgets to tell me how, immediately after the liberation, his small town was quick to burn down every *fascist palm tree* planted there by the new Italian authorities at the beginning of the occupation. Well, in Ukraine, formal, legally justified, as well as informal processes of de-Sovietization, de-communizing, and de-russification have been fast developing since the beginning of the war in 2014 and especially since 2022. In short: they cannot wait to *Get away from Moscow!* as Mykola Khvylovy (1893–1933), a Ukrainian writer and victim of Stalin's repression, who was both an enthusiast and a critic of the new Soviet power, emphasized in the 1920s. The authorities purposefully change the names of streets, places, and towns, and tear down memorials or public symbols that recall the former regime. New legislation forbids any totalitarian symbol, which includes the Nazi and communist symbolism, but also symbols that they believe to be Great-Russian. To be sure, the other side is doing the exact same thing on occupied territories: total numbers of angry renamings and dramatical tearings down/puttings up of memorials to *theirs/ours* are reaching thousands.

Just like everywhere and everywhen in the Ouroboros of history. On the Ukrainian side, those dedicated to Lenin, of which there were about 5,500 at the time of independence (their dismantling is called *Leninopad, Leninfall*), and other Soviet leaders are falling, red stars, hammers and sickles, Soviet state coats of arms and those of Ukraine from the Soviet period are disappearing from buildings. A good month after the total war erupted, the impressive symbolic statue under the *Arch of Freedom of the Ukrainian People*, which had since 1982 symbolized the solidarity of Russian and Ukrainian proletariat, was also dismantled — along with the sculpture honoring the Pereiaslav Agreement, which the Ukrainians today find controversial, as it stands for the agreement with which the Zaporizhian Cossacks led by Hetman Bohdan Khmelnytsky pledged allegiance to the Russian tsar. The arch spanning the two monuments survived. In other cases, the monument was preserved, but its symbol was modified: a year younger but no less majestic, a more than 100-meter-long titanium sculpture of *Mother Motherland* was renamed into *Mother Ukraine*. Until July 2023, the monument's shield bore the coat of arms of the Soviet Union, now it bears the Ukrainian trident. Elsewhere still, only the pedestal remains to carry new monuments, remain empty, or bear the symbol of victory.

The *decolonization of toponomy*, as the Ukrainian authorities call the derussification of public spaces, also means purging the names of streets, institutions, and monuments dedicated to figures not only from Soviet but also from Russian political history. An impressive monument to the founder of Odesa, Empress Catherine II of Russia, and her companions was erected on Katerynska Square, right next to the famous Potemkin Stairs, in 1900; 20 years later, the Bolsheviks tore it down, and in 2007, the city authorities restored it — it lasted until the end of 2022. I took a photo of an enormous Ukrainian flag now stuck in its pedestal. The de-russification fervor even reached names from the world of culture, art, and science. Street names have been changed or monuments removed, for example to Leo Tolstoy and Yuri Gagarin.

And Aleksandr Pushkin (1799–1837). "We don't like him anymore!" I was surprised by the casual response of one of my companions when I pointed to his name being crossed out from the street address while we were strolling through Kyiv. In another city, we were walking past an empty pedestal, until recently occupied with his bust, and she commented: "In school, we spent so much time on him and on other Russian authors that we ran out of time to study our, Ukrainian writers." I took a photo of its empty pedestal; for years before Pushkin was dismantled, the name of Joe Dassin has stood above his name — the statue was said to resemble this famous hairy French singer more than the Russian poet. On my walks through these towns and cities, I saw many more spontaneous interventions like this one, things being crossed out or renamed, a *Ukrainization* of street signs and inscriptions. This is also what happened to the trilingual entrance sign to the Pushkin Museum in Odesa; how meaningful it was that the sign was written in Russian first, then in Ukrainian, and finally in English. Across it, somebody wrote *Get out of Ukraine!*

Much more serious is the official, systemic cleansing. I read the lists: since the beginning of the war, in a year and a half, Ukraine demolished or removed between 30 and 40 statues and memorial plaques dedicated to Pushkin. Similarly, Latvian authorities removed his statue in Riga.

Leninopad was followed by *Pushkinpad, Pushkinfall*. What people resent from his entire oeuvre (and his prompt comment of the current political activities) are his imperial poems — but, truth be told, these are much more anti-Polish than anti-Ukrainian. Among the most discussed are those from the bloody crushing of the Polish Uprising of 1830–1831: *To the Slanderers of Russia* (in which Pushkin asks: "[s]hall Slavonic streams meet in a Russian ocean?") and *The Anniversary of Borodino* (in which he claims Kyiv is the "ancestor of Russian cities"). But the most infamous is the previously mentioned *Poltava*, in which he severely slandered the "Little-Russian" hetman Ivan Mazepa as a traitor to Emperor Peter the Great, because he had joined the Swedish army of Charles XII and been defeated with them at the 1709 Battle of Poltava. The poem calls Mazepa "Judas," claiming that he had "changed sides, betrayed the Russians." Well, on Ukrainian side, this "Judas" basks in glory: Mazepa is a hero, a fighter for a Ukraine independent from Russia. This is why his image can be found on a banknote; he inspired literary authors and musicians all over the world, from Lord Byron and Victor Hugo to Pyotr Ilyich Tchaikovsky, Franz Liszt and many others.

Oh no, not again! I exclaimed hearing about this erasing of history, another reminiscence of the Balkans with thousands of its memorials of the partisan resistance and the cohabitation of Yugoslav nation destroyed. During the most recent war, Croatian nationalists even took on Tesla. New post-Yugoslav authorities performed an ethnic and ideologic cleansing of memory geography, but also of library collections. In her 2022 study, Berlin-based cultural historian Dora Komnenović showed how draconically unwanted books were disappearing from libraries after independence: loudly in Croatia, more silently — how typical — in Slovenia. I believe that the anger at the attackers — justified as it may be — goes too far, and, as is often the case in such situations, aims at the wrong targets, the convenient ones. But Pushkin is no Putin, and neither are other literary classics. Another one to suffer is Mikhail Bulgakov: in 2022, there were calls for his museum in central Kyiv to be closed down on the grounds that he opposed Ukrainian nationalism. Despite reproaches, his creativity cannot be unambiguously reduced to advocacy of the Great-Russian ideology or support for the emperor's repressive regime (as is also emphasized by Bojanowska in the article and book that I have already mentioned). My recipe for addressing these authors is critical reading, not simple removal.

Especially because Putin's, um, subcontractors, the empty rhetoric of the new pro-Russian authorities in the occupied territories of Ukraine now finds it even easier to instrumentalize the memory of this same Pushkin. I follow news on raising flags with his image, on a new Pushkin memorial recently unveiled in Sevastopol, on only his Russocentric poems being recited in celebrations, on memorials to Taras Shevchenko being removed, and on Ukrainian books being systematically destroyed. And on the erection of a new memorial to Lenin to replace the one removed by the Ukrainian authorities in the occupied Henichesk. In the recent wars in Croatia and Bosnia-Herzegovina, similar things happened with the appropriation of the image of Nobel Prize winner Ivo Andrić, and others.

But "manuscripts don't burn," claims Bulgakov through Woland's mouth in *Master and Margarita*.[7] They survive, they cannot be destroyed — just like the monuments. The destruction only makes them burn more vividly in the memory of not only the losing side, but also the winning one. Without being too familiar with Freud's theory of suppression, one can find confirmations of the thesis that the repressed sooner or later comes back, stronger than before. I am aware how controversial memory politics are, and I can understand why this is happening. Nevertheless, I firmly believe that either unplanned or systematic destruction or renaming of monuments to the past, no matter how traumatic, is worse than a mature confrontation with the past. You simply cannot erase history, not even if you rename every street and every institution and destroy every monument. Actual change takes time, it takes public and academic discussion, and at the same time and foremost it takes social engagement. This is the only way to transform monuments to problematic personalities into a reminder of the tragic past, to transform the glorification of the past into a warning. But, of course, the old story repeats itself: it is easier, however completely counterproductive, to destroy something than to critically reinterpret and recontextualize it. Instead, everything stays the same: a disturbing memory that doesn't even need a memorial to exist.

From dismantling now to erecting monuments. In every political transition, the destruction of old memorials always, simultaneously, and linearly happens with a boom of new ones; historian Eric Hobsbawm calls this process *statuomania*. Everywhere, I saw impressive monuments to Ukrainian victims of various tests of the recent history. To those fallen in the Ukrainian War of Independence after WWI, to victims of *Holodomor*, to victims of Stalin's purges (that also reached the peak of the Ukrainian artistic and cultural scene of the 1930s and acquired name *Executed Renaissance*), to the fallen in WWII, to anti-Soviet resistance post-WWII, and to those who fell during the Soviet-Afghan War. The majority, however, refers to events from the past decade: there are monuments to the victims of Euromaidan Uprising, the victims of the 2014 unfinished limited war with Russia, and the victims of the unlimited war raging since February 2022.

Some statues are general, others dedicated to important individuals, such as Avhustyn Voloshyn (1874–1945, Carpatho-Ukrainian politician killed just after the war in Moscow) or composer Ihor Bilozir (1955–2000, who died in a bar fight resulting from using Ukrainian vs. Russian). In Maidan, a low improvised brick wall is home to photos of people killed during the *Revolution of Dignity* or the *Euromaidan* in January and February 2014: these *Heavenly Hundred* have posthumously been called the *Heroes of Ukraine* and every February 20, commemorations are held in their honor. Close by, you can find graffiti of enormous wings spanning a crowd of protesters and two inscriptions: *They protected us with their wings* and a dedication *To the known and the unknown ones*, as not every victim of the protests has been identified. Not far away, along an entire street, a similar homage can be seen to fallen soldiers: The Wall of Remembrance of the Fallen for Ukraine was erected in 2014. The fallen have been listed chronologically, following the events of the war, and every photo also lists all the main data of the soldier. Every city that I visited, regardless of how lively the vibe is in it, is also a necropolis where death is present also in the most populated areas.

While the remnants of the unwanted past are disappearing, remnants of an unwanted present are erupting. Destroyed Russian war machinery is displayed in two places in Kyiv: one next to the National Museum of the History of Ukraine in the Second World War, the other downtown, on Saint Michael's Square (*Mykhailivska ploshcha*), in front of the Saint Michael's Golden Domed monastery. The same morbid scene is on display in the centre of Mykolaiv, another city hit severely by the war. These rusty war trophies, metal *scalps* of vanquished opponents, are sites for pass-ers-by to vent by writing and drawing anti-Putin sayings and signs (e.g. *Onto Moscow!*, *To Ukraine!*, *Glory to the Ukrainian Armed Forces!* etc.) or by tying on Ukrainian ribbons. On Independence Day in 2023 and 2024, this machinery was even exhibited on the main street in Kyiv; like in a pro-cession, it was delivered there on trailers. A *défilé* of the defeated. Again, such displays are not very foreign to us although we haven't had a long war in some time. Since 2011, Medvedjek, Slovenia, is a site of a captured BOV3 armored personnel carrier of the Yugoslav army from the times of the Ten-Day War in 1991, clearly visible from the highway. In 2012, another such trophy, a T-55 tank was finally moved from the entrance to the Ljubljana Museum of Contemporary History to the Pivka Park of Military History — but not before *unknown perpetrators* painted it pink and stuck a bouquet of flowers in its barrel to commemorate March 8.

Along with the previously mentioned concerts and public events, many cities across the world — from Tirana and Gdansk to London and Toronto — renamed a few streets and squares, especially those overlooking Russian Embassies, into *Ukrainian*, *of Ukrainian Heroes*, *of Boris Nemtsov*, *of Free Ukraine*, etc. Expectedly, Russian authorities reacted by renaming the *Great Devyatinsky Lane*, home to the American Embassy in Moscow, into *Donetsk People's Republic Square*. Protests are held in front of many

Russian Embassies around the world with anti-Putin graffiti and those expressing solidarity with Ukrainians on nearby buildings and posters, stickers, ribbons and small pictures posted or tied up on fences protecting them. The ones in Tallinn in summer of 2022 that I saw and took photos of cover half of the street, dozens of yards in front of a well-protected Russian Embassy.

Stand with Ukraine! can be read in symbolic lighting or decorating of important public buildings and memorials around the world in Ukrainian colors, e.g. the Eiffel Tower, the Roman Colosseum, the World Trade Center, the Empire State Building, New York Kosciuszko and Mid-Hudson bridges, Sydney Opera House, London Eye, etc., or flying Ukrainian flags on Berlin museums and many other public buildings around Europe. What I find much too harsh are the attempts at rejecting Russian literature in general or to ban Russian artists from performing (opera singer Anna Netrebko, for example, despite her condemning the war and distancing herself from the Kremlin) go quite far over the edge. This merely reinforces Putin's arguments about *Russophobia* and the threat that the West poses to Russia.

The descriptions of war don't need metaphors or adjectival acrobatics, I read in a few statements by Ukrainian literary authors, everything is here and now. One of the most awful consequences of war is the fact that it has become normal in everyday life, I heard from the people I spoke with: the state of emergency becomes self-evident, tragedy something ordinary, *how-is-this-possible* is replaced

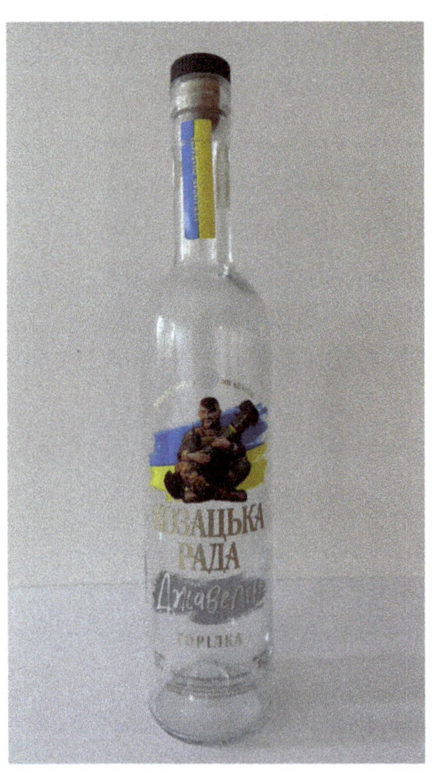

"Cossack Council 'Javelin' Freedom Edition" vodka featuring a Cossack holding an anti-tank weapon, Lityn, June 2024.

   Ukrainian Vignettes: Essays on a Culture at War

by *that's-just-the-way-it-is*, patriotism turns into *daily plebiscite*, to quote Ernest Renan, *banal nationalism* turns into *banal militarism*, to reference Billig. People start to feel being constantly under the siege. This "new normal" gets literally under their skin: those I hosted in Ljubljana or that I met elsewhere, out of their homeland, said to me how surprised they were when they were waking up ("What's going on tonight, no alarms?) —before realizing they are in the safe place.

Nevertheless, with the people I met — I dare not generalize this — a forward-looking optimism was more than obvious: not stemming from some romantic impulses but from basic human, survival reflexes. There was no blind determination but a project-based, realistic, engaged kind of *this-is-what-we're-going-to-do-when-the-war-is-over* determination. A lot of dismay, hurt, disappointment, anger, but no numbness. A restless certainty that they are right.

NOTES

1 Kurkov, Andrey. *Death and the Penguin*, 2001. 71–72.

2 Chkvanava, Gela. *Toreadors*, 2013. 133.

3 Plokhy, Serhii. *The Gates of Europe: A History of Ukraine*, 2021. 314.

4 https://teronlyfans.com/english/ has since disappeared from the internet.

5 See, e.g. https://www.youtube.com/watch?v=Q5RsQWm3rOY .

6 Menon, Rajan and Rumer, Eugene. *Conflict in Ukraine: The Unwinding of the Post-Cold War Order*, 2015. 53.

7 Bulgakov, Mikhail A. *The Master and Margarita*, 2012. 292.

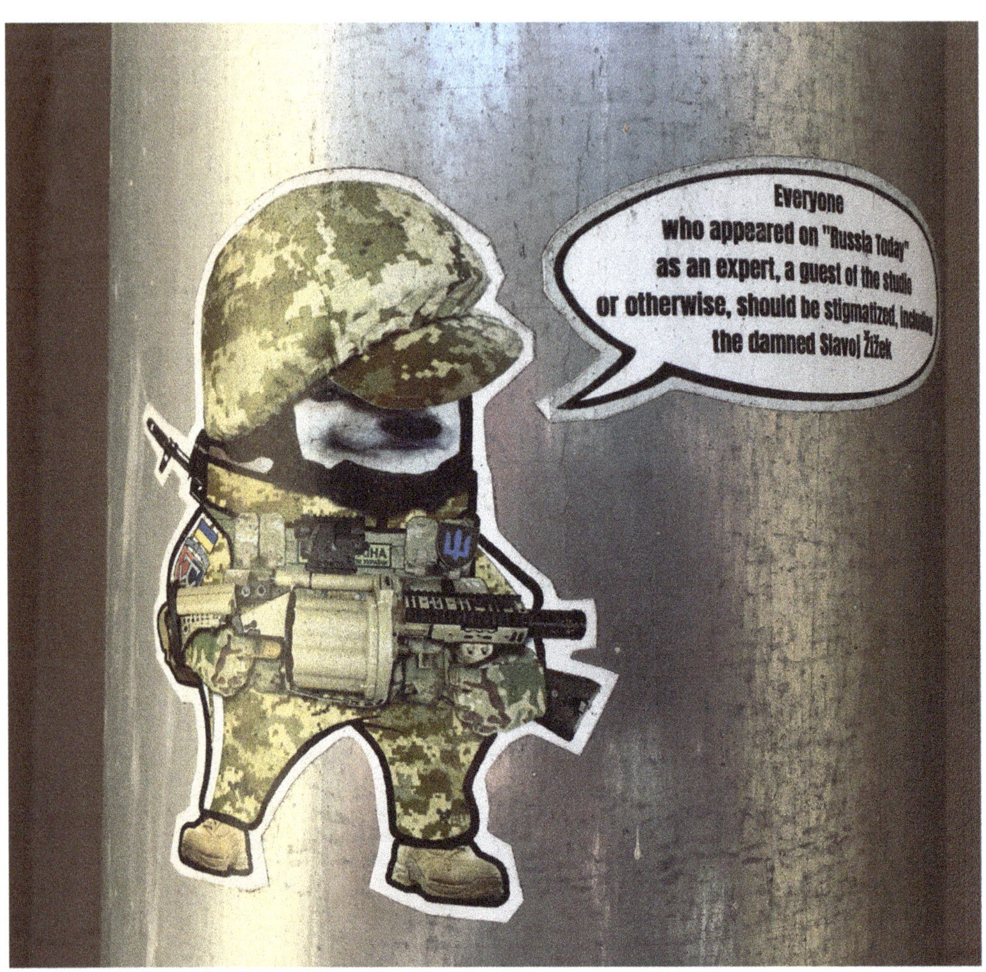

Odesa, May 2023.

VI

WAR IN ACADEMIA

> *"Learn Ukrainian — The Language of Freedom!"*
> *Flyers for a Ukrainian language course pinned to the*
> *bulletin board in the hallways of Columbia University,*
> *New York, early spring of 2014.*

The Anglo-Saxon way of learning and approaching science in general is radically different to the continental, *Germanic* way, which includes the Slovenian system of education and research. Speaking broadly, the latter mainly focuses on continuity, a linear explanation and research from A to Z, accumulating and memorizing knowledge by upgrading existing knowledge, a strong and presupposed theoretical and methodological background, and a pre-designed order of learning programs and their topics. The Anglo-Saxon system is more adaptable, open, theoretically and methodologically more flexible, and especially more focused on issues or topics — it follows the situation in the world, immediately reacts to it with new projects, courses, or curricula. They both have their good and their bad sides, their advantages are simultaneously their disadvantages; lately, I have noticed more and more combinations between the two ways, searching for a middle way on both sides of the ocean.

Until a fatal event happens. That spring semester of 2014, when I was teaching a few courses at Columbia, New York, I was surprised at how quickly attention was focused on what was happening in Ukraine: the Sochi Winter

Olympic Games were over, Putin suddenly, overnight occupied Crimea, the pot started to quietly simmer and then loudly boiled over in Donetsk and Luhansk. All at once, various study programs and research groups came alive with lectures, *ad hoc* discussions, guest lecturers, round tables, movie screenings, field reports. For the first time after the Cold War, historians and other experts on Eastern Europe — Russianists, Kremlinologists, were again popular, each with their approach ranging from serious academic methods to more apologetic, immediately distinctive, biased styles.

The 1990s Balkan story all over again: experts — and "experts" — hurriedly wrote books that their publishing houses hurried to publish. Some were focused on a single issue or topic, others were longitudinal, systematic; some were critical and in-depth, others apologetic and instantaneous. I will list the most typical ones. An example of the first approach is the already mentioned book by Yekelchyk, the very title of which reminds of a high-school history course: *Ukraine: What Everyone Needs to Know®* (2020). Its brief subchapters begin with questions: *Is it ...? Who are ...? How did ...? Why did...?* and contain useful information, especially from the American point of view (as foretold by the title of the first chapter: *Why did Ukraine become a key reference point of American political struggles?*). The explanations are concise yet understandable and clear but at times tendentious. As such, they follow contemporary dominant interpretations of the Ukrainian past, and avoid sensitive and controversial issues, as is usually the case in national historiography. The book mostly deals with national and political questions and pays little attention to social history and even less to class. It is a sort of *Reader's Digest*, which must be urgently and rapidly complemented by serious and in-depth historical studies.

In the shadow of the current war, *old demons* (as Michnik described the compromised historical figures and armies in an interview from the early 1990s) are reinhabiting bookshelves, too. In historical revisionism, the Balkans operate with a more or less successful rehabilitation of the whole — to reference Michnik's metaphor, *pandemonium* of WWII quisling leaders and their formations: the notorious Chetnik and Ustasha units,

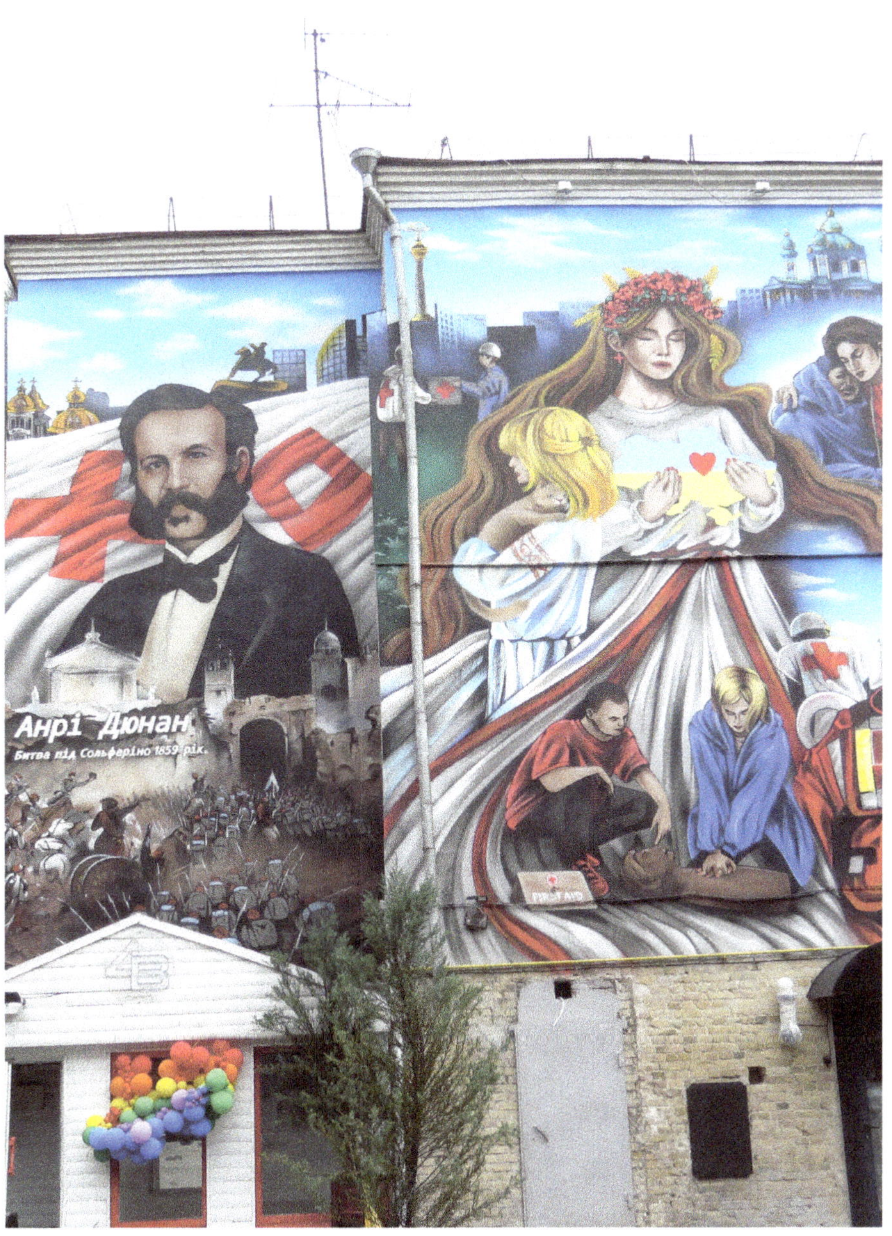

Kyiv, June 2024.

Slovenian Home Guards etc., the list is too long. Similarly, some people are trying to exonerate certain Ukrainian figures and groups for their collaboration with Nazism and for their role in what are undeniable crimes. In *Operation Payback* (2021), Canadian historian Lubomyr Y. Luciuk ascribes the persecution of Ukrainian Nazi war criminals (adding "alleged" to the description) in North America solely to a Soviet propaganda campaign.

In his *Short History of War in Ukraine* (2023), the aforementioned Lampreht expanded on and further substantiated his radio shows that he broadcast from 2021 to early 2023. Written with a diarist's meticulousness and from a mostly political and diplomatic, but also military perspective, this in-depth chronology sadly reads like a true-life crime novel with an open end. Although he unmistakenly condemns Putin's attack, he is also intolerant of mistakes and excesses on the Ukrainian side, clearly emphasizing that he believes "the West, both the USA and the EU member states to be de facto already at war with Russia."[1] His conclusion is pessimistic: "[t]he wounded declining empire [...] can yet prove to be very dangerous." I am sad to say that, months after his publication, this is coming true.

An example of the second approach is the vast, meticulous, and multi-sourced study by the historian Serhii Plokhy *The Gates of Europe* (2021), an A–Z of the Ukrainian past *from the beginning to today*. It is a highly instructive treasure trove of historical and comparative knowledge, but almost entirely focused on political and national perspectives of Ukrainian history and very little on class, culture, gender, minority, etc. It was written in a distinctively teleological approach, based on the *development of the nation* and directed towards the end goal of the *national state*. A typical *longue durée* national historiography. Ukraine sees its future in Europe; Plokhy believes that its realization of full sovereignty is "closely associated with the aspiration to join the European community of nations"[2] and "oriented itself toward the West in its geopolitical aspirations and social and cultural values."[3] I often felt that he was minimizing certain delicate situations, tendencies, and excesses on the Ukrainian side, dealing with them in only a few paragraphs and justifying them with exclusively external reasons

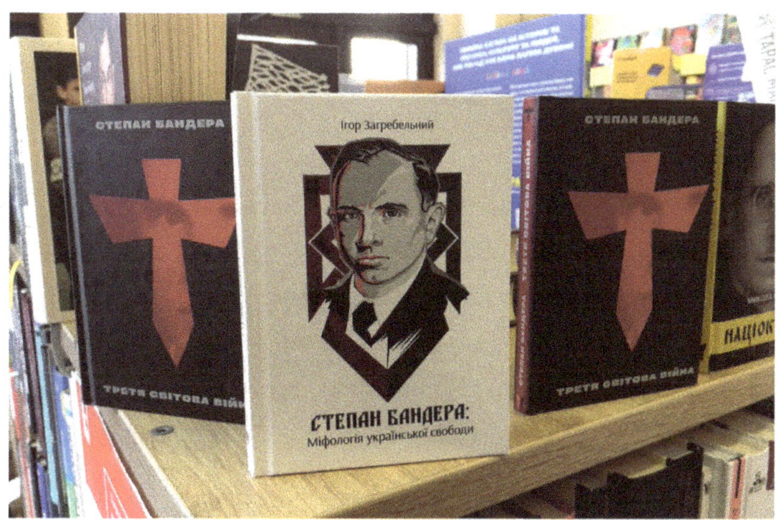

Lviv, May 2023.

and pressures — with a reaction of the victim, not with an independent view of their protagonists.

The impressive comparative work *Forward, To The Past — Studies about the Politics of History in Poland, Ukraine and Russia* (2019) by a critical Serbian researcher of Eastern Europe and author of this book's Foreword, Milan Subotić, analyses respective ethnic ideologies, interpretations of political histories of these nations and continuous waves of historical revisionism, sequences of inventing different ethnic traditions, painful dialectics of heroism and victimhood in their histories, and changing attitudes towards their most controversial historical personalities. He is not interested in history as such, but "in the ways it is (re)*presented* in the present through historiographic *narration* and collective *memory*."[4] Each of the three parts of the book is followed by an extensive list of bibliographical references in a number of languages. History's *white spots* & *black holes* — this is a delicate topic to research, but dealt with comprehensively, revealing Subotić's detailed knowledge of that part of Europe and ability to identify general trends and individual specifics of its history.

The ambitious collection *Ukraine's Many Faces — Land, People, and*

Culture Revisited (2023) edited by Olena Palko and Manuel Férez Gil is a comprehensive textbook of the Ukrainian past and present. Written by researchers of different provenances, generations, and social sciences, its chronologically listed chapters speak to the reader with different kinds of texts: historical spreadsheets, transcriptions of original documents, declarations, letters from the fateful periods of Ukrainian history, poems, interviews, and research articles (on historical, geographical, sociological, ethnic, economic, and religious topics, as well as the war). This variety of texts together with images, photos, and maps make the collection easy to read. Their main aim is, as summarized in the conclusion "let Ukraine speak": to include it in the school curricula and place it on the mental map of students, the academia, and general public. Along with a few other studies — allow me to mention the two colossal works by Timothy Snyder *Bloodlands* (2010) and *Black Earth* (2015), which comprehensively deal with the oppressing history of this part of Europe in the time of Hitler's and Stalin's empire — have offered me a scientific perspective on the current situation in Ukraine.

From books to experiences, from the distant gaze to everything I lived first-hand. At universities where I was invited to lecture and at other institutions that hosted the presentations of my book (libraries, galleries, and institutes) I was met by the initially mentioned surreal, completely Buñuelian duality, a simultaneous *war and peace*, to reference Tolstoy. On the one hand, everything was normal or even better. Their *Yes, We Can!* enthusiasm matched mine perfectly. Lecture rooms and halls were full of mainly young people, students, which made me especially happy on both late spring visits (2023, 2024) as the end of the semester and the summer vacations were close. They were joined by professors, even heads of department as well as president of the university and faculty deans, as well as the wider public, coming well-prepared with clear ideas and questions. During and after the presentations, which lasted longer than scheduled, we engaged in excellent and exhaustive debates that — I was told — sparked great interest on social media (which I avoid). We were discussing future collaborations, exchanges — four of them are already in process during my writing these lines. With the majority, I sensed the desire to engage a wider sphere in the future, not limited to academia. Based on the attention my graffiti book received, a publisher offered to translate another one — on nostalgia for Tito — which was published exactly one year after the first one, in late spring of 2024.

Both of my books were first launched at the Odesa National Library. Its team was especially welcoming and prepared at the promotion of the first two exhibitions from their archive materials: one on Slovenian authors from France, Prešeren and Srečko Kosovel, to brothers Milan and Josip Vidmar; the second on books and publications on graffiti. Promotion of the second one was even more intense: it was organized as a part of the annual Odesa Book Fair taking place in early June. Despite the wartime conditions and occasional alarms — a night before neighboring Chornomorsk was again under attack — dozens of publishing houses presented their works at stands inside or in front of the library, with hundreds of different and well attended events and thousands of visitors, booklovers. No electricity — no problem! Many events took place outdoors, with roaring generators and street traffic. My book on nostalgia for Tito attracted quite some attention and opened intense discussion there, but also in a few other places where it was promoted, mainly for two reasons. First, I got questions about the two socialist multiethnic federations, the Soviet Union and Yugoslavia: among a few similarities and much more differences I was pointing out how Yugoslav society was ethnically much more balanced, no ethnic group had decisive majority or enjoyed more political power than others. And the second one was about Yugoslavs' — and Tito's — successful resistance first against Nazi occupation 1941–1945 and then against Stalin's pressures from 1948 on. I was repeatedly asked how did they — and he — manage to succeed in both cases. Both of these queries were in one way or another connected to the harsh recent and present-day situation in Ukraine. (I found out few days later, when I already left Odesa, that it got the Book Fair's award in the category of scientific books.)

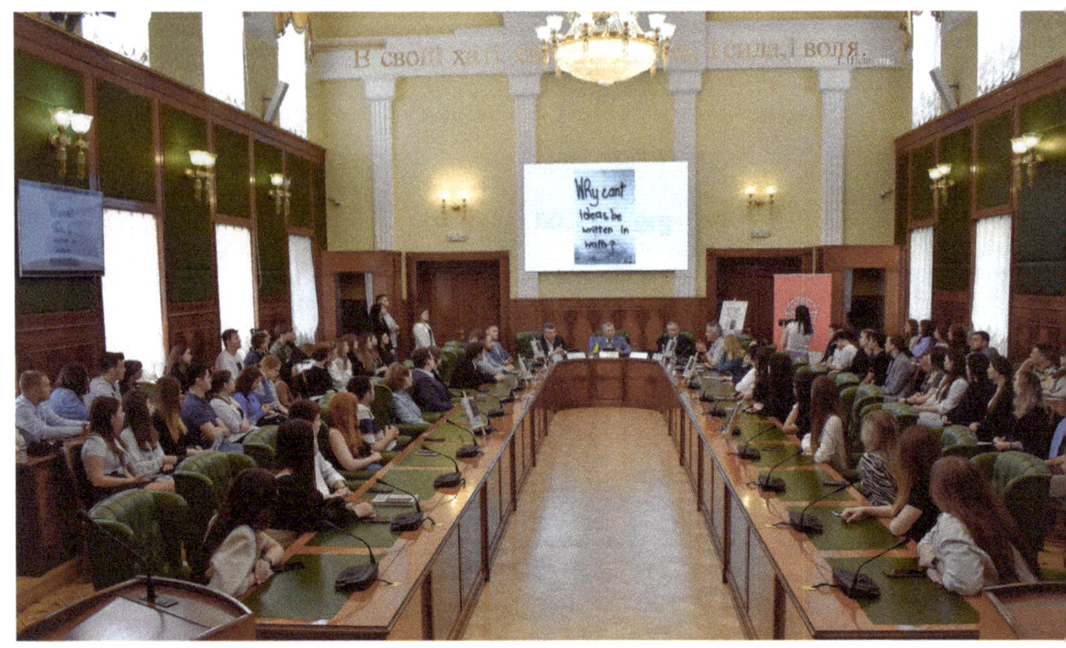

Odesa, May 2023.

Before, during, and after every event, there were so many pictures taken (which I wasn't prepared for): wider with everybody, select with the organizers, of the book signing (which I was even less prepared for!), of comings and goings, of presentations, shaking hands, talking. "Everybody enjoys having their picture taken here …," a host whispered into my ear. As proof, social media was apparently full of photos from every event, and I received dozens by e-mail after them with all kinds of questions and information.

At the beginning of my first lecture, I finally realized how abnormal the situation really is: students spontaneously welcomed audiences with *Glory to Ukraine!* followed by a loud and unanimous, *To the heroes — glory!* Corridors and rooms in general were full of flags and other national decorations; there were pictures of (fallen) soldiers hung in some places, apparently their students and staff. I later learned that one of the events had a small hitch; at the time, they did not want to bother me with it, as I

   Ukrainian Vignettes: Essays on a Culture at War

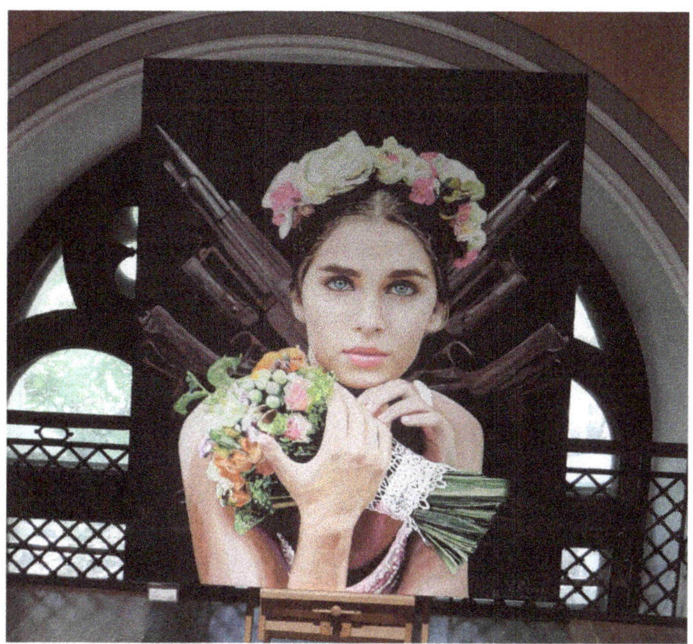

Odesa, June 2024.

was their guest. At first, the organizer designed the paper and electronic invitations with a Slovenian and a Ukrainian flag. Then somebody realized how similar Slovenian and Russian flags were — only separated by the clumsy, really unfortunate symbol in the top left corner, called the Slovenian coat of arms. To avoid any controversy, both flags were removed, and the invitations sent without them.

Before and after the events, I was hosted by the heads of these institutions, even by the rectors and directors of the universities, which took me by surprise: I am completely unaware of *high academic politics* (I hardly know who the rector of my home university is, and I have not been in the dean's office of my faculty for more than four or five times in the good three decades that I've worked there). I was really caught off guard. I don't have a single suit jacket in my wardrobe and the last time I wore a tie was when I served in the Yugoslav army ... if you don't count — if I remember correctly — wearing it as a bandana at concerts in my youth. I believe that people were this interested in me because I was — as my hosts told me — the first foreign lecturer or author that visited Ukraine since the total war erupted. In such circumstance, every attention, every support, every planning of future collaboration is more than welcome. If it had not been for the shadow — better, darkness — of the war hanging over it, I could say that everybody, they and I were more than happy with the whole thing.

As was expected, I encountered a rather typical Eastern-European academic culture with extremely visible hierarchies of leadership, professors, younger staff, and students. Back home, at least, this has become much less formal. But there, it can be seen in the way people dress, in how they address each other, in the long academic rituals, in the sequences and intonations of speaking and asking questions, in the age scale, in seating arrangements for interviews and group photo sessions. Certain leading figures still dressed classically, in suits, accompanied by *alla vecchia* stance and facial expressions, in which there was something so vehemently Brezhnev that they reminded me of the eternal headmaster of my primary school. Everything else had a patina of some other time: from the perfectly blond PR lady to the pyramidal protocol at lunchtime toasts (at one occasion, lunch consisted of game from a hunt, featuring all meat that its rector had caught and shot himself!), from enthusiastic greetings (during which I was glancing around to see who the fuss was all about) to strong handshakes in front of the camera and symbolic gifts.

Some senior academics were also in high positions within local and state political structures and therefore especially well protected: along with police officers, they were surrounded by their personal mean-looking security guards. "Chechens," an expert whispered with a nudge. Perhaps they were, but this ethnic name has become a generic appellation for ruthless army mercenaries. Other senior academics, the younger ones, were dressed modestly, casually, as if they were running morning errands, going to the market or to the post office. They explained that they believed any kind of formal wear during a time of war to be "tasteless," of which I immediately made note.

What I found the most valuable was talking to Ukrainian students. Involuntarily, I compared them to American students, whom I lectured exactly twenty years ago at the International Program of European Studies at the Jagiellonian University in Poland's *Coalition of the Willing* led by the United States. Literally overnight, those students changed, became more serious; the class atmosphere suddenly became harsh, curt, not relaxed. I went to an anti-war protest to the Main Square, *Rynek Główny*, attended by no more than thirty people in total — for the first time, none of my students were there. I am used to seeing them at every anti-war and other progressive demonstrations. In Ljubljana or elsewhere, we grin when we spot each other in the crowd. "We are at war …," one of these American students explained when I asked why the change in their behavior. Well, with Ukrainian students, I noticed no such war attitude — sooner a combination of rage and optimism, encased in the determination to persevere, to resist with a reason.

Older university buildings had the typical smell of building materials from another time, of worn parquet floor, of slightly moldy air, and of disintegrating paper. Yet this is always well balanced with the bubbly student youth in the corridors and the familiar blue light shining from the screens in offices and libraries. Some rooms, lecture halls, and offices were new, practical, shiny; others had a patina of a patina of antiquity, high ceilings, and thick walls; others yet were like artivist centers around the world — fun, with graffitied staircases, provocative posters, random chairs, and a barely working photocopier and coffee machine. However, this idyllic panorama was interrupted by the sacks of sand stockpiled in front of the lower-floor windows that revealed that we were in a state of war. Get real!

On every level, students at Ukrainian schools are taught either live or in hybrid mode, depending on the danger. War made numerous institutions and organizations — educational, cultural, and scientific ones, entire universities with all their infrastructure, *tutto completo* — move from the east to the west. Now, professors and students continue following the same programs but in a different location. They include foreigners, who mainly come from third-world countries. "That's a sign that there's peace here, at least," my Uzhhorod host told me when we came by cricket players on one of the campus fields. We exchanged a few words; they introduced themselves as Pakistani and Indian and were friendly to one another while they were chasing around their leather balls with their odd bats. They probably purposefully never told us who comes from where. Another Balkans analogy — funny if it weren't tragic. Abroad, the Pakistani and the Indians obviously hold no ethnic grudges or religious issues against each other, just like *our people* don't. But back home, in their quarrelling homelands and on their bloody borders, the story would be completely different. True, they also measured against each other on that grassy field — but in a game that brings them together, not tears them apart.

Based on my experience from elsewhere, I immediately spotted another difference between the hosts at universities, institutes, and libraries — the current academic and linguistic environment. In short: one accepts your work and makes it known, the others unjustifiably less so or not at all. Knowledge resembles the waves made by a stone thrown in a pond: in concentric circles, it spreads where it can. In the southern Balkans and in Central Asia, the academic epicenter is Turkey, the Turkish academia,

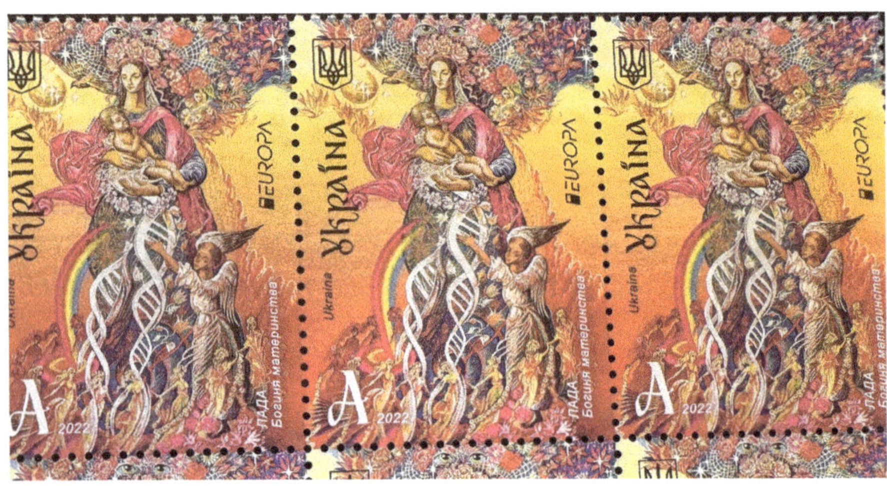

Uzhhorod, June 2024.

    Ukrainian Vignettes: Essays on a Culture at War

Istanbul; everything tends mainly towards this city on the shores of Europe and Asia. In the Francophone world, from Romania to Central Africa, everybody is oriented towards Paris. On a smaller scale but nevertheless, the former Yugoslav space is directed to the larger and academically more established centers like Belgrade and Zagreb. In Slovenia (after independence) and elsewhere in the West, things are completely tied to the Anglo-Saxon academia type, its publishers, journals, institutions, to the unwritten rule of *Publish in English or perish*. The post-Soviet world remains Russocentric, Russian academia and language are still the most important. Russian is spoken by 260, 270 million people, and a large part of publications, publishing houses, relevant journals, conferences, scientific and pedagogic activities in general remain tied to the Russian space, academia, and language. Until lately, so still around 2010, the situation was the same in Ukraine, explained Ukrainian philosopher, activist and editor Olha Mukha at her well-attended lecture in Ljubljana, organized recently by the Slovenian branch of the PEN writers' association. After independence, scientific textbooks and studies have increasingly been published in the Ukrainian language, replacing Russian as the first language in academia. But still: writing in Russian was absolutely necessary

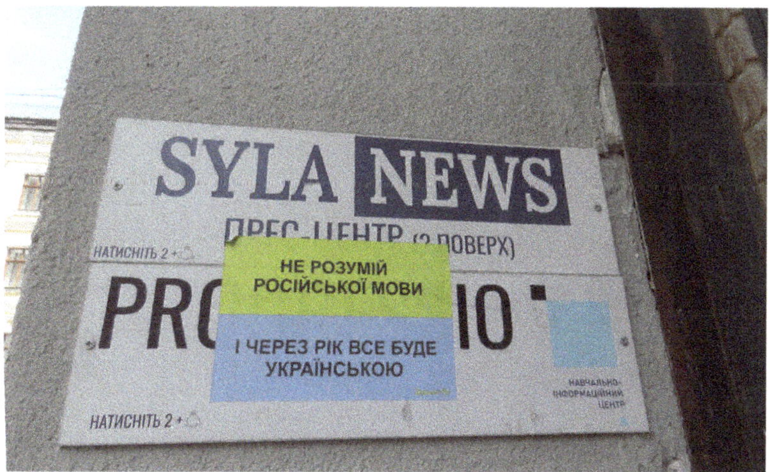

"I do not understand the Russian language – and in a year, everything will be Ukrainian," Lviv, May 2023.

for real academic breakthrough and academic recognition. As it is the case in Slovenian and other smaller languages — and smaller academic environments.

All my Ukrainian colleagues speak perfect or nearly fluent Russian; some of them are only now learning the correct, literary Ukrainian. Formally acknowledged or not, Ukraine is a deeply bilingual country, in some regions also tri- or even quadra-lingual. No matter their age, many struggle with other foreign languages, which is why some events during my visit were being interpreted. (Unlike in Slovenia, even the young-sters, the teenagers, even waiters speak very little or almost no English. I often asked some 16-year-olds for directions, and we struggled with even the most basic words. Or when I asked waitresses to help me decipher the menus written in Cyrillic alphabet.) Russian, however, is present at every step. "Ukraine is full of Ukrainian Russian-speaking nationalists," claims Kurkov in his diary (2022).[5] I heard and read about numerous cases of people in Ukraine who ethnically define themselves as Russians and politically as Ukrainians; or about the divisions withing families — one part (usually, but not always, the younger ones) choosing the Ukrainian side, while the other (usually, but not always, the older ones) chooses the Russian or the pro-Russian one.

Locals told me that Russian is often the language used by the police officers on the home front and soldiers at the front — just like by their enemies in the opposite trench. Even many ordinary chats are in both languages: they begin in Ukrainian, the answer is given in Russian, etc. A really absurd thing happened when I met one of the co-authors of the act on public usage of Ukrainian language: during the interview, for which we needed an English interpreter, he spoke in Russian! In every city that I visited, even my ear, not used to any of these two languages, could hear *spasibo*, not just *dyakuyu*; *khoroshiy*, not just *dobre*; and *da*, not just *tak*. A Ukrainian colleague told me a typical story about her family, similar to the one I heard from another colleague in Georgia: she is of Jewish and middle-class origin, but her parents enrolled her in Russian schools,

  Ukrainian Vignettes: Essays on a Culture at War

just like they have been doing for several generations, although they also understood Ukrainian, the language of their neighbors. Very similar to President Zelenskyy's situation. Just like in other European countries, Jews have been speaking the language of the ruling nation.

If anywhere, in Slovenia we can understand how politically sensitive the issue of language is, as the Slovenian national ideology is fundamentally a linguistic one despite various political connotations. We know its mantra, Slovenians are created by language. Since 1996, Ukrainian is the only official language in the country, while Russian is included among its minority languages. However, since 2000 and especially after the Russian attack of 2014, Russian has been increasingly marginalized. Posters around the cities and television adds invite people to attend Ukrainian courses, use it in daily life, and in celebration on *Mother Language Day*. In other countries with fresh wounds from recent wars, in Bosnia-Herzegovina, Croatia and Kosovo, extremists from both sides are removing signs or road markings in *foreign* language, the language of the *enemy*: in Republika Srpska those in Latin alphabet; in Croatia and in the Federation of Bosnia-Herzegovina those in Cyrillic; the Kosovo Albanians remove those in Serbian and the Serbs there those in Albanian. Here, Ukrainian deal with signs in Russian, while Russians do the same with signage in Ukrainian.

A few of my academic colleagues have explicitly told me that it is time for them to also look elsewhere, to redirect towards Western academia — and have doubled down on learning foreign languages, especially English. I expressed my opinion clearly: the issue of academic imperialism, the domination of the West also in the field of research, should not be neglected. The largest part of journals and publishing houses that have high impact factor are either from the Anglo-Saxon world, or from the areas that tend toward it, or anywhere else provided that they are in English. This is why we should balance our articles and academic engagement in general among various academic worlds and publics and lecture and publish complimentarily, non-exclusively, in different places and in different languages: Eastern, Western, Southern, in more of them at the same time. As I try to do this myself, I was delighted to have my first academic article published in Georgian and to speak at their annual humanities symposium just last summer, while I was writing these essays.

So, as soon as I returned home, I connected the academic circles in which I am active with my new Ukrainian colleagues to help them publish, visit, and be funded. Together with a few enthusiasts from University of Ljubljana and several Ukrainian universities we organized winter school for Ukrainian students in Ljubljana entitled Voices of Ukraine in the week around the second anniversary of the attack. Twenty of them came, together with their professors, for a series of lectures, presentations, talks, exhibition of artworks of Ukrainian students of the Fine Arts Academy, round tables and — for the *Grand Finale* — a movie evening and artist talk with the young Ukrainian director Antonio Lukich along with a screening of his two films: *My Thoughts are Silent* (2019) and *Luxembourg, Luxembourg* (2022). On my third trip to Ukraine I brought, combining different means of transport, four boxes full of books in English with total weight of about 170 pounds that I collected from my colleagues and Slovenian publishing houses. I donated them to the university library in Mykolaiv which suffered two direct missile hits back in 2022: those that were not burned were later destroyed by water and other extinguishing agents by firefighters. Librarians, scholars and students couldn't hide their surprise and excitement about the unexpected act of solidarity by their unknown Slovenian colleagues. I connected a few of my new Ukrainian colleagues with editorial boards of some social-science journals for the possible publication of their articles: some of them are now already in the process. This is where I can help: school, education, creating and disseminating knowledge, these are my little utopias. To counter the justified Foucaultian reservations that *knowledge is power*, it works *for* the authority, I always add the same affirmative words of the Enlightenment thinkers: *knowledge is power*, but *against* the authority, it is the power of emancipation. This is why I am so involved in education: here, I can make a fundamental change, elsewhere I cannot.

NOTES

1 Lampreht, Miha. *Kratka zgodovina vojne v Ukrajini,* 2023. 347.

2 Plokhy, Serhii. *The Gates of Europe: A History of Ukraine,* 2021. 326.

3 Plokhy, Serhii. 2021. xix.

4 Subotić, Milan. *Napred, u prošlost: Studije o politici istorije u Poljskoj, Ukrajini i Rusiji,* 2019. 95.

5 Kurkov, Andriy. *Diary of an Invasion,* 2022. 175.

"Internet Party of Ukraine," a stencil promoting a small political party based in Odesa, whose anonymous candidate for the presidential elections in 2014 dressed as Darth Vader, Odesa, June 2024.

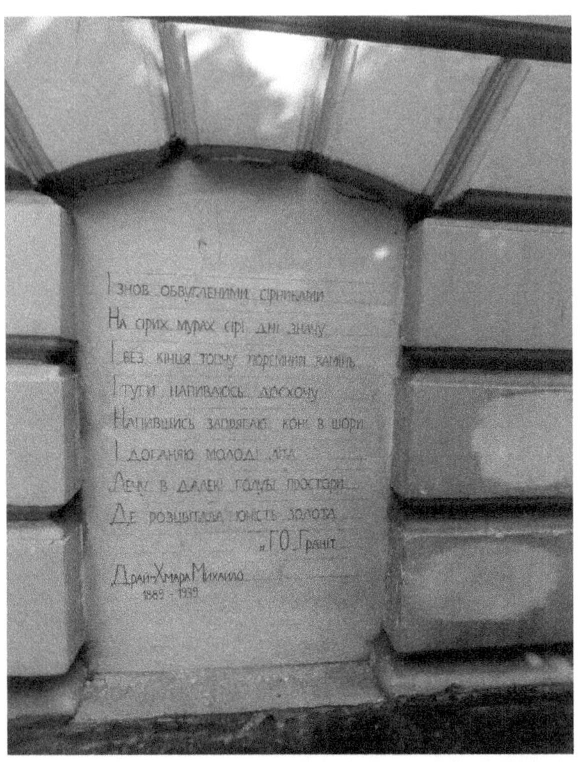

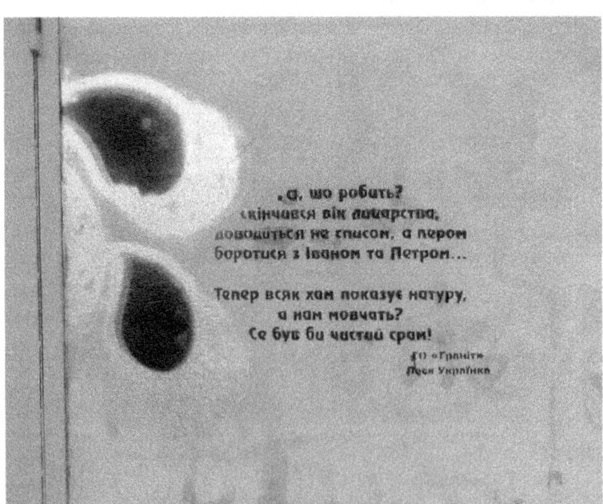

Top to bottom: Verses from a poem by Mykhailo Drai-Khmara (1889-1939), Lviv, May 2023; verses from a poem of Lesya Ukrainka (1871–1913), Lviv, May 2023.

VII.

WORDS OF WAR

"But what will you do with yourselves?"
"What? Oh, don't worry about us. We will live."
Tamara Duda, Daughter, 2021.[1]

When arms speak, muses are silent is a peace-time cliché — they actually become furies. Every war is a cultural struggle, *Kulturkampf,* too. If art is usually criticism and alternative to the history of the victors, to the *status quo* of current politics, to the prescribed taste and ruling morale, this can change during the war. On the one hand, the radical situation narrows the possibilities of creating, but on the other it also encourages creators to reach for what was unimaginable, to surpass the existing even more than in peace. Art can serve *our side* loudly or quietly, it can become one of the (non-)intrusive forms of *soft power*; or it can keep problematizing, criticizing, and subverting reality around it, regardless of sides. It can support the war or is engaged against it — or overcomes this forced dilemma. In both cases something is clear: just as weapons are changing through history, so are artistic media. During the era of spears and sabers, images of war were found in frescos; during the era of rifles and cannons, they were described in books; during the era of fighter pilots, they were recorded on film; and, finally, today, in the era of drones, they are posted on social media. Immediately posted on social media.

Bosnian French writer Velibor Čolić concluded a recent interview by saying that even war cannot stop poetry: "Winners write history, losers write books." (2023) To avoid this bitter fact, history in Ukraine is already being interpreted by the artists themselves. In this essay, I write about the literature of war, of literary works, both prose and poetry, that directly address the experience of war in Ukraine; the next essay is on artistic manifestations and visual metaphors of war, on exhibitions, graffiti and street art; and the ninth essay on music, on the local war soundscape.

Ukrainian literary authors immediately responded to the beginning and the continuation of the war in their novels, poems, graphic novels, collections of short stories, diaries, readings, and performances live at home and abroad. Some works were written under occupation — they speak of authentic experience living under the authority of the attackers and separatists; some recount the stories of their armed and unarmed resistance; others are genuinely personal, autobiographical records, mostly from the first months of the war, angry and optimistic at the same time. I was surprised to see poetry on the walls, too, whole excerpts of it. I (in)voluntarily compared these fresh works with the classics of contemporary Ukrainian literature and found parallels and meaningful premonitions of what is happening today.

In *Daughter* (2021), Tamara Duda uses no grand words to movingly describe true stories: her own and other people's testimonies, from the time of the occupation of Donetsk in 2014 and 2015, and the transformation of her circle of people into active resisters against the separatists and Putin's militias, the *little green men*, as they called them because they didn't wear any military insignia. The narration of the novel gradually spans from a perfectly normal life before to a complete domination of humiliation, deprivation, pain, and death. In short: war. Duda compares it to a nightmarish fall down the rabbit hole ("Everything which you once could have relied upon crumbled into dust in your very hands"[2]). The cruel *crescendo* out there is pierced by the protagonist's affective hardships and existential dilemmas "between panic and apathy, hope and despair,"[3] as well as by patriotic maxims. Despite the apocalyptic situations — she is even mistakenly declared dead —, the novel ends as it should: optimistically. The *daughter*, the orphan adopted by the protagonist, is safe.

The metaphor of being an orphan is also central in Zhadan's above-mentioned novel *The Orphanage* (2021), maybe most concisely, "If you think about it, it's like we're all living in an orphanage. Abandoned by everyone, wearing too much makeup and whatever clothes we come by," and "Abandoned, neglected, forgotten. Aggrieved."[4] Being outcast by everyone is also a feeling I got from many people I talked to in Ukraine. The novel takes place in the confusing start of the war and tells the story of an uncle who's on no one's side and just wants to rescue his nephew from the orphanage in a besiged town. The atmosphere among the people reflects the atmosphere of the devastated urbanscape: apocalyptic chaos, complete confusion, danger at every turn, both from bombs and from people, anxiety and shortage that lead to acts of unimaginable cruelty and equally unimaginable solidarity and love. Toward the end, Zhadan outlines the sad and inevitable omnious consequences of war: "Nope, nobody'll forget anything, nobody'll leave anything in the past, and the kid, no matter how things play out for him, will keep carrying these memories, like bags filled with rocks, and the smell of torn skin and men's salty tears will pursue him until the end of his days, and the shadow of the orphanage will linger behind him, no matter where he goes, no matter how sunny those places may be."[5]

In 2016, Ukrainian journalist Mykola Semena from Crimea, who stayed there in 2014 to whip the new Russian authorities, was found guilty of *separatism*, which provoked harsh reactions from the international community. *Crimean Report: Chronicle of the Occupation of Crimea* (2018) is a collection of more than 100 commentaries, articles, and notes that he was publishing under various pseudonyms and range from the complex history of this peninsula to the false promises of rapid development after 2014. He focused on the devastating political, economic, social, international political, tourist, health, and educational consequences of the annexation,

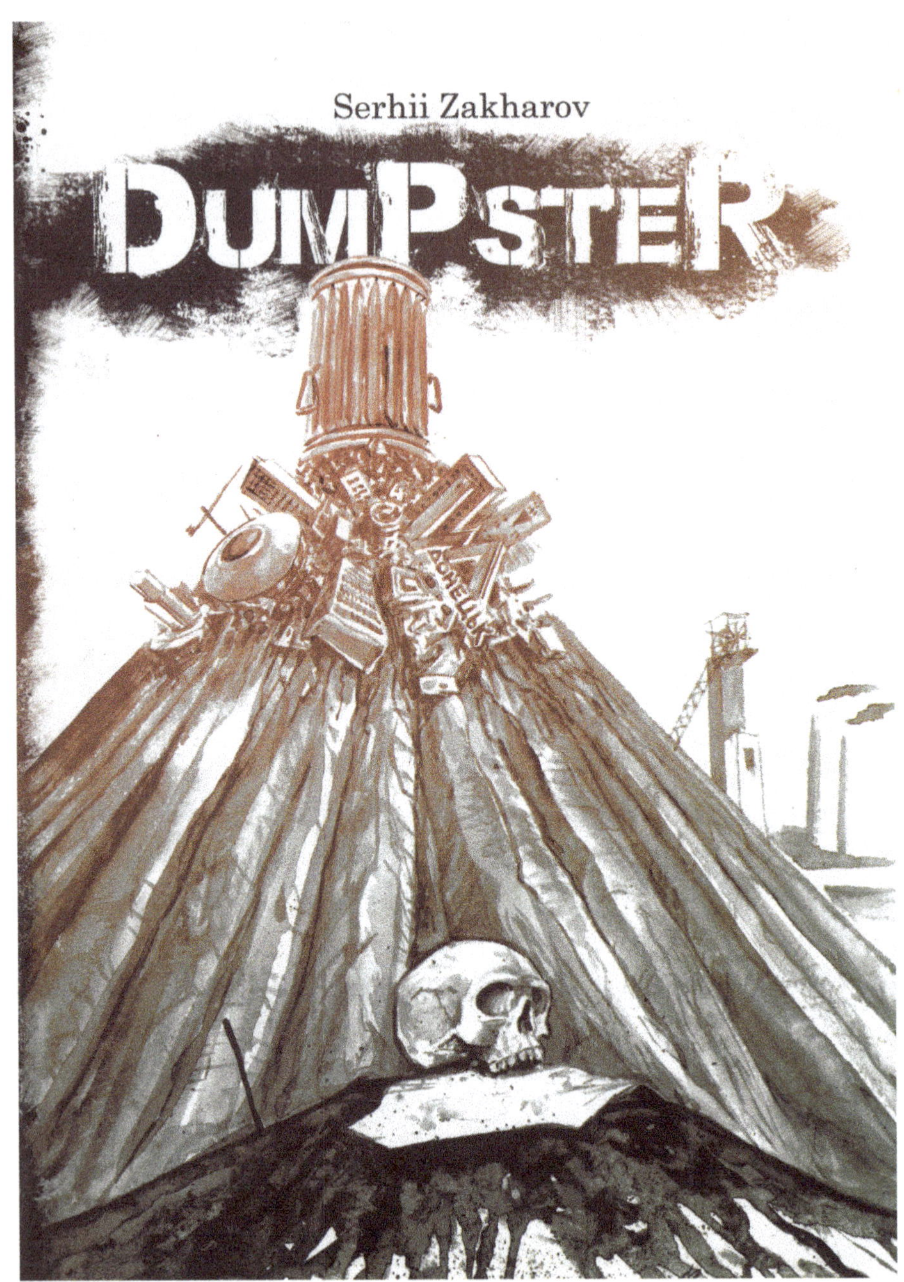

Serhii Zakharov graphic novel DumPsteR cover, 2018.

as well as those concerning freedom of speech and the media, art, culture and, last but not least, official Russian historiography. ("In the blink of an eye, the invaders took Crimea out of the 21st century and back to 1937"[6]). He admitted having no idea that he would become a *reporter from the front*, like those who were praised during WWII. And that he neither realized the coming danger nor expected that something like this could even happen.

In *The Ukrainian Night* (2017), an expert on the intellectual history of this part of the world, Marci Shore (first writing in Vienna, then in Ukraine), described her close encounter with the Maidan Revolution and Putin's subsequent occupation of parts of Ukraine through a prism of recent history, current politics, and culture. She prefaced the book as "a history of a revolution as it was experienced by those who chose to take part in it. The purpose of writing history is like that of writing literature: to allow the reader an encounter with alterity, an imaginative leap into another time and place, a possibility of understanding the Other" (xvii). Shore described the scenes of dramatic events from 2024 and 2015 in a vivid, sometimes zealous literary tone, interweaving excerpts from literary works with her personal reflections and shocking first-hand testimonies. These were recorded in numerous encounters with her friends, colleagues, acquaintances, and strangers, with a multitude of newly introduced or perfectly random, passing people, the protagonists in these events.

In his graphic novel *DumPsteR* (2018), visual artist Serhii Zakharov reveals his political conviction in the very title of the English translation: *DumPsteR*, DPR, *Donetsk People's Republic*. He describes his story of artistic resistance: when his home Donetsk was occupied, he filled public spaces with life-size cardboard cutouts of grotesque separatist soldiers and their leaders with stupid facial expressions — *paste-ups*. He was quickly traced, as he published photos of it on his social media. (In an interview, he later admitted, "I thought that no one would look for an artist who was just painting things. I thought nobody cared about that. ... I was wrong.") Twice in a row, he was caught and spent weeks in prison, accused of *terrorist propaganda* and tortured (repeating the question I remember from my days in the Yugoslav army that arose if someone did something bad: "On whose orders did you do this, who is paying you to do this?"), and was exposed to a fake execution more than once. His story combines the ordeals of his fellow prisoners with whom he shared interrogations, cells, and torture chambers. Now, back in Kyiv, he is pursuing his artist's career and is active in the program for the rehabilitation of Ukrainian war prisoners and others released from Russian prisons and camps.

Italian comic-book writer and illustrator of Russian descent Igort (Igor Tuveri) took another step back, to the "roots of the conflict," as he subtitled his graphic novel *Ukrainian Notebooks* (2022). This wonderfully designed book collects, summarizes, and visualizes the testimonies of elderly inhabitants of the land, whom he met during his two years of living and traveling there, some 15 years ago. He was interested in the shards of the difficult fates of real and simple people caught in the wheels of epochal changes that shook Ukraine from the 1920s to today (Holodomor, dekulakization, forced relocations, gulags, WWII, poverty, Chernobyl). Each of the rather impressionistically set stories is presented as a martyrdom, while Igort cuts the integrity of the narration in a Brecthian fashion with the images of the culprits: the pan-Soviet and local Ukrainian leaders of the time. The novel ends with an ominous forecast of the new decade, when huge billboards, gigantographs, with the image of Stalin appeared around Moscow in honor of Victory Day in the beginning of April 2010.

The short novel *My Grandfather Danced the Best* (2020) and short stories collection *Happy Naked People* (2024) by the Ukrainian writer and poet Kateryna Babkina deal with the contemporary situation in her country in a quite different way. She's stitching together fragments of people's lives, insights of chronicles of families and friendships, notes about romances and childhood memories, flashes from little personal dramas with the past and present tragedies of Ukrainians (again: Famine, conflicts and wars, troubled post-socialist transition, political unrest etc.). In her writing, these latter ones seem secondary, marginal, sporadic — they are in fact always ominously close, important as a persistent dark frame of protagonists' quotidian lives and their life paths. Babkina's lyrical, bitter-sweet stories are far from easy reading, since — what wonderful metaphors! — her "dancing grandpa" and "happy naked people" are perfectly aware of the world in which they are living. For example, how afraid protagonists are to admit that death of a young relative "in the East" in the ongoing war is not as terrible as it is terrible that it happened without any sense (in her short stories collection). But still: both books end in an optimistic tone, with the very last words "smile" (in *Happy Naked People*) and a steady gaze forward because, "in principle, this is the only thing that needs to be done in their place" (*My Grandfather Danced the Best*).

Books on the second stage of war, starting in February 2022, appeared practically instantaneously, in a few months. "Sad, angry, strong, brave words," I wrote in pencil on the first page of the anthology *State of War* (2023) together with the date marking when I had put the book down. The anthology collects five-to-six-pages-long reflections by prominent Ukrainian authors and is prefaced by a short note by a Supreme Commander of the Ukrainian Armed Forces (while the cover features *The Angel of the Armed Forces of Ukraine* by Ukrainian artist Matvii Vaisberg). It's no good for a book if it's not introduced by a writer, I thought, even though it is the middle of the war. Apart from a few exceptions, the sketches contained are not written from a fan perspective, but are intimate, existential, with a strong emphasis on the shocking fragments of the experience of war (and also on small pleasures, like having a cup of real strong coffee after a couple of weeks, reading novels during the lulls in the tunnels, etc.), while they are also full of determined statements about the future perspectives.

How to put horror into words? While I was reading these works, I was involuntarily, yet constantly reminded of *Apocalypse Now*; perhaps because I find it the best ani-war movie I have ever seen. As the film concludes, Colonel Kurtz, the mostly hidden antagonist, explains: "It's impossible for words to describe what is necessary to those who do not know what horror means. Horror... Horror has a face... and you must make a friend of horror.

Horror and moral terror are your friends. If they are not, then they are enemies to be feared. They are truly enemies!" In this exact vein, Vakhtang Kebuladze, one of the authors featured in *State of War*, is asking, "Can new, unknown words be found to express the endless horror and infinite sadness?"[7] Another author, Max Kidruk, states that we need to find the strength to speak out loud, "despite the pain, insults, and anger,"[8] while the third, Serhiy Zhadan, adds that "speaking remains necessary — even in war, especially in war."[9] Halyna Kruk comments on the everyday realities of war: "we have no time to work on our trauma now"; authors now "bet on realistic, documentary, essayistic writing, not fiction."[10]

I had the pleasure of meeting her contemporary, poet Iya Kiva in Kyiv after a long tour she had in Western Europe. Sad again for my lack of knowledge of Ukrainian I was unable to read her newest book of poems she gave me at that occasion, entitled *The laughter of an extinguished fire*, published only in Ukrainian. *So far* only in that language, I thought, hoping to read it soon translated. Expelled from her native Donetsk, Kiva claims in one interview that since wartime she has since written "completely differently": "luxuriant metaphors seem superfluous to me" because "difficult times demand simplicity in speaking. But that's just formal minimalism. I don't mean semantic simplification. I mean something like the inability to put on a beautiful, expensive dress if everyone around you is a beggar." That's something I noticed also in works of other Ukrainian writers, and artists in general. Despite their various approaches, the language of the descriptions of tragedies, distress, desires, and hopes of these authors is simple, clear, intense, concrete, void of comfortable peace-age escapades into the abstract, metaphysical, sentimental magniloquence, pure lyricism, superfluous sophistication. In short: theirs is a literature of naked survival.

A special genre is the war diary, full of autobiographical images and details of catastrophic events: to mention only the three prominent Ukrainian writers: the aforementioned Kurkov, Belorusets, and Zhadan. Kurkov titled his work *Diary of an Invasion* (2022), covering the period from a little before the war until the early summer of the first year of the war and focusing mostly of the end of winter and spring. Dedicated to Ukrainian fighters, the diary uses genre-typical descriptions of everyday situations and reflects on the general events of daily politics and war; Kurkov combines personal experience and the fates of his nearest ones, friends, and acquaintances with the historical insight from his environment and wider. His records are full of current and political references, which occasionally glide into exaggeration (e.g. "Ukrainians are individualists, egoists, anarchists who do not like government or authority"[11]) and — not typical for Kurkov — a slightly unusually robust language. Despite the will and resilience he displays, the current situation scares him; towards the end, he writes, "I do not know what will happen tomorrow. To be honest, I find this lack of certainty about the future almost unbearable."[12] Yevgenia Belorusets, who's also a photographer, described the first month and a half of the war in 2022 in her hometown Kyiv, suddenly "a changed city," as she sees it now. She collected her thoughts, impressions, fears, feelings and reflections day by day in a book with a simple title *War Diary* (2023). Black and white photos that she took and included in the diary only deepen the gloomy atmosphere in which "peacetime seems unattainably far away. New laws and a new reality are unfolding," and in which everywhere she looks, she sees war: "a total, all-encompassing way of life that swallows up everything."[13]

Serhiy Zhadan also published a war diary titled *Sky Above Kharkiv — Dispatches from the Ukrainian Front* (2023). It is a chronology of Facebook posts from the first four months of the war, instantaneous diary notes, and photos of the besieged town as well as this charismatic poet and singer in it. A telegraphic style, one could say, with an analog vocabulary. His collection is much angrier and sharper that Kurkov's, which can certainly also be attributed to the fact that he spent most of his time in this city directly on the front. His notes celebrate the resistance of the Kharkiv people, fighters, activists, civilians, the solidarity among them; commemorate dead fellow citizens; express gratitude for the support they are

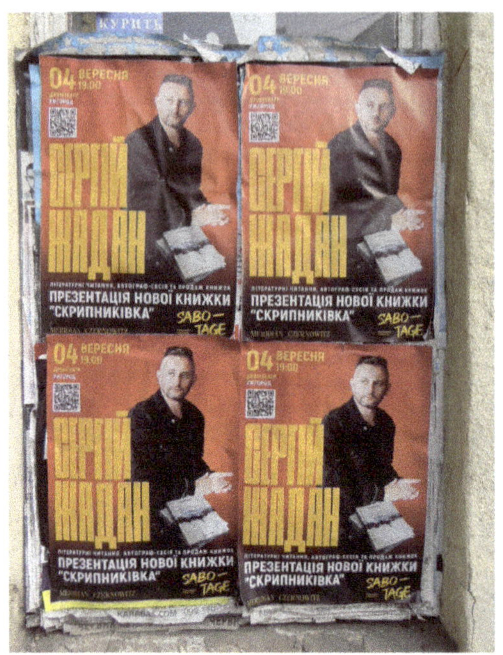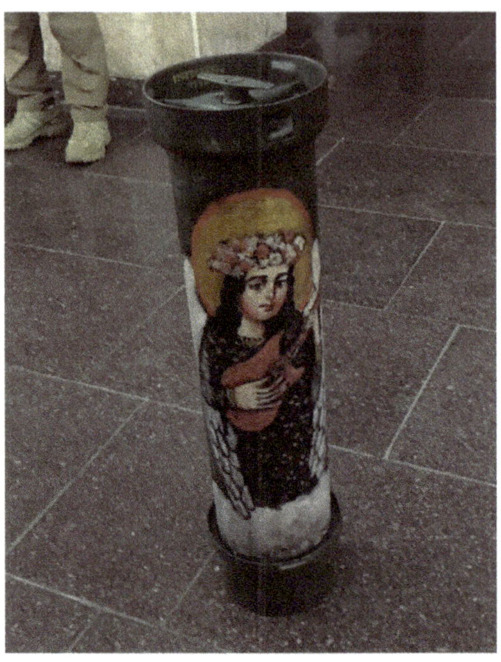

Left to right: poster for Serhiy Zhadan's poetry evening; Propelling charge with painting, sold this same poetry evening, Uzhhorod, September 2023.

receiving; appeal for donations; and describe not only the bombardments but also the cultural life in the besieged town (children's exhibitions, concerts, performances, etc.). The diary pages are full of unfiltered emotion, rock'n'roll one liners, poems that flowed on paper, patriotic rhetoric, and the glorification of soldiers and everyone engaged in defense. Along with, of course, the romanticizing and the encouraging of his compatriots; many posts end with "Tomorrow, we will wake up a day closer to victory," "Greetings from Ukrainian Kharkiv," or with excitement expressed over the Ukrainian flags flying high over the ruins. On the other hand, there are also countless severe exaggerations, such as repeating, "The Russians are barbarians,"[14] *en bloc* attacks on Russian culture and art with no attempts of differentiation. All Russians? I was asking myself when reading that. Everything Russian? A photo of a bombarded bookstore is, for example, cynically subtitled, "Does anyone still want to talk about Dostoyevsky?"[15] Such statements only mirror the Great-Russian "Ukrainians-are-Nazis" argument and encourages exactly what the attackers want. Such oversimplifications and collective condemnations are unfortunately not rare also among some most critical minds of contemporary Ukrainian literature. Albeit written in spasms of rage and resistance, non-selective judgements of this type take away credibility from otherwise sincere and justified criticism of the Russian attack and Putin's ideology and discourage critical readers. With all due respect to his or their work and engagement, I was discouraged, too.

First-hand war experience is also recorded in war novels; I was sadly unable to read them all but only had a good leaf through them, squatting in a corner or leaning against the walls of a Lviv, Kyiv, Odesa, or Uzhhorod bookstore. These, in short, are action-packed. In her book *Heroic Cities of Bucha, Irpin, Hostomel* (2023), the aforementioned war reporter Podobna, who has been reporting on the war since day one, describes the experience of the inhabitants of these cities, fighters and prisoners, civilians and journalists, before and during the war. She is also a contributor to *Heroes*, a show featuring short, 15-minute portraits of great feats achieved by simple nameless Ukrainians, those at the front or those on the home front. Journalist Daria Bura has written several books on this topic: in *Heroic City of Chernihiv* (2023), she wrote on the weeks-long unsuccessful siege of this city at the beginning of the war, a city in the way of Putin's military advance into Kyiv. In *Journey to the Beyond. Mariupol* (2023), editor and journalist Yevhen Shishatskyi described the painful events he experienced on his one week Odyssey into this besieged city, i.e. his hometown, and from it; a journey he made to see his family at the beginning of the war in a van carrying humanitarian aid. These three books were published by the Kharkiv-based Folio publishing house. Much more controversial is *Valhalla Express — the story of a nationalist, revolutionary, and volunteer,*[16] full of original photos and signed with the callsign Woland. It describes the protagonist's political transformation from activist during the Maidan Revolution into a fighter of the notorious Azov Brigade in 2014 and 2015. In bookstores, especially in their windows, these war novels are accompanied by various patriotic children's books and comics, and books glorifying achievements of *our fighters*.

These books all contain real references to actual places and original testimonies, are systematically chronological, and often feature photos, which is a documentarist upgrade of fiction. This is also the case in the theatre play *Azovstal — Voices* directed by Valeria Demchenko (2023), the aim of which is to raise awareness of the captured defenders and civilians, as well as of the steel works transformed into a fort. Performed at home and abroad, profits from this play support the families of people in captivity. *Not Born for War* is a kind of a military stand-up by Yevhen Avdieienko, a former actor who joined the army in February 2022, in which he shares his and his comrades's experiences from the frontline. This show started in Odesa in February 2025 and is followed by American tour which is scheduled for the spring following it. As in many similar events and shows, earnings will be used for supporting Ukrainian army.

Even more documentarist is the approach of the feature length war drama that is apparently regularly screened on Ukrainian TV channels, *Cyborgs: Heroes Never Die* directed by Ahtem Seitablayev (2017). The film focuses on one of the most militarized episodes of the Ukrainian war, the selfless defense of Donetsk airport between September 2014 and January 2015. *Cyborgs* was the name given to Ukrainian defenders by the separatist Donetsk People's Republic attackers as they were putting up an inhumanly strong resistance. The response of the Russian side is their first film on the war, *The Witness* by David Dadunashvili (2023), which focuses on the experience and perspective of a Belgian musician who happens to be in Kyiv when war erupts in February 2022. As a foreigner, i.e. an *objective observer*, he is supposed to tell the *truth* about the events. In reality, he repeats every main motif of Putin's propaganda: Ukrainian soldiers as contemporary Hitlerians, drug addicts, etc. In contrast to the Ukrainian film, which proved to be a hit, the Russian one was apparently a financial flop.

If the documentarist approach aims to emphasize the authenticity, the previously mentioned author Chkvanava's novel *Toreadors* (2013), which I

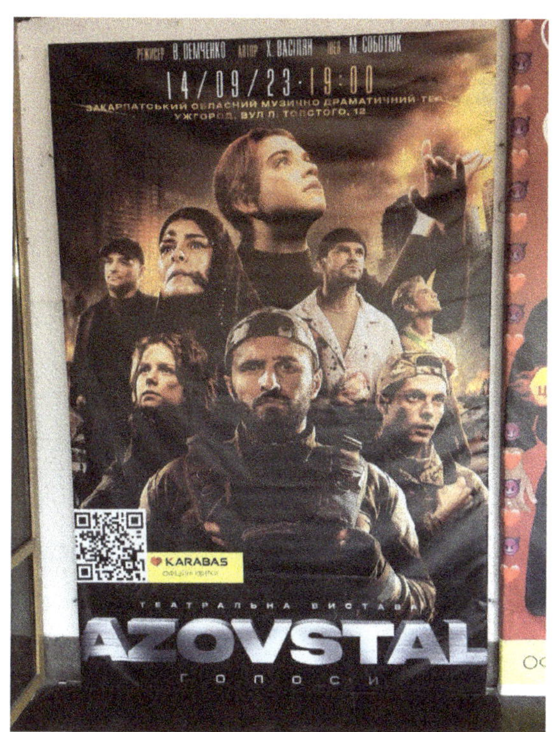

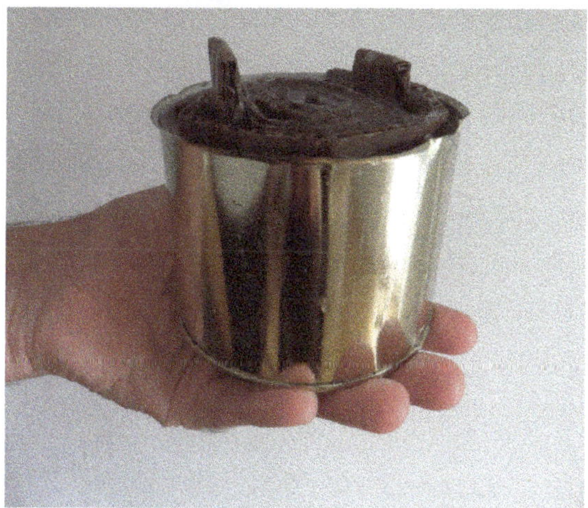

Top to bottom: Poster for the theater play "Azovstal – Voices," Uzhhorod, September 2023; My hand holding a 24-hour improvised D.I.Y. candle gifted by a friend from Kyiv showing the kind used during the first days of the war when there were common blackouts. People saved used candle wax, melted it, and poured it into small cans with used cardboard.

coincidently studied that same summer, reads completely differently. As the author was a soldier in the 1992–1993 War in Abkhazia, he experienced these events directly. Yet the novel contains no temporal, spatial, or political references, and definitely no patriotic morals or appeals. To use the language of cinema criticism, this is essentially a buddy story of two soldiers fighting their way back to their side and who only wish for the most basic: to survive. It could be happening anywhere, anytime, on any side, and to any two *comrades*.

Poetry is as sharp as prose. I've read numerous statements and verses by Ukrainian poets proclaiming how war changes language, how the ordinary way of writing prose and poetry cannot capture these atrocities, how words fail them. "The war drank you dry," begins one of the poetic lines by Yuliia "Taira" Paievska, who is an activist and medic captured during the battle of Mariupol (the poem can be found in *State of War*[17]). "In such a case," said Halyna Kruk in the previously mentioned Berlin speech, "poetry takes on peculiar forms of either spontaneous prayers, sparing testimony, lament or even a curse upon the enemy." Silent poetics of pain. Similarly, Zhadan, on the first pages of his journal, wrote, "War contends with language. During times of war, you constantly catch yourself thinking that you lack words. It's like you've had your breath taken away, the wind knocked out of you, so words get lost, spill all over, and seem misplaced."[18] In times of war, literature is thusly *recalculating*, if you allow me to use this succinct GPS navigation prompt: the *lyrical subject* is not meditating but wants to survive.

With a very telling title *Kyiv-Nanjing*, the most recent collection of *war poems* by the established Ukrainian poet Iryna Shuvalova, sadly only available online, answer the challenge she poses in one of their titles: *a poet can't write about war*.[19]

    neither victim
    nor participant
    nor defender
    nor observer

nor outsider

so who

the war gave everyone a role—what's yours?

covering your mouth with your palm?

...

she texts you

"I can hear explosions close by,

fighter jets flying"

you don't know

how to respond.

A new poetic sensibility is also apparent in literary performances, completely different to those I am used to. A colleague told me to go see Zhadan, performing incidentally in her city in those days. "What a coincidence," she wrote, "And right when you're here!" I thanked her warmly and added that we create our own coincidences if we harmonize with the right, interesting, inspiring people. Coincidences just find us. An old hall in a maximally functional and impressively brutalist late-socialist building smelling of pale old wooden seats covered in worn-out red velvet, suitable more for a local party congress than for a (celebrity) poet night, was pleasantly full. After an introduction of the local organizer, Zhadan appeared with a casual, yet extraordinary beatnik stage presence interlaced with stand-up skits, waves of applause after every poem read, and, finally, a standing ovation akin to trance. He filled more than two hours himself: on a disproportionately large stage were only him and a reading stand. One could tell that he also performs as a singer in a ska band with his *dogs* (the full name of the groups is Zhadan and the Dogs): his poetic performance was honest, unpretentious and strong, convincing, spiced up with an impromptu rapping at the end. He constantly alluded to the war in the east and south — especially because this is his home, where he still lives now. At a point during the reading, his host, the local master of ceremonies, held a humanitarian auction: brought out were signed flags and parts of military equipment. The audience were very generous, often collecting twenty, twenty-five thousand hryvnia (or $550–$650) per piece. The most attention — and the highest price — was attributed to a propelling charge (experts later told me what it was) with a painted angel with a crown of flowers on its head and a guitar in hand.

The performance of the other prominent poet and multimedia artist I attended, Yuriy Izdryk, differed a lot from the former. Taking place in the restored, beautifully decorated old synagogue turned to concert hall, it attracted a different public: a bit older, more serious and more restrained. He also performed alone on that large stage — but having different stage charisma, he recited his poems slowly, like hymns, in almost rhythmical sequences, creating a specific, almost meditative atmosphere. Recognizing only a few of them I read previously in English, I let myself enjoy more this parallel, but equally important element of his act.

Andriy Lyubka, one of a handful of Ukrainian authors whose work is translated into Slovenian, had recently a literary event in Ljubljana. The audience was almost exclusively female — I always remember only afterwards that men can hardly ever leave Ukraine and that only women can go abroad. Lyubka read his works and spoke about volunteering and other ways of resistance practiced by the Ukrainians on the home front, especially about his own actions, and also about how urgent it is to deprovincialize and decolonialize their culture not only from Russian, but also Western influence. He argued for more direct contacts between smaller nations and languages outside the current filters that the larger ones impose. Lyubka emphasized the fact that is well-known in Slovenia, too, that most of the literature — fiction or scientific writings — is read in the languages of larger or more dominating nations: here once in German and Serbo-Croatian and now in English; there in Russian. His arguments and his conclusions were actually similar to the ones of Mukha, calling for "fairer representation" of literary and scientific works of smaller nations in the wider intellectual arena. In her words, "now it's time to put Ukraine on the global map of culture, after it was put on a political map of sovereign states."

Ukrainian poetry also landed on the walls; for example, the verses by the member of the *Executed Renaissance*, Mykhailo Drai-Khmara (1889–1939), and the verses by poet and feminist Lesya Ukrainka (1871–1913). Zhadan's heart-wrenching verses from *As long as your thirst guards you* (from the book of poems *The Life of Virgin Mary*, 2015) were painted on a park wall, together with an image of an unborn child in a bomb falling from a plane.

The stars should rise above you
or explode like hand grenades.
The heart must be filled with blood
and distill it, distill it.

Bones must grow firmly.
Scars should add anger.
Something must happen to you.
Something has already happened and is still going on.

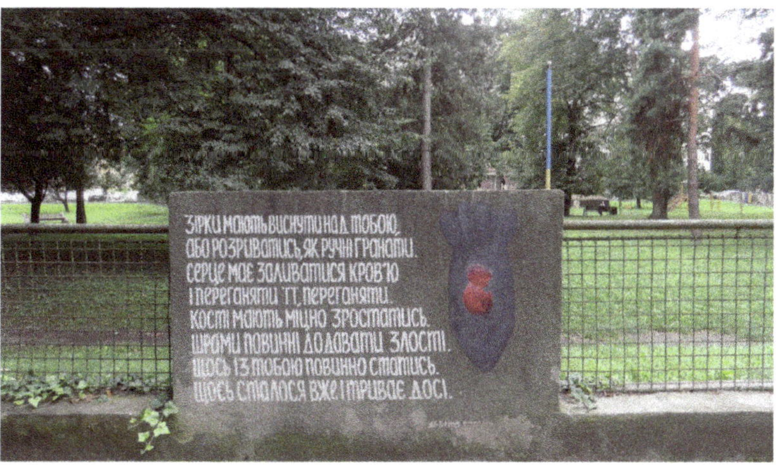

Quote from Serhiy Zhadan's poem "As long as your thirst guards you," on a graffiti mural, Uzhhorod, August 2023.

When I was reading these poems, (graphic) novels, and shorter literary writings, I was constantly reminded of other Ukrainian writers and how critical and self-reflective they thought of the Ukrainian past and present before the war struck. In *Fieldwork in Ukrainian Sex* (first published in 1996),[20] an autobiographical novel focusing on the (im)possibility of love between a poet and an artist torn between Ukraine and the United States, Oksana Zabuzhko offers sharp insights into the environment from which she originates. She mentions how Ukrainians are eternally condemned to nonexistence; how Ukrainian choice is a choice between nonexistence and the existence that kills. She explains: "Eastern fatalism, oh yes — the Russians have it; we're in worse shape, we, actually, are neither here nor there, Europe has managed to infect us with the raving fever of individual desire, faith in our personal "Yes I can!" — however, we never developed a foundation for such faith, those structures that might support that "I can!" and thus have tussled about for ages at the bottom of history — our Ukrainian "I can!" helpless and alone. Amen."[21] This despondent view on the inevitability of their own fate is later only deepened: "in general all that Ukrainians can say about themselves is how, and how much, and by which manner they were beaten" and that "it's not such a great thrill to belong to a beaten nation."[22]

Yurii Andrukhovych, another world-famous contemporary Ukrainian author of novels and essays, is another sharp critic of such hopelessness and sad surrender to the power of fate, who swaps self-victimization for self-evaluation, and searching for the blame for a miserable situation with accepting the blame for it in oneself. In a more sophisticated and less obvious manner, he does so in his complex and eclectic novel *Twelve Circles* (2015).[23] Through the perspective of an Austrian photographer, who journeys through the Carpathians and meets a grotesque company of archetypal characters of the Ukrainian transition, Andrukhovych claims: "This country had excellent opportunities to change and to leap, lightening -like, from the state of permanent monstrosity and oligophrenic helplessness to a state of almost *normalcy*. It turned out the numbers of those people who did not want this, who did not even want this country to exist as such, greatly exceeds all acceptable limits."[24] Janja Vollmaier Lubej, one of the authors of the Slovenian translation, claims that the novel "shows Ukrainian reality and the past and present filled with evil," which hints that "the circle of the history of evil is promulgated in the new, independent Ukrainian reality, too."[25]

More directly critical words can be found in Andrukhovych's *The Moscoviad* (2008),[26] first published two years after the independence. The (anti)hero of this grotesque novel, written with dark humor and — hmmm, how shall I put it — recognizable magic realism of the East-European type, is a student of literature and poet, who is wandering around the decadent parts of Moscow during the age of the disintegrating Soviet empire (i.e. dormitory, supermarkets, toilets and sewerage, metro, banquet, etc.), hangs out with bizarre fictitious and historic characters, and ends on a train to Kyiv. "At the helm of freshly-baked, forgive me, independent governments there will appear executives tested and appointed by us. Chaos will generate more chaos. [...] Everything will drown in gray mediocrity. In monotony. In vileness. The great wave of entropy that has shattered the Great Empire will utterly destroy these little, forgive me, independent states as well. All this will look like a cartoon: these presidents appointed by us, these parliaments bought by us. [...] These heroic attempts of Western bankers to teach madmen about freedom. These hungry petty squabbles, mutinies and strikes. This mass-production of churches and bordellos. The great obscenity of directives, constitutions, and declarations. [...] This is our program of action. More and more often will the people look back. And see in their deceived visions the Great State — cosmic, fiery, all-encompassing, millennial. All this, pardon me, independence of theirs will look worse and worse in comparison with it."[27] In short, "Millions of people are only waiting to be proclaimed slaves."[28] The novel ends in resignation: "And what remains for us is the most persuasive of all hopes, passed on to us from our glorious ancestors — that it will work out somehow."[29]

In his most famous novel *Death and the Penguin* (2003), Kurkov sketches the new normality of the post-Soviet society permeated by media outlets with shady intentions, mafias, inhumane competitiveness, and cold interpersonal relationships. The focus is on the one authentic symbiosis: the one between the two protagonists, a failed writer who earns a living by writing newspaper obituaries for future deaths and his domesticated penguin. And even this is more a complementarity of two solitudes, as Kurkov describes the relationship early on. The author's satirical approach with Kafkaesque elements proves to be not only literarily convincing, but also critical of what is lately and unjustly been taken for granted: "Today's battles were all for material gain, anyway," he writes, "The crazy idealist was extinct — survived by the crazy pragmatist…"[30]

In *Carbide* (2023), written after the — well — first half of Putin's attack, Lyubka is even more relentlessly critical. The grotesque describes entering the European Union in an innovative Ukrainian way: "unofficially", "illegally", "smuggling", through an underground tunnel. The idealism of its initiator, who meets a miserable end, overcomes the ruthless pragmatism of those who take his idea and turn it into another criminal undertaking. The author's more than obvious affection for his homeland is constantly confronted with its realistic image: "Ukraine's caught in a spider web of governance woven from mob money and backed by police sadists,"[31] he writes, often describing is as a mafia state. The bitter point the novel makes is that *Euro-integration* is no noble idea but essentially a profitable undertaking for the elites on both sides of *European* border.

When I was reading these works, I was constantly wondering how Russian writers and poets are reacting to the war, what is their war literature like. I would love to know more about it. I'll look into it, I've decided.

NOTES

1 Duda, Tamara. *Daughter*, 2021. 309.

2 Duda, 2011. 56.

3 Duda, 2011. 179.

4 Zhadan, Serhiy. *The Orphanage*, 2021. 141, 208.

5 Zhadan, 2021. 298.

6 Semena, Mykola. *Crimean Report: Chronicle of the Occupation of the Crimea*, 2018. 4.

7 Kebukadze, Vakhtang. *State of War*, 2023. 86.

8 Kidruk, Max. *State of War*, 2023. 92.

9 Zhadan, Serhiy. *State of War*, 2023. 238.

10 Kruk, Halyna. Interview. *Svet je od nekdaj ujet v neravnovesje med vojno in mirom*, 2023. 19.

11 Kurkov, Andriy. *Diary of an Invasion*, 2022. 136.

12 Kurkov. 251.

13 Belorusets, Yevgenia. *War Diary*, 2023. 49–50.

14 Zhadan, Serhiy. *Above Kharkiv: Dispatches from the Ukrainian Front*, 2023. 10–11, 16.

15 Zhadan, *Above Kharkiv*, 2023. 30.

16 Woland, *Valhalla Express: the story of a nationalist, revolutionary, and volunteer*, 2017, Markobook, Kyiv.

17 *State of War*, 2023. 148.

18 Zhadan, *Above Kharkiv*, 2023. vii.

19 Shuvalova, Iryna. *Kyiv–Nanjing*, poem *a poet can't write about war*, translated by Amelia Glaser and Yuliya Ilchuk.

20 Zabuzhko, Oksana. *Fieldwork in Ukrainian Sex*, 2011, translated by Halyna Hryn.

21 Zabuzhko, 2011. 23.

22 Zabuzhko, 2011. 88–89.

23 Andrukhovych, Yurii:. *Twelve Circles*, 2015, translated by Vitaly Chernetsky.

24 Andrukhovych, 2015. 144.

25 Vollmaier Lubej, Janja. *Ukrajinske družbene spremembe v romanu Dvanajst krogov Jurija Andruhoviča*, 2018. 144.

26 Andrukhovych, Yurii. *The Moscoviad*, 2008, translated by Vitaly Chernetsky.

27 Andrukhovych, 2008. 176.

28 Andrukhovych, 2008. 177.

29 Andrukhovych, 2008. 189.

30 Kurkov, Andrey, *Death and the Penguin*, 2001. 61.

31 Lyubka, Andriy, *Carbide*, 2023. 215.

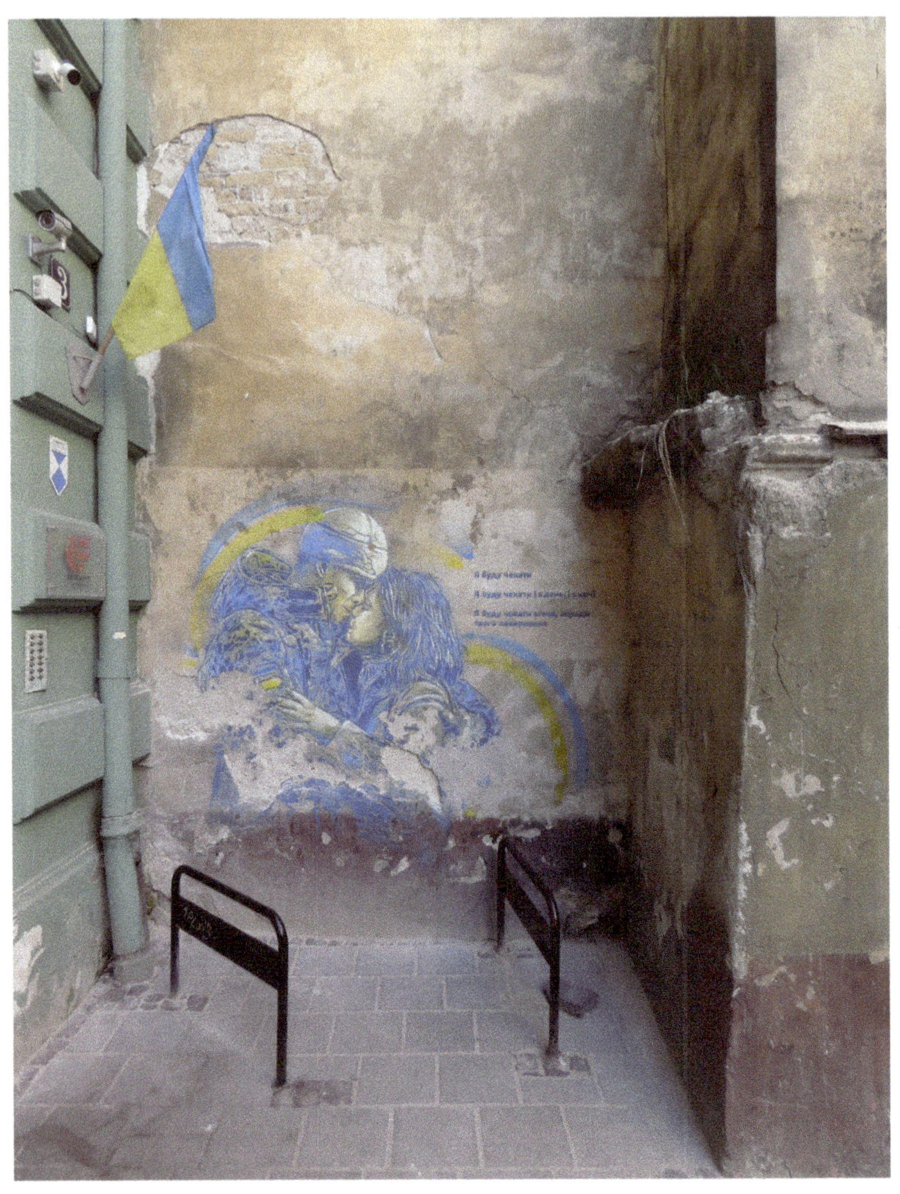

Waiting room mural, "I will wait for you – I will wait for you day and night – I will wait forever, for your return," Lviv, May 2023.

VIII.

IMAGES OF WAR

"In times of physical destruction, we will create physically."
Lesia Khomenko, an artist of the group exhibition
Forms of Presence, *Kyiv, 2023.*

The veil of war also has a visual component: on my Ukrainian travels, I could see practically no space not covered by it. To borrow Pasolini's terms, I am moving from *lisegno* (language-sign) in the previous essay to *imsegno* (image-sign) in this one. I have already mentioned the flying flags, the new monuments, the flower beds in Ukrainian colors, the encouraging ads and shows, the ruins of buildings, the various uniformed people, the patriotic dress code of even, hmmm, civilians. I will now add the war visualia found in ordinary sites (galleries, museums, street displays) and outside them, spraypainted on walls (graffiti and street art) and displayed in public and state institutions (schools, post offices, etc.).

In the spring and summer of 2023, the prestigious Kyiv Art Arsenal hosted the exhibition *Forms of Presence*. It aimed for an artistic reflection of the past year of the war. Due to a sense of irreversibility and loss, material creation has become a way of resisting and witnessing the war, wrote its curators. The exhibited works were accompanied by the personal stories of their creators (usually beginning with: *Since the beginning of the full-scale Russian invasion, I have ...*); with a strong presence of documentarist elements, they build a sense of authenticity and directness. As such, they are introduced as expressing "war's presence and acts of defiance against injustice and violence, through which life pulsates as opposed to the void of absence." Most works were minimalist, monochromatic and made of accessible materials, which made them even more confessional and innovative: they reminded me of the neo-avantgarde trend of *arte povera*, as improvisation, explicitness, and determination in them easily overcame the distress and lack of means.

The exhibition hall of the Kyiv Modern Art Research Institute, active as a part of the National Academy of Arts of Ukraine, where I presented my book, hosted a temporary exhibition of prints and collages on the topic of war. These, too, were aesthetically very simple and effective, and their content was one-sided and convincing. Blue and yellow were, of course, the dominant colors supported by black and red, while the motifs included Ukrainian heraldry, folk costumes and other patriotic imagery, angels, civilians persecuted and killed, images of devastated landscapes, soldiers, and the front. Included were, obviously, the dedications to their armed forces with an occasional insignia of a controversial military unit. *The Disasters of War*, to borrow the title of Goya's series of etchings. In terms of art, if not in terms of content, the most striking of these was a very realistic, almost life-size statue of a ballerina wearing a suicide vest full of dynamite sticks and pointing a Kalashnikov gun. "Literally Guns N' Roses," I thought.

Also, a few other exhibitions I've been to were totally dominated by war motifs: again, omnipresent war, war, war. In many of them, the "exhibition" began already on the exterior of the gallery: sandblasted windows, windows crossed with adhesive tapes, militant graffiti, flags waving at the entrance, plaques dedicated to fallen employees in the entrance hall. The one I saw in Union Gallery Odesa — I forgot to write down its title — again showed different faces of "the state of war": portraits of soldiers, "still lifes" of war devastation (I thought to myself, the Italian translation of the term is much more adequate, *natura morta*), images from the trenches, *Pietà*-like scenes from the operating tables in military hospitals, shots of destroyed military equipment, pictures of piles of military boots from the fallen soldiers, etc. As a rule in many similar exhibitions, the concepts and contents of works are more important than the techniques used, that's why we find, side by side, documentary and art photos, oil paintings, watercolors, collages, digital-art pieces. And another thing is also very meaningful: most of these are group exhibitions, bringing together artists whose works would otherwise not be exhibited together. Making a collective out of separate voices, views and means of expression is a message in itself. War separates, but in galleries it unites.

Kyiv was also full of stickers with a motif of peaceful life before the *Big Bang* of February 24 and falling bombs marked Z — they were invitations to the exhibition *24. Before and After* by young Kyiv painters. Furthermore: moving children drawings depicting war are displayed in many public spaces, not just schools: in waiting rooms, post offices, and elsewhere. They portray the various ugly faces of war, devastation, suffering, refugees, mothers with children, and calls for the war to end. Kyiv hosted a documentary street exhibition comparing the complete devastation of two war-stricken cities: Warsaw during WWII and Mariupol in this war.

Resourceful local artists used the wide fiberboards protecting certain public buildings of Odesa to hang picturesque prints and A4 drawings. Their almost graffiti-like simplicity and directness expressed the fighting spirit and the anti-military stance of their authors. Hundreds were pasted one next to another, from extremely sharp (burning New York Twin Towers with the inscription *In Ukraine, every day is September 11; Russia is a terrorist country*; a drawing of Putin hiding behind a mask of a bloody skull) to witty ones (the horses without their famous bogatyrs from the well-known painting by Viktor Vasnetsov and the inscription *Fuck off!* or Putin behind bars with *Time for Haag!*). In one of the bookstores, I took a picture of a Ukrainian version of the famous 1930 Grant Wood's painting *American Gothic*: it featured Lesya Ukrainka and Taras Shevchenko — wearing a papakha. In a restaurant, I saw its more drastic upgrade: Ukrainka and Shevchenko stand in the foreground with Putin's head on the pitchfork, while Moscow is burning in the background.

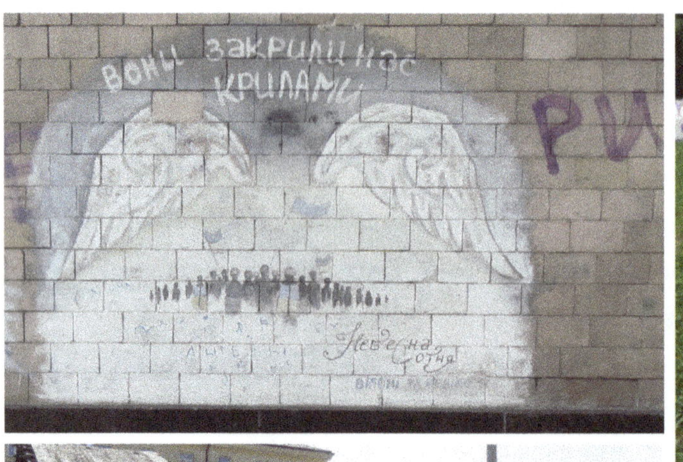

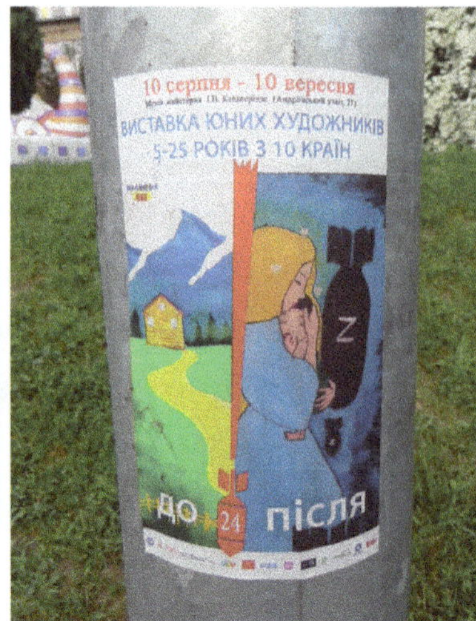

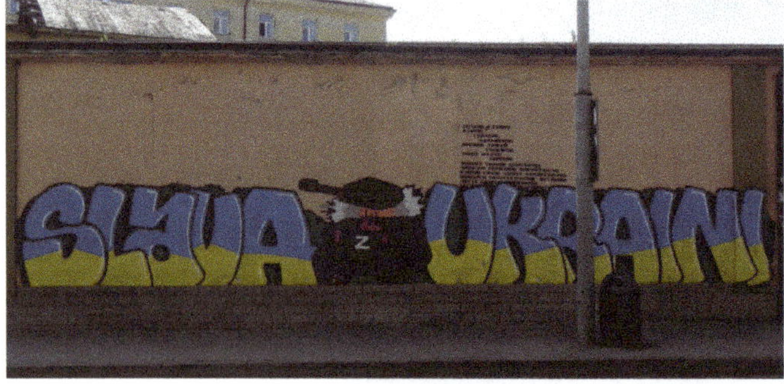

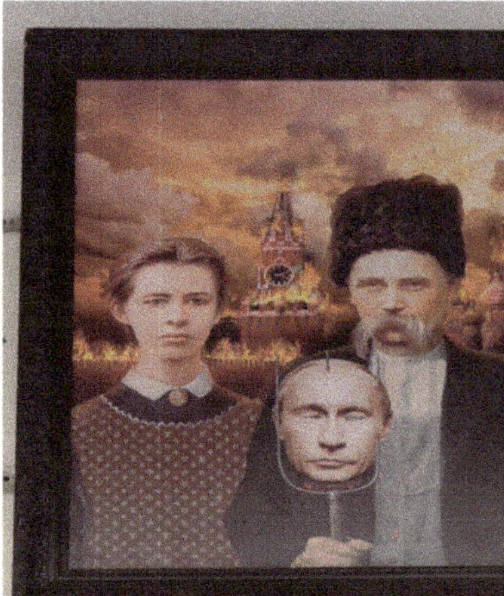

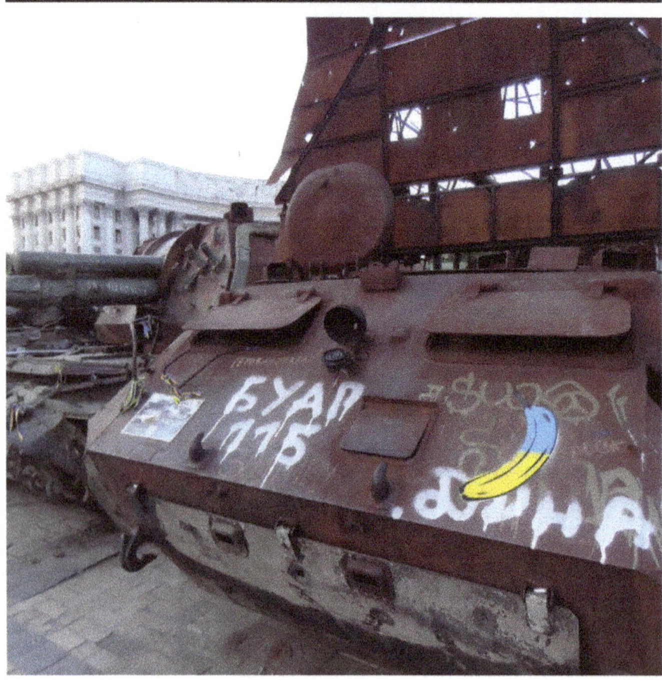

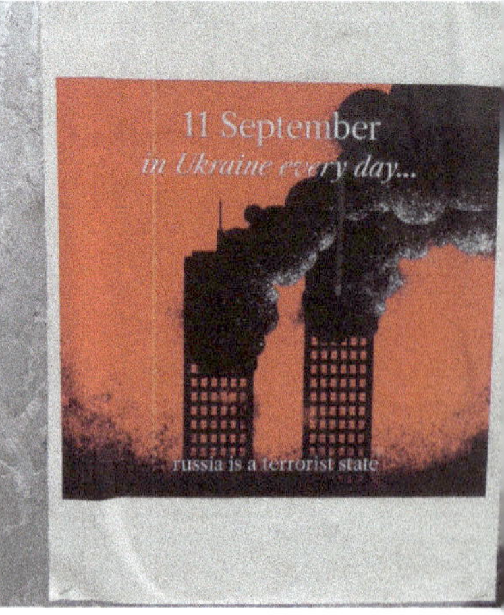

Top to bottom, left: "They have covered us with their wings – Heavenly Hundred - Known and Unknown, Kyiv, May 2023;"Glory to Ukraine," Lviv, May 2023; Kyiv, May 2023.
Top to bottom, right: "Before – After February 24," Invitation sticker for an exhibition of young painters from ten countries, Kyiv, May 2023; Lviv, May 2023; Odesa, May 2023.

A a researcher at Kyiv National Academy of Arts of Ukraine, Natalia Moussienko, documented numerous examples of protest art during the so-called *revolution of dignity* and initiated the travelling exhibition *Art of Maidan*. Following it, she published an eponymous catalogue (2016) where she meticulously collected and described photos and reproductions of posters, sculptures, paintings, postcards, various installations, theatre plays, films, concerts (also on the famous blue-and-yellow *freedom piano* which was played during demonstrations), street exhibitions (e.g. *Women of the Maidan* and *Photos from Maidan*), and performances created on the spot, literally on the barricades or just behind them. The second part of the anthology is dedicated to reports and photos made at the openings of this exhibition, which travelled through Ukraine and the United States, from Vinnytsia and Chernivtsi to Washington, D.C., and Arkansas. Especially valuable is the final index of artists, art groups, festivals, and institutions. On page 7, the author claims that the exhibition and the book covers "the road from carnival to sacral and organically combined in itself elements of avantgarde, mass culture, and high classicism that is characteristic of our era of post-modern." The works collected are innovative, improvised, sharp, witty, decisive — offering themselves to be described as *action art*.

The Museum of Ukrainian Military Uniforms presents a cornucopia of ethnographic material including weapons, heraldry, insignia, old photos, patriotic leaflets and paintings, original uniforms or their exact replicas. First are those of various Ukrainian units of the Austro-Hungarian army from the early 20th century and WWI, then those of the 1917–1921 Ukrainian states, the Insurgent Army from 1942 and the post-war period, ending with uniforms from the current war. This included the collaborator's uniforms and uniforms that are historically controversial — but not those from the Soviet period. But that was something I said nothing about. The curator was very charmingly trying to tend to us rare visitors although we didn't speak his language and were improvising in four others. Similarly to other dominant historical discourses, he explained the suffering and yet heroic fate of the Ukrainians in the last century and a half. The walls were full of maps of *historically Ukrainian territories*, some located way beyond the borders that are today recognized internationally (and breached by Putin's regime).

Artistic interpretations of the war have also reached Slovenia — the walls of its galleries and other walls. In less than a year, Ljubljana-based young Ukrainian artist Svitlana Ryabishchuk put up two smaller exhibitions, both concerning the topic of war, both raising issues, both having a question mark at the end of its title. *Did you know you can get killed while waiting for bread?* was displayed at the Ljubljana Faculty of Art's Bookstore (and later at the Alkatraz Gallery), its minimalist prints reflecting the massacre of civilians waiting in line for bread in Chernigov and confronting the facts that Ukraine is the granary of Europe and at the same time its only battlefield. The contrast between life (bread) and death (ruins) could not be more painful. A few months later, she followed up with the installation *Where Should the Russian Warship Go?* in the Ljubljana gallery Dobra vaga. The installation was composed of everyday objects from the Ukrainian and Soviet past piled on a simple wooden board (raft?) and a model of a passenger aircraft model stuck into an old fake-leather suitcase. The title referred to two well-known events, repeated and reproduced in the current war and popular culture a thousand times: to *Go fuck yourself* — the answer of Ukrainian border guards at Snake Island given to the Russian warship Moskva; and to the warship's later sinking. As the content has almost nothing in common with its title, I understand them as a current conflictual coexistence of the recent Soviet and Ukrainian past and tragic present; a peaceful life and the war of today.

From the white walls of Ukrainian exhibition halls to the grey outer walls of Ukrainian cities. A few rapid presses on the nozzle of the spray can and there you have your street truth, a condensed statement that others need whole paragraphs to express, an entire poem, or the big screen. When I was wandering through these cities, older layers of paint revealed that street art and the graffiti scene of the region is strong and varied. The first challenge in studying graffiti in general is that it is impossible to even count, much less study all of them: here today, they may well be gone tomorrow. More than any other visual from of culture, they avoid quantification.

As expected, a great majority of newer graffiti, murals, and various forms of street art (stickers, stencils, posters, paste-ups, various inscriptions, latrinalia, 3D installations) is connected to Putin's aggression. The more severe or even harsh the conditions in each environment, the harsher and more brutal such street resistance becomes. Gloves off. The cities are quite literally flooded with it: in a technical sense, they are of every possible dimension; in an aesthetic sense, they explore every style and genre; in terms of content, they are more or less variations on the topic of war. Other, non-war art, which is otherwise predominant in the graffiti landscape elsewhere, is almost non-existent here; only once in a while could I spot an anarchist A in a circle, the omnipresent *ACAB*, one or two *Go Vegan*, a handful of soccer fan graffiti, but almost no art dealing with identity, feminism, LGBTQ+, alter-globalism, anti-system, ecology, etc. And again, how symptomatic, no graffiti pointing out social injustices and painful social divisions originating in post-socialism: I saw no anti-corruption, anti-oligarch, or anti-tycoon graffiti, none that would rage against the new poverty. The only one that I photographed was a mural dedicated to the murdered activist Kateryna Handziuk (1985–2018), who investigated such crime in her home city of Kherson.

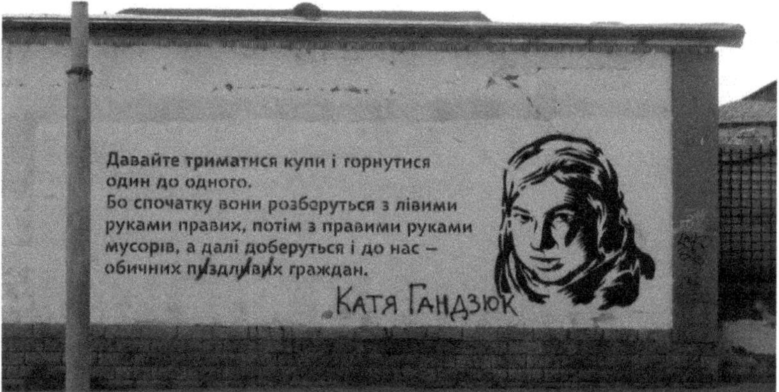

Mural for murdered activist Kateryna Handziuk, Lviv, May 2023.

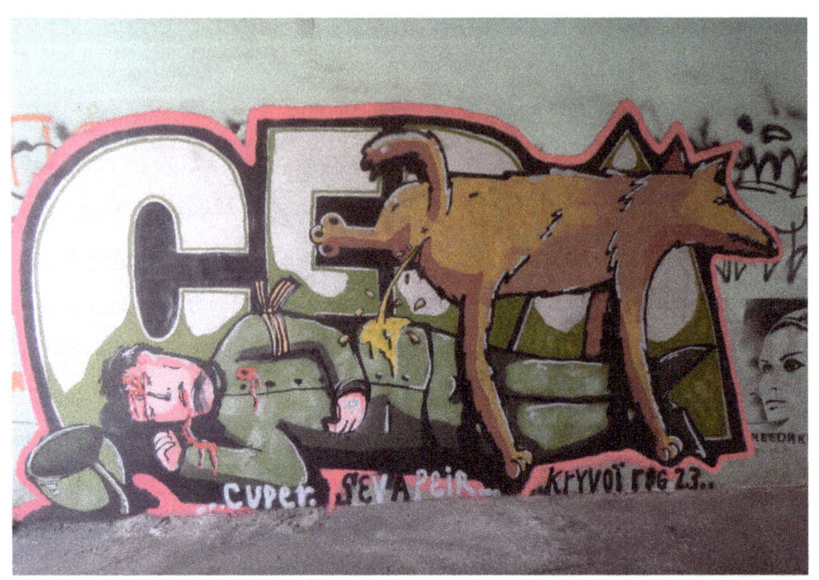
..cuper. SEVA peik... kryvoi rog 23..

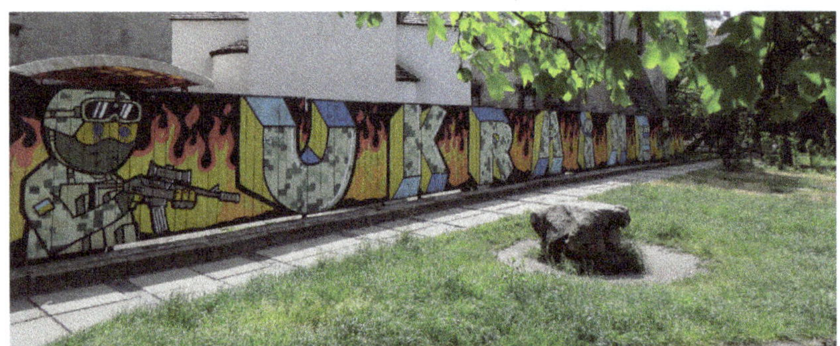

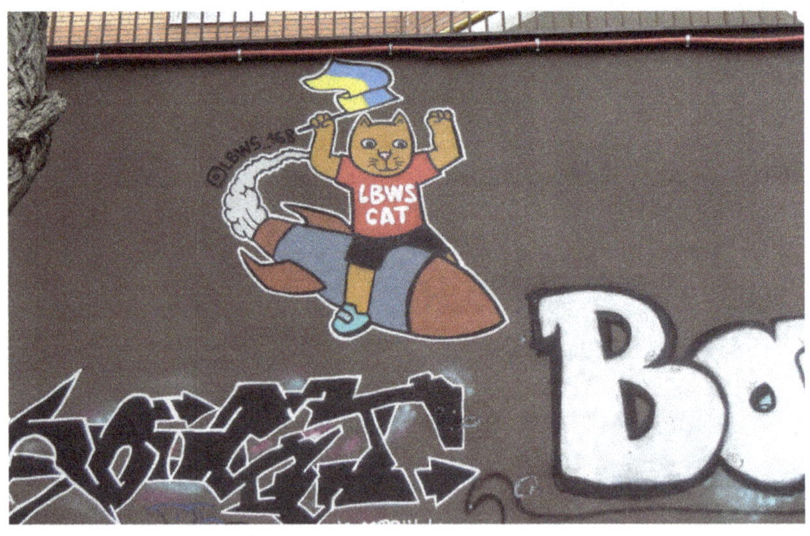
LBWS
CAT

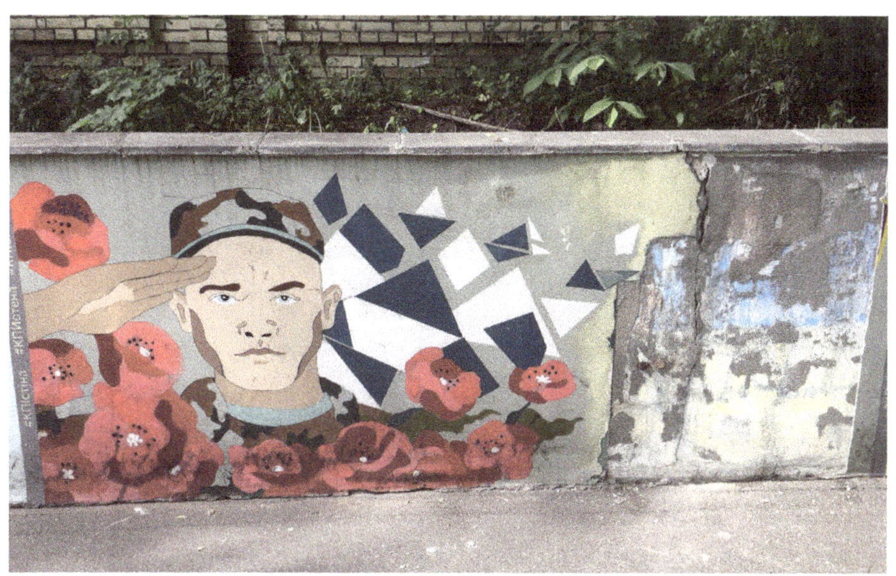

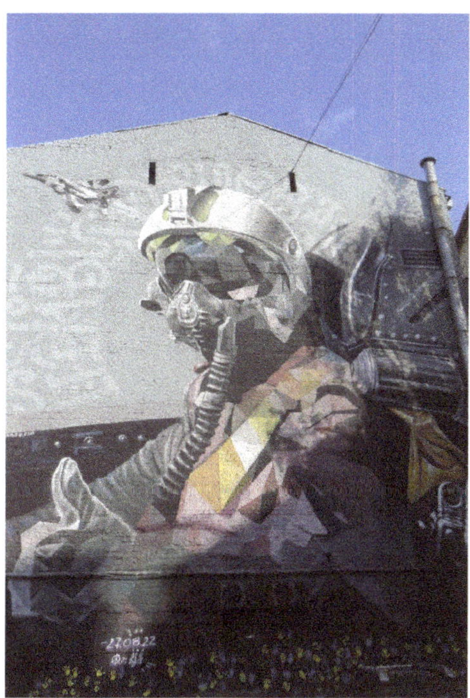

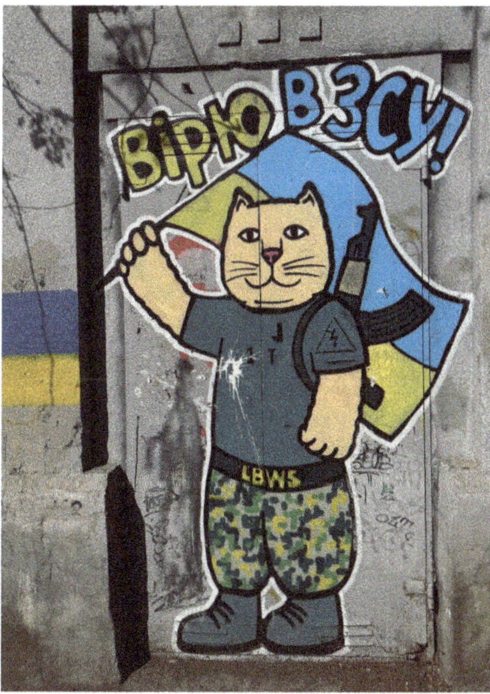

Opposite page, top to bottom: Kyiv, May 2023; Kyiv, May 2023; Odesa, June 2024.
Top: Kyiv, May 2023; bottom left: Kyiv, May 2023; bottom right: Odesa, June 2024.

The second, more substantial issue in their study is the fact that many of them are more than obviously allowed, encouraged, or even commissioned by the authorities or the ruling politics as another medium of the public space, which is already monopolized with the ruling ideology. If we follow the strict definition of graffiti and street art as illegal visual interventions in public space that can only be understood in their own temporal and spatial context — these fail to make the mark. On the other hand, they are still *a weapon of the weak*, to borrow anthropologist James C. Scott's concept; they are a communication medium of the attacked side. And thirdly, to anticipate the question that I was sometimes asked when I returned: I encountered no more openly Nazi graffiti there than elsewhere around the world where this cultural scientist's camera has snapped street art.

Ukrainian (anti-)war graffiti would most definitely deserve a separate study; I personally photographed more than fifteen hundred of them, while I saw many more online or in messages by my Ukrainian friends. Like I said, radical social circumstances are reflected in radical diction on the walls. It makes little sense to telegraph their extremely various content, techniques, messages, or sizes, but I would like to focus on a few main emphases. If I start with the *ordinary* political graffiti: I found an impressive one of a frowning Cossack with a typical hairstyle but a contemporary uniform; on one side is a squad automatic weapon, and in his hands, he holds a traditional Ukrainian instrument, the bandura. The second and the most explicit one I found is of a dog (a wolf?) urinating on a dead Russian soldier. The third and the simplest one is composed of hundreds of handprints in yellow and blue. The next graffiti put the American and the Ukrainian flag side by side with the flag of the European Union. The graffiti of a large bird carrying a Ukrainian flag in its beak is overwritten with the expressions, names, and places that are constantly in the news (territorial defense, sword, Cossack, Azovstal, fate, Ukraine, Shevchenko, air defense, etc.) and encourages with *Who if not you? You can do it!*

Let me continue with the simplest or apparently extremely impulsive visual diversions. Many one-way traffic signs pointing east bear the word *Putin*: they instruct him to go back home. On a language school window inviting passersby to join language courses with flags of various countries, the Russian flag was covered with the Ukrainian coat of arms. At the exhibition of world puppets (yes, I also wonder if there is anything that I don't go see...), orderly displays in glass cases by countries, the Russian case received a sticker: a traffic sign with a crossed-out Putin. Those memorials from the Soviet era that have managed to survive, like Mykola Shchors on horseback, a statue to this Soviet commander of Ukrainian descent, who fought against Ukrainian independentists, Germans, and Poles, feature graffiti writings such as *Oppressor* or *Let's tear it down*. Everywhere, anonymous authors vent by hastily spraypainting or writing in marker slogans like *Fuck Putin — Fuck War — Viva Ukraine* and the classic *Glory to Ukraine! To the heroes — Glory!*

The more sophisticated forms of street dissensus are stencils, of which there were incredibly many: walls celebrate the *Robin Hoods of Kharkov*, who drove vans with aid to the city; the aforementioned Lesya Ukrainka; President Zelenskyy (with the inscription *Glory to Ukraine*), the short-lived Carpatho-Ukraine (of 1938), the *Ukrainian* St. George killing the dragon (with the inscription *Free yourself to be free!*) and the National Corps. Here and there, they also feature the *88* neo-Nazi code (for *Heil Hitler!*), included in the name of the city that is home to the volunteers of the Carpathian Sich unit: *Uz88orod*. One *14/88* textual graffiti (combined global white power and neo-Nazi code) was immediately covered by the yellow-blue graffiti of the Ukrainian flag. I found a replica of Banksy's famous girl frisking a soldier with an added *Frisk the Orc*; and I discovered various appeals, such as *Free Azov from its captivity, Freedom to patriots!, Support Ukraine* inviting people to contribute to this humanitarian fund, *Freedom to Kharkov patriots*, etc. ad infinitum.

Yet another infinitum is that of stickers. They are either generic, in the colors of the Ukrainian flag or with the trident, or have concrete content, e.g. photos of the front and slogans like *Ukrainian Resistance, I support*

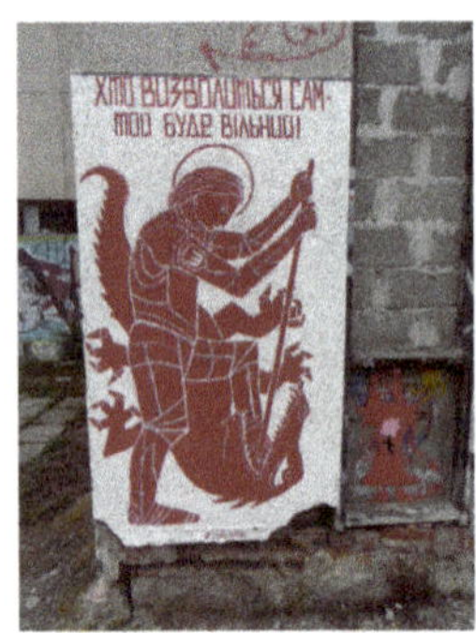

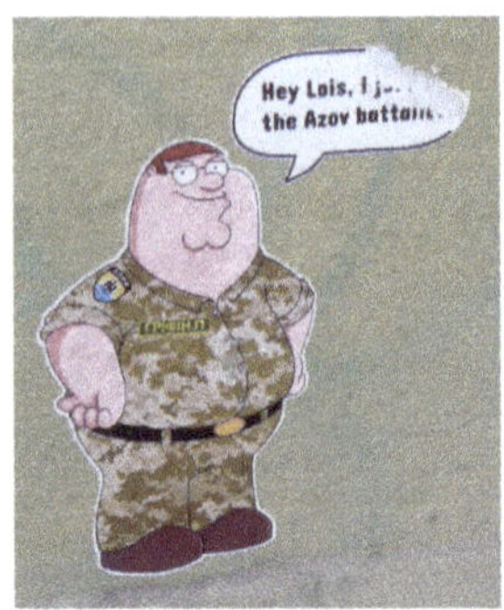

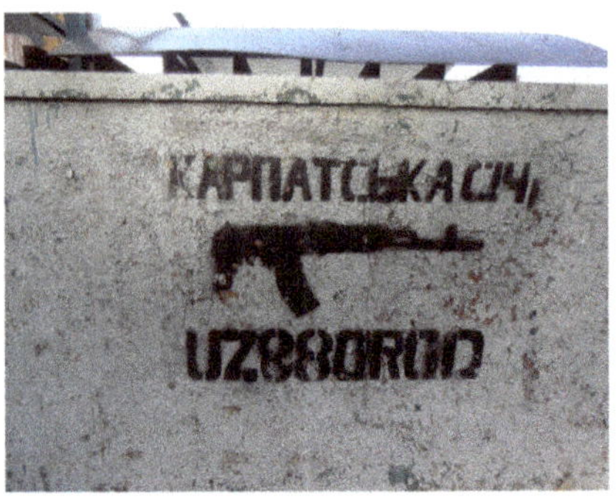

Left to right: "Whoever frees himself will be free!" Uzhhorod, August 2023; Kyiv, May 2023; Carpathian Sich, Uzhhorod, September 2023.

Ukraine, and *This will all be Ukraine* with the outline of the entire country, including the besieged east and south, or those of militant groups such as Centuria or Carpathian Sich. Many mock Putin using what my translators told me were puns that are difficult to translate. Some include a QR code leading to webpages that provide more information; others encourage donations; those with the image of author and founder of a nationalist movement Ivan Franko (1856–1916) appeal for signatures on a petition to decorate specific fallen Ukrainian soldiers or celebrate the anniversary of Azov. Others still refer to popular culture: on them, even the animated character of Peter Griffin from Family Guy joined this paramilitary unit. The Italian far-right has printed and pasted stickers that express their brotherhood with its Ukrainian counterpart: a stylized fascio with the symbol of the Azov group (these probably commemorate the Ukrainian supporter of the Italian neo-fascist youth movement CasaPound, Dmytro Yakovets, who died in a tragic accident in Italy ten years ago). Solidarity with the attacked Ukrainians is expressed also in the stickers that combine Ukrainian national symbols with, for example, Polish, Georgian, or Turkish ones (the inscriptions on them are in the style of *Two nations, one heart*).

Other techniques of street art are also abundant. Especially obvious are posters of various sizes, most of them again with war motifs; such as the one with a group of soldiers and two slogans in English: *Bring Them*

Home Alive! Stop the War Now! and *Azovstal — Free Mariupol Defenders*. In a series of similar posters, surrounded knights defend a mother with a child from monsters (again, an allusion to orcs) with an appeal to *Stand with Ukraine*; on another, civilians keep the door shut from these same monsters, now armed with rockets, while *Game of Thrones* is referenced in the slogan: *Hold the Door! — Help Ukraine!* Others simply demand *Stop Putin*. Frequent are posters with patriotic motifs, like *You are the future of Ukraine* by an organization of young right-wingers; *Power in community — Support Ukrainian armed forces!*; or a poster for the Ukrainian army with a photo of blue-and-yellow fish.

I also saw paste-ups: one was sending Putin behind bars (*Put In Prison*), the other portrayed him on a pyramid of skulls. Or 3D installations; for example, of a yellow gypsum Christ with a spray can with *Stop War* spray-painted across it in blue. Especially interesting was a technique that I had previously not seen in the universe of street art although it is popular in the commercial world of advertising for services, whereby half of a pasted sheet of paper is dedicated to the description of the service (such as cleaning, guitar lessons, selling cheap bikes, etc.) and the other half is cut into slips with phone numbers. I have started calling this the *ripper*. These sheets of paper pasted on public surfaces were obviously in patriotic colors, featured a QR code that led to further information, and the obligatory *Glory to Ukraine* and *Glory to the nation!*, while the slips were first equipped with anti-Great-Russian calls such as *Air attacks on Russia until the war ends* or *Moscow is burning*, then with calls for *our side*, such as *A hug for our armed forces* or *Victory to Ukraine*.

In the graffiti landscape of Ukrainian towns, it is murals, the new media of memoryscape, that are especially prominent. Memoryscape always turns into muralscape, I explain to my students. Appearing on extremely busy streets, they are enormous, mostly technically perfect (and untouched!), which must mean that they are allowed or supported by municipal or state authorities. These memorial urban frescoes include motifs of heroes and martyrs, e.g. the mentioned *Ghost of Kyiv*; one of the first Maidan victims, Serhiy Nigoyan, a Ukrainian activist of Armenian origins; Pavel Skoropadskyi (1873–1945), hetman or leader of the short-lived 1918 Ukrainian State installed by Germany; a bare-chested knight with a Cossack hairstyle defending the country. A mural with children playing on the map of Kyiv without any fear of being hit by bombs expresses a wish for peace. Another, just as huge, features a portrait of a girl in a yellow-and-blue combination with a flower crown and a quote from President Zelenskyy's 2019 inaugural speech. The speech, which includes "I don't want my portraits to hang in your offices, because the president is not an icon or an idol. Hang pictures of your children there and look them in the eyes before every decision," broke with the tradition of hanging pictures of heads of state in public spaces, which dates back to Stalin. But some murals are also lyrical, e.g. the stencil of a girl and a soldier saying farewell with the inscription *I will wait for you — I will wait for you day and night — I will wait for you, always, until you return.*

I photographed signs in Ukrainian colors looming tens of meters high that say *Independent, Glory to Ukraine, Mariupol — Hero City, Azovstal,* or simply just *Ukraine* surrounded by fire and stylized Ukrainian soldiers demolishing armored vehicles with the symbol Z — or, sometimes, the highly controversial and non-confronted Nazi symbols like Azov's *Wolfsangel.* Elsewhere, giant signs in English and Ukrainian appeal: *World, help!* Especially impressive are more than 10-meter-long, almost comic-book-like murals, real visual odes with strong stories. One represents the entire Mariupol battle: Ukrainian defenders, the devastated Azovstal complex, civilians on the run, on foot or in a convoy of vehicles leading away from the ravaged city, past minefields, the dove of peace flying away. Another combines the flag of Ukraine with the flag of the interwar insurgent army, depicts a fighter from each period, and comments *In honor of Ukrainian heroes.*

Graffiti battles in 2014 already foretold the first conflicts and then armed conflicts. The pro-Maidan side spraypainted messages such as *Donetsk is Ukraine, I love the Ukrainian army,* and *Putin is a terrorist.* The first studies of graffiti and inscriptions on the walls of the *liberated territories*, i.e. the towns and villages reclaimed by the Ukrainian army, have already been made. One of them, *Wall Evidence*, can be found online (wallevidence. mizhvukhamy.com), "An open archive of the inscriptions of the Russian occupiers of Ukraine." Far away from the front, the pro-Russian side is producing graffiti and murals celebrating Soviet and Russian history. For example, one such example online that I just received from someone is a Sevastopol graffiti depicting a hero from WWII and one of their heroes from the current war.

My Ukrainian — how should I say it? — *informants* pointed me to a graffiti platform (rather than a classical graffiti crew) called ETC, which either stands for *Enjoy the City* or for *Erase the City*. Its members are active in tagging in various techniques, styles, and shapes on the usual urban surfaces at home and abroad — but also on destroyed Russian military mechanization. They also leave their tags on vehicles and weapons of the Ukrainian army, as well as the projectiles it sends to the Russian side (similar to WWII practice, when this was done by both sides). The platform regularly publishes its feats on its Facebook profile. I can't tell if my camera caught any works of graffiti writer Sociopath who gained lots of attention and respect depicting three main Ukrainian cultural figures — Ukrainka, Franko, Shevchenko — as being prepared to join protesters during the clashes in central Kyiv in February 2014. Removal of these stencil graffiti in 2017 caused strong reactions from the public, considering them by now an informal monument to those fateful events. I'm wondering if his next work "War Trilogy" — again, three stencils (Putin as Hitler, a spray can with a Kalashnikov inside, a Misfits-like skull under a helmet), made the same year in Lviv — survived. (I wrote down in my notebook, "Ask my new Lvivian acquaintances about that next time, yes?")

A crew of five graffiti artists from Odesa with the enigmatic name LBWS CAT or LBWS_168 decorates their city, but also some others, from the beginning of war with the image of a smiling, confident cat. He usually appears in all sorts of military or patriotic situations, like waving

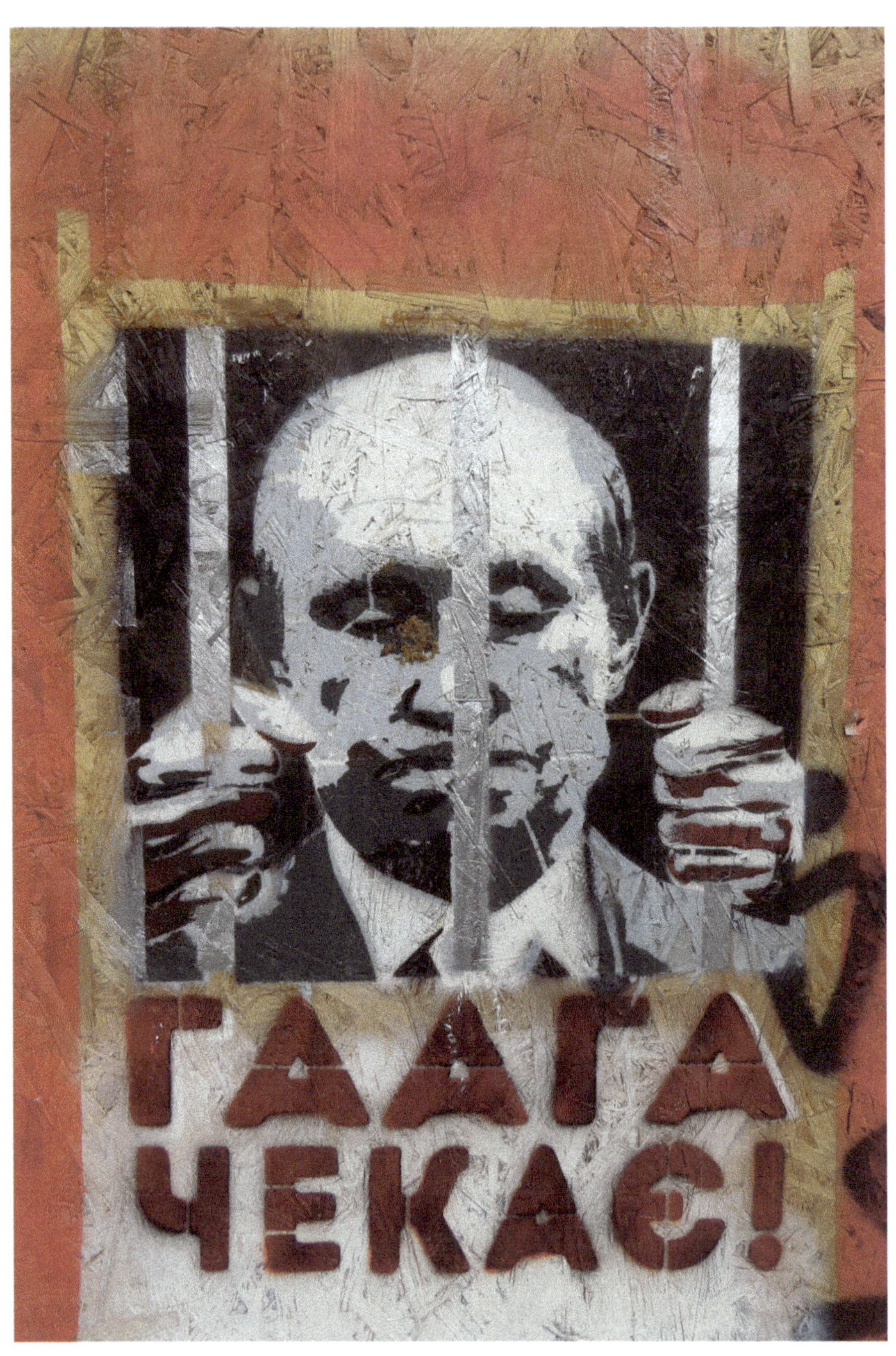

"The Hague is Waiting for You!," Odesa, May 2023.

   Ukrainian Vignettes: Essays on a Culture at War

Ukrainian flag, carrying weapons, wearing a uniform and carrying weapons, smashing the enemy armor and warships, calling for victory, posing with the aforementioned dog Patron, catching missiles with a fishing net, etc. etc. In some cases, he also refers to Ukrainian folk tradition by wearing *vyshyvanka*, playing *bandura* and eating *borscht*. The city center is literally flooded with these cat-themed graffiti on the walls and other public spaces, but also on some vehicles (cars, buses, etc.). This crew's simple, but highly elaborated works that juxtapose relaxed and funny images with deadly serious content are regularly updated on social media — worth a look, I guarantee.

War is therefore not happening only on the front but also on the walls — and not only on Ukrainian walls, but around the world, as well. Wherever I have travelled since February 2022, I could find this graffiti: a large majority of them were pro-Ukrainian, but I could also see some pro-Putin ones. Immediately after the general strike, I found a sticker in Ljubljana with the Russian tricolor and a swastika in the middle; similarly in Tallinn, where its author appeals *Stop! Russian peace*, e.g. ironically commenting on what Putin envisages as peace; Manhattan became home to numerous *Stop Putin — Arm Ukraine* stickers.

The Russian leader is also the target of graffiti with predictable messages (*Fuck Putin!!!!* can be found in Skopje, *Fuck Putin — Love Ukraine* in Berlin), *paste-ups* (Zagreb features one with blood-shot eyes), stickers with his crossed-out portrait (Padua); he is depicted in the passionate Brezhnev/Honecker kiss with Salvini (Modena), or with a Poo Tin written next to a telling pile on his head (Zagreb). In Maribor, Zagreb-based artists Yo.Pecador and Lunar stenciled *Ukrainian boy*, inspired by a photo of a boy with a cap in Ukrainian colors saving a cat in the middle of ruins. A Kyiv friend showed me an enormous Paris mural with a protagonist of Delacroix's *Liberty Leading the People* with a Ukrainian flag trampling over a defeated Russian dragon. There are also many street interventions calling for peace: such are the New York and Zagreb graffiti sidewalks (with a Ukrainian bicolor, peace sign, and white dove) or two-toned hearts and

doves of peace in various street art techniques (Tallinn, Zagreb, Ferrara).
Just recently, a few pedestrian traffic-lights around Union Square in New
York have changed their colors of a walking man icon from green to blue-
and-yellow by simply by using a transparent adhesive tape. Bitterly funny
is the stencil from Budapest, showing a bare-chested Putin riding a horse/
donkey with EU-ally Viktor Orbán's head.

Maribor is the first Slovenian city to host a mural dedicated to the war
in Ukraine and join dozens of other towns across the world to do so. The
largest number of such giant wall paintings can be found in Polish cities,
as well as in the United States and Great Britain, while they also occupy
prominent public spaces in Paris, Prague, Vilnius, Riga, Amsterdam, and
elsewhere. The Maribor mural occupying the empty wall of a car park next
to the city hall was spraypainted by the visiting street artist Konstantin
Kachanovsky. It represents *young Ukraine*, as the author called her — a
young woman dressed in a traditional costume (again) with the corresponding head ornamentation standing in a field of wheat and holding a
bouquet of poppies shaped in the form of the country.

Due to the more than thirty-year-long feud about two occupied territories forming one fifth of its lands, Georgia is especially angry about Putin's
imperialism. In contrast to its current authorities, which are extremely
servile in regards to their mighty northern neighbor, wall tapestries of
Georgian streets all support the Ukrainian side: *Boycott Russian goods,
Fuck Ruzzia, Fuck Ruzki, Moscow will burn, Russia kills, Good Russian —
Leave Georgia, Fuck Russia — Putin falos, Georgia is occupied by Russia*
(writings in Georgian are accompanied by those in Italian, French, Polish,
and Russian), *No to war* (in Russian), *Fuck Russians* (too many to count!),
*Russia is a terrorist state, Rus go home, Putin get out, No Russian is welcome,
good or bad, Putin* (with a giant penis), *Russia is an occupier, Stop Russian
aggression, Fuck Putin* (whereby the letters *uc* are replaced with a Georgian
and a Ukrainian flag), images of Putin and inscriptions *Hitler Kaput, Fuck
Putin—Stop War, Russian whores, Never back to USSR, Visas for Russians,
Fuck bloody Ruzzia, Resistance to Ruzzian imperializm!, Russia kills, To*

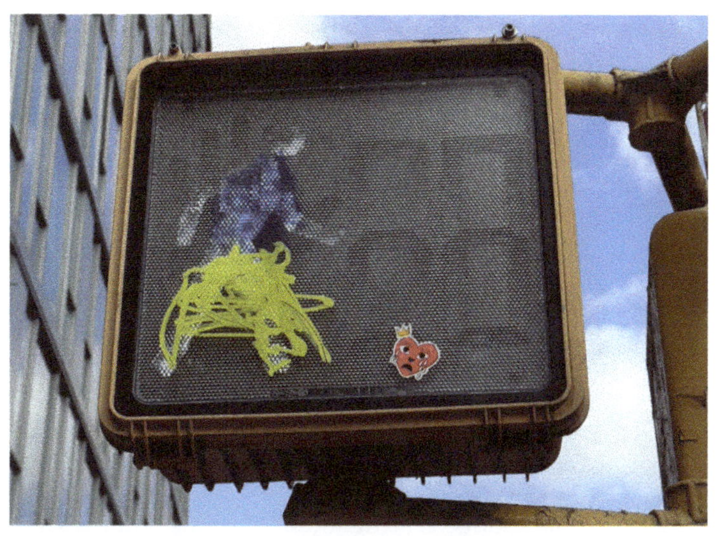

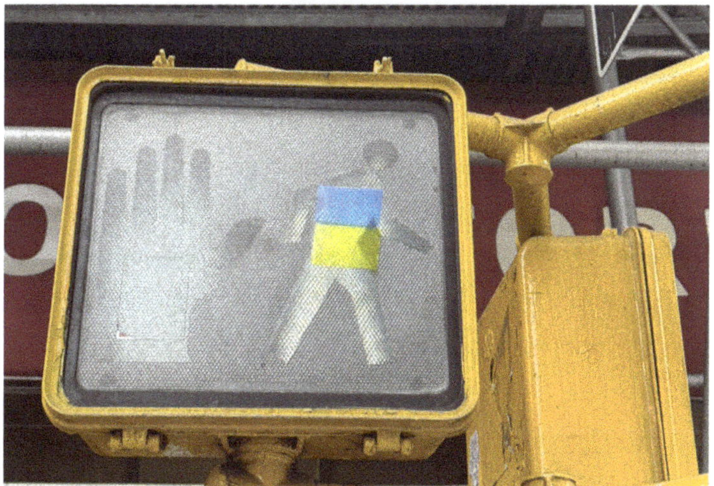

Top to bottom: East Village and Union Square, New York, February 2025.

brave Ukraine from Georgians, Ukrainian victory is the whole world's victory, Belarus against war (with a Belarus and Ukrainian flags), *USSR* (on a garbage bin), everything. And also *Glory to Ukraine, To the heroes — Glory,* a neo-Nazi sign with the name *Azov* and an appeal to *Support Azov* with their QR code. Some bars are equipped with signs declaring *YOU are more than WELCOME here if you agree that PUTIN is a WAR CRIMINAL, and you respect the independence of PEACEFUL nations* and an added *Stand with*

Ukraine. Especially strong are the images of two tortured and killed war prisoners, the clips of which the pro-Russian sides have even published online: Georgian Giorgi Antsukhelidze (2008) and Ukrainian Oleksandr Macievskyi (2023). They are undersigned with *Never, never surrender!*

Images follow with no comments in all graffiti and street art techniques: a Ukrainian refugee family setting off into the unknown with a small house in hand, while the boy is reproachfully staring at the viewer; a crossed over pig in Russian colors; a crossed over Russian passenger airplane (a reaction to the mass of Russian tourists and/or refugees with free access to Georgia); a mural with a panorama of Kyiv on Kyiv Street in Tbilisi; Putin as Hitler on a torture device; a Ukrainian trident; a Georgian wolf with a Ukrainian badge tearing a leg off of a soldier with a Russian flag on his army boot; a crossed over army boot in the colors of the Russian flag, etc., etc.

The flags of Georgia, Ukraine, NATO, and the EU, spraypainted closely together, expressed what should be each country's foreign policy. While there are numerous Ukrainian flags all over, they have also invented new flags: one shaped like that of Georgia (a large red cross and four white fields with smaller red crosses) but in Ukrainian colors and with blue hearts replacing the small red crosses; another shaped like that of Georgia but in Ukrainian colors and with an inscription *Today we are all Ukrainians*. And finally: the light blue street signs are given a spraypainted yellow reflection on the bottom to make a Ukrainian flag. Georgia was also the only place where I took photos of calls for the Russians as a nation to be dealt with brutally: *Death to Moscovians* (in Russian), *Good Russ = Dead Russ*, and *Kill Russians*. Hmmm. I found the most original street intervention on a tourist street. A currency display was running the selling/buying rate for dollars and euros, while the rate for rubles was — *Glory to Ukraine!* Instances of this spraypainted, pasted, or performative anger are everywhere — I had a feeling that they are even more intense in Georgia (which fears being attacked again) than in Ukraine.

However, I have also often encountered support for Putin's politics. Let me start with my home in the Balkans again: for almost a decade now, the main Ljubljana transversal is home to the graffiti *Pahor + Poroshenko + EU = swastika.* The sports club in its southern periphery was marked by the letter *Z*, by *Russia,* and by *Fuck Ukraine.* The recent *Putin, throw that bomb already* from the center of Ljubljana was immediately upgraded into *Rasputin, throw that bonbon already.* In Trieste, two hearts surround a graffitied *Russia.* In Zagreb, the graffiti *Stop NATO wars* was transformed into *Stop Z wars,* with a small swastika added to the middle of the letter Z. In the past two years, the Copenhagen statue of *The Little Mermaid* was also a target of anti- and pro-Russian interventions.

In Belgrade, the *Z*'s and the glorification of Russia are strong: since 2022, my connections there have been telling me how shocked the Russians who fled Putin to Serbia are. Everywhere, both sides engage in graffiti wars, in cross-out wars. During my last visit there, I took photo of a mural dedicated to a young Serbian volunteer and member of extreme right-wing groups, killed on Lugansk front in 2022, juxtaposed with anti-Putin stickers with his face combined with characteristic Hitlerite mustache and hairstyle. Overnight, the now infamous crossroads in the Belgrade neighborhood Vračar, which is *decorated* with images of Ratko Mladić (leader of the Bosnian Serb army), Draža Mihajlović (WWII collaborator) and similar characters, sported a mural of Putin, a connected Serbian and Russian flag, and inscriptions *Glory to Russia* and *brother.* Its opponents soon reacted, *bloodying* Putin's eyes, mouth, and ears with red paint, crossing over the inscription, correcting *brother* to *war* (Serbian: *brat* to *rat*), and adding, in Russian, *No to war* and *Shit.*

In Ukraine, the vibrant, convincing, and varied home graffiti production was almost overshadowed by the (anonymous) Banksy visit in the fall of 2022, which at the same time contributed to media around the world finally coming to their senses and starting to report also about everything else that is drawn or written on the walls of Ukrainian towns. After Banksy's social media authenticated seven stencils of anti-war and anti-Putin murals in Kyiv, Irpin, and Borodianka (a gymnast on a pile of

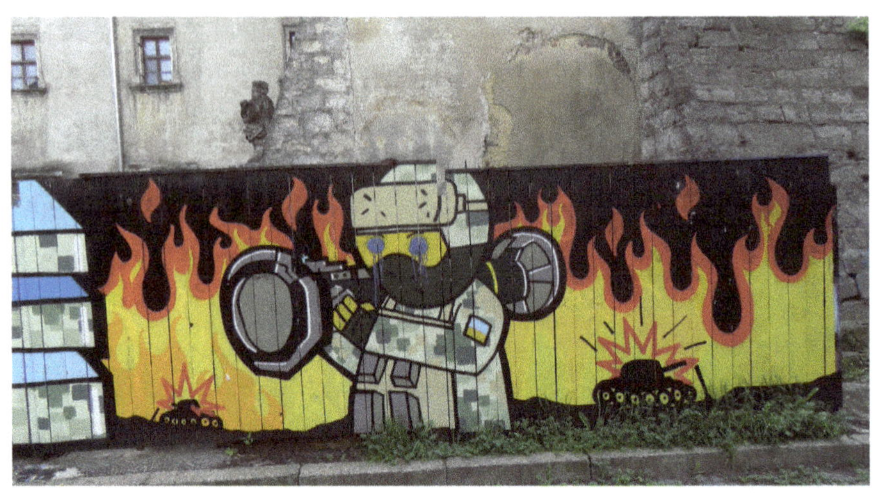

Lviv, May 2023.

rubble, a child on a swing, a giant penis-rocket on a Russian military vehicle, etc.), a destroyed wall of this last town became the scene of a young boy defeating a grown-up judoka — a tried-and-tested motif of *David and Goliath*, which often serves as a description of this war at home and abroad. Although the defeated *Goliath*'s face is semi-covered, Banksy obviously portrayed Putin, as he made his judo skills well-known — together with a series of photos on which he heroically defeats one opponent after another. This time, he seemed to fail. And for the first anniversary of the general strike, the Post of Ukraine reproduced this stencil on stamps and postcards bearing a postscript *Putin, fuck off!* (This is not the first time a political institution adopted a street image: a few years ago, Roman street artist Alessia Babrow sued the Vatican for unauthorized use of her Jesus Christ stencil on its stamps.) Other famous graffiti artists who created works in Ukraine include Thomas Baumgärtel aka Bananensprayer, who finds his main inspiration in a banana: he dealt with Putin in a similar way to another autocrat, Donald Trump, a few years ago.

After the large paintings, either hanging in buildings or spraypainted on the outside walls, let's turn our attention to the small images with rippled edges. I am sadly unaware if there is anybody researching post as a

   Ukrainian Vignettes: Essays on a Culture at War

medium of political propaganda and the complete monopoly the state has over this ideological apparatus. It would be wonderful if someone is — as the post is a discrete and omnipresent institution completely conforming to the ruling politics.

On all three trips, one of my missions was to find a post office to buy stamps. (Yes, I still choose, buy, write, and send postcards. This usually takes me half a day: the easiest thing is to find postcards — tourists still buy them as souvenirs. Stamps, on the other, hand, are another story; not only in Ukraine but in many other countries, they can only be bought at a post office. Once both items are procured, you are left with the safari of finding a post box. It's as if someone is trying to tell you "Man, are you realizing how passé this whole affair is?" and instead to make a selfie in front of a cathedral or a full plate of an unpronounceable dish and send it through your phone. Or, even better, post in on social media for all of your hundreds of friends to see — but I am not on social media, and I can count my true friends on the fingers of my hands.)

At every news stand, tourist shop and post office, one can buy patriotic postcards and any paraphernalia one can think of (from posters to decorative helmets, everything in Ukrainian colors), which almost exclusively commemorate the important moments of history and war or prominent Ukrainian people. Especially post offices fill their windows with commemorative stamps and commemorative envelopes (memorializing the day that the stamps are issued). The first group are history stamps: they feature reproductions of paintings by the older generation painter Ivan Kuchmak (1899–1977) or Nil Khasevych (1905–1952), who is famous also for his propagandist woodcuts for the Organization of Ukrainian Nationalists — years after WWII, he kept creating those in Ukrainian bunkers until the Soviet secret police tracked him down and killed him. New prints of some of these can be bought on stands and in museums. A postcard commemorating the 65th anniversary of Ukrainian Insurgent Army shows an image of Yevhen Konovalets (1891–1938), a leader of interwar Ukrainian emigration, who was also killed by Soviet agents.

The second group is composed of completely contemporary images depicting protests from the Orange Revolution onwards and fallen or injured soldiers from the current war (on the back side of some of them, there is a QR code explaining what their feats of bravery were). Their authors are contemporary artists such as Andrii Sahach and Viktor Grudakov. Boris Groh's famous painting *Russian Warship Go Fuck Yourself* with a motif of a Ukrainian soldier shooting a middle finger to the Russian warship Moskva, sunk in April 2022 close to Snake Island, ended not only on commemorative postcards and stamps but also on the walls of Ukrainian towns as graffiti and on T-shirts. On the next stamp, a sunlit Ukrainian tractor pulls a Russian tank, with the words *Good evening, we're from Ukraine!* The *cyborgs* from the Battle of Donetsk Airport were given their own stamp, while series of postcards are also dedicated to military units or forces, e.g. air force, air defense, special units (commandos), etc. A reaction to the reductions in electricity consumption during the first winter of the war is commemorated on a dark-blue postcard with a worker, an electrician, who manages to find light, find energy, and an inscription saying *Life will defeat death, light will defeat darkness.*

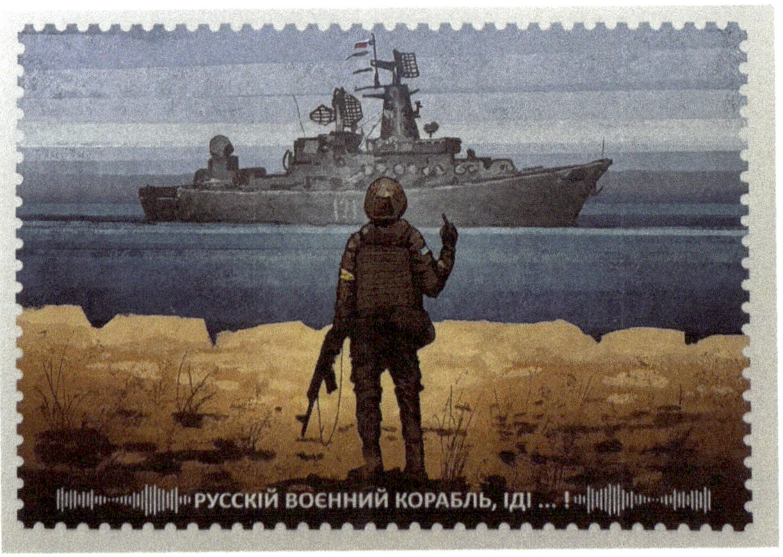

Envelope with stamp motif, "Russian Warship Go Fuck Yourself," 2022.

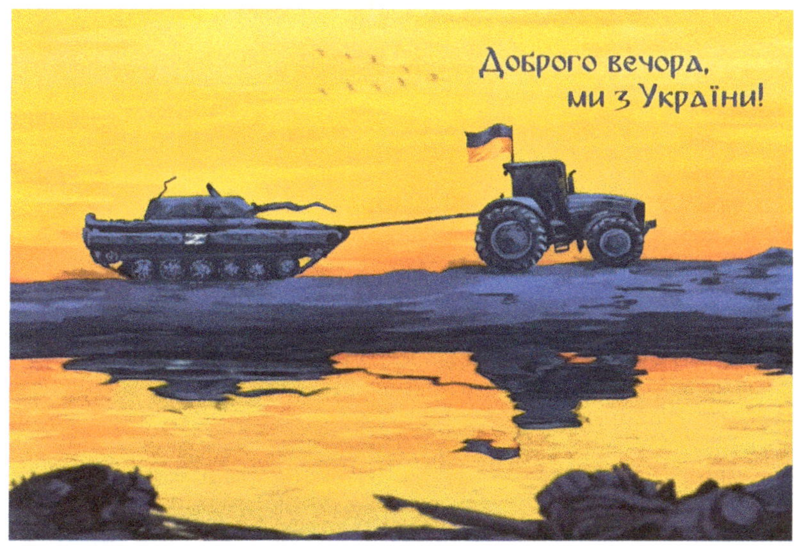

Postcard, "Good evening, we're from Ukraine!" 2023.

The third group brings together those postal works that are more abstract in their patriotism; they include, for example, the motif of the aforementioned colossal Mother Ukraine memorial with the inscription *Hope*; a motif of a stylized sun with a Ukrainian trident in the middle, shining down onto a yellow-and-blue landscape; or a children's painting of a field of grain on which a mother wearing a *vyshivanka* and carrying a child is waiting for her husband returning home from the front in his uniform. And finally, the connection between war culture and popular culture is established by the postcard that features a fighting soldier and the frontman of the Eurovision winners Kalush, together with the refrain of the winning song, a nostalgic tune dedicated to his mother Stefania.

Image flows into sound, which is the topic of my next essay.

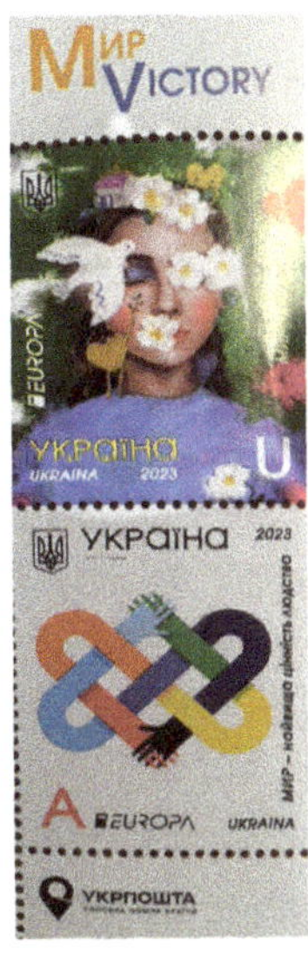

Stamps from Ukraine, 2023.

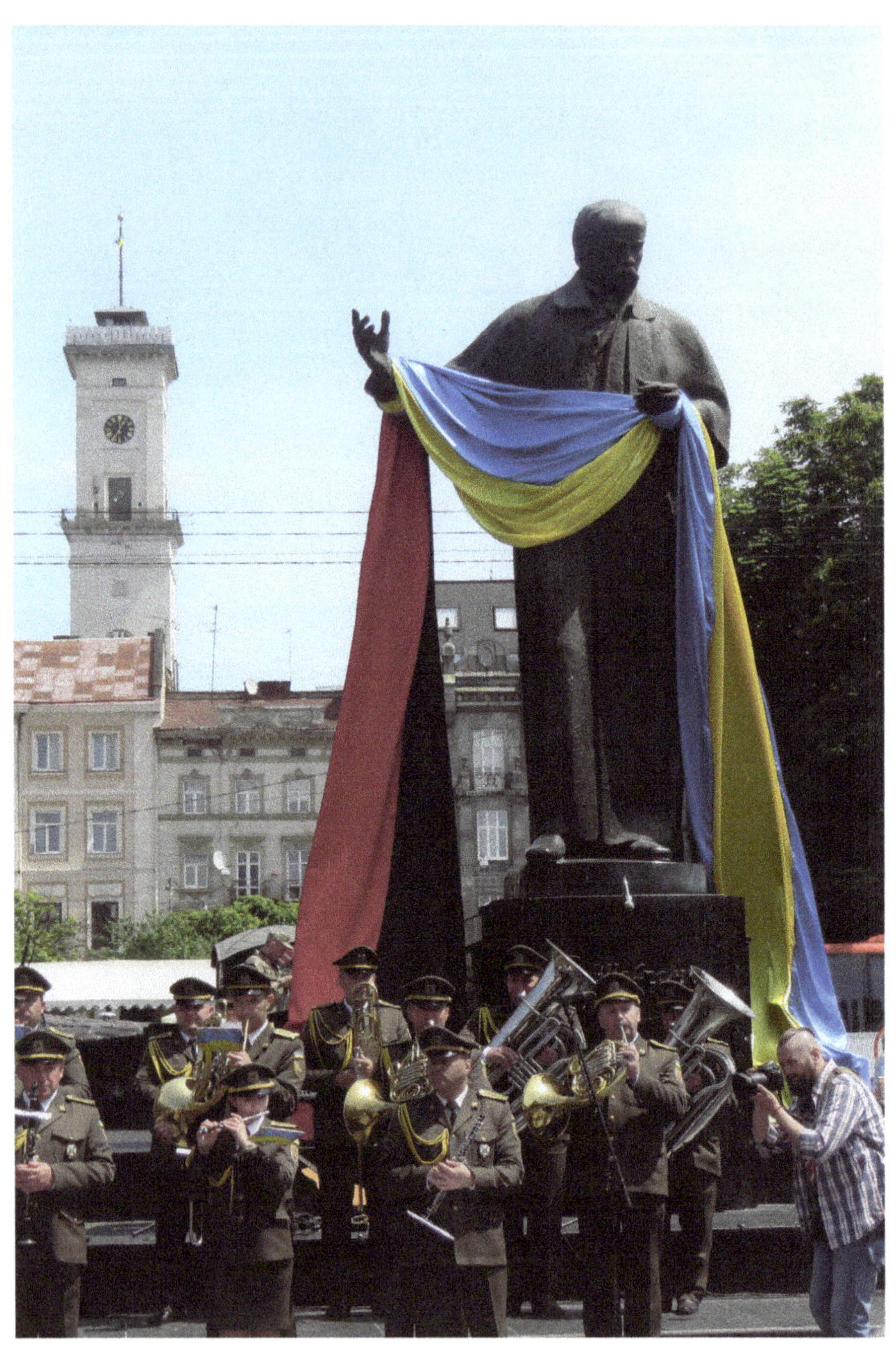

Open air concert, Lviv, May 2023.

IX

VOICES OF WAR

> *"Scream for me, Ukraine!"*
> *a greeting from my correspondence with a heavy-metal fan*
> *from Kyiv, April 2023, in reference to the documentary film on*
> *a Bruce Dickinson (lead vocalist of Iron Maiden) concert in*
> *besieged Sarajevo.*

"Make noise from our frustration," is a verse by American indie rock-ers Gossip, blasting through my earphones on long rides (the song is "Pop Goes the World" from the album *Music for Men*). It reminded me that war is also a scream, a voice, a sound, a noise, a whisper, a melody. Shocking me once more with how self-evident for them the culture of war is, a piece of information my hosts gave me very early on concerned the hum of the projectiles that were aimed at them. Regardless of the blaring sirens on TV and in various apps, their trained ears were recognizing the sounds of various types of cruise missiles swooshing, air-launched bombs murmuring, or drones whirring. At night, war cannot be seen, but it can be heard.

During that short time, I couldn't sharpen my hearing enough to be able to differentiate them myself, but I did listen to a lot of other things. "War is always radically loud," claims Ukrainian writer and editor Oleksandr Krasovytskyy in his dystopic, dark humor novella *Tomorrow*.[1] I encountered (anti-) war and patriotic songs either live, in concerts, through my hosts' recommendations, or by reading articles on Eurovision episodes with Ukrainian winners (2004, 2016, and 2022). Radio and TV programs cycled patriotic marches and just as patriotic pop, rock, and ethnic tunes. Those were also blasted through speakers for improvised concerts in public spaces; especially popular were, as I could understand, *Oi u luzi chervona kalyna* (Oh, the Red Viburnum in the Meadow) and *Batko nash Bandera, Ukraina — maty* (Our father is Bandera, Ukraine our mother). One of those May mornings, the city promenade in front of the gigantic statue to Taras Shevchenko, wrapped in a ten-meter flag combining the blue-yellow and the black-red combination especially for that occasion, hosted an open-air concert of the military orchestra with singers and a similarly motivational program. "Dammit, why can't I speak Ukrainian," I said to myself. I had, however, mastered the bare basics and managed to grasp the repeating phrases such as *dlya Ukrayiny* (for Ukraine), *boh z namy* (God be with us), *heroyi* (heroes) here, *heroyi* there, *slava* (glory), *khloptsi* (boys), *voroh* (enemy), *dobrovil'nyy* (volunteers), *bat'ko nash Bandera* (our father Bandera), *Ukrayina syl'na* (strong Ukraine), *maty Ukrayina* (mother Ukraine), *vil□na* (free) back and forth — if the entire pompous arrangement and the matching military visuals weren't enough. Excited, the mass sang along, while the hair on the back of my neck stood up — like every time and everywhere when anybody out of any reason starts exclaiming *My!* (We!) or *Nashi!* (Ours!) — and I couldn't stay long. A few mornings, when I was still in bed, tired from everything that happened during the night, I was awoken by a patriotic wind band that also played marches and similar anthemic songs — I still don't know if it was played live or if it was just a recording, as the music disappeared as quickly as it appeared only a few minutes in. I hadn't heard those brass sounds from marching band live, especially not in the early morning, ever since I last witnessed a May 1st morning parade in my childhood in socialist Yugoslavia.

Lasting for eleven years now, the two half-times of the war in Ukraine have left their mark on the world music scene, as well. During the war in Croatia, Croatian band Let 3 used *Detonation — inspiration!*, a typically borderline, sarcastic and punk exclamation, to fill the breaks between their songs on their concerts — while the public could only muster a bitter smile. May is Eurovision Song Contest month and so *our region* (another witless euphemism for the territory of former Yugoslavia) was buzzing with the expectations over the song ŠČ! by this infamous band — but so was Ukraine, especially in the light of their recent victories. In 2016, the Eurovision winner was *1944* by electro/ethnic pop singer Jamala, who sang in English and in the language of the Crimea Tatars (she is a descendant) to recount their bitter post-war fate and deportation due to their supposed collaboration with the Nazis. Six years later, this song contest was won by ethnic rap group Kalush Orkestra with the song *Stefania* (at the national level, the group came in second, but it was later discovered that the singer of the winning song illegally visited occupied Crimea in 2015). Since then, Kalush Orchestra has been regularly performing on world stages, raising awareness for the situation in their homeland. The 2022 event did not escape war references, either: their lead vocalist appealed to people to help Ukraine, Mariupol, and the defenders of Azovstal. The group sold their Eurovision trophy and had the money used to buy military equipment. Both cases obviously provoked accusations of politicization of the event: the Eurovision stage has also become a Ukrainian battleground.

Ukrainians in Slovenia made me aware of the YouTube sensation Jerry Heil, a young singer whose posters I saw on my Ukrainian travels later. Born Yana Oleksandrivna Shemaieva, she started a YouTube channel singing covers; today, she is an acclaimed singer regularly performing also abroad. Often using now ever-present ethnic motifs in her vocally strong minimalist arrangements, her newest compositions (as well as the accompanying visuals from clothing and promotional photos to concert looks) reference the current situation: a typical song is *Blahoslovenna zemlya* (Blessed land), while another, *Kozats'komu rodu* (to the Cossack people), glorifies the former — and the present — Cossack bravery, disobedience, and the fight for freedom. I strongly suggest searching her out on YouTube.

During the mind-numbing drives across the Ukrainian plains, I fought boredom by trying to remember the anti-war songs from my (crazy, I'll admit it) music collection that includes everything from mainstream (like

War Pigs by Black Sabbath, *Love and War* by Neil Young, *Peace Dog* by The Cult, or *The Holy War* from the last Thin Lizzy album) to alternative (400 by Borghesia, *Bleed for Me* by Dead Kennedys, *War Ensemble* by Slayer). Practically all of them share the message of *Slušaj 'vamo* by the Belgrade antiwar super-group Rimtutituki: *Peace, brother, peace.* Just before I left, a friend, a Prague-based *neo-dada dark noise industrial and-a-lot-more artist*, after a performance in Ljubljana's new autonomous cultural center Plac, gifted me with *Chomu ne vyyshlo?* (Why didn't it work?) (2018), an album by the Swedish anarchist black metal band Trespasser, who are inspired by somebody I also find to be one of the most interesting personalities of Ukrainian history: Nestor Makhno (1888–1934). In 1917–1921, especially in the south of Ukraine, his strongly rural anarcho-communist movement took to weapons and resisted various armies. They fought the German and Austro-Hungarian troops during their final offensive on the Eastern Front; against the White movement, i.e. against various anti-Bolshevik armadas; against the Ukrainian People's Republic; and against the Red Army (with which they first sided to conquer the Whites). Today, his name is almost completely forgotten in Ukraine, apart from a few marginalized anti-authoritarian and anarchist groups that have joined the Ukrainian defenders in resistance to Putin's invasion. Among countless characters on walls, I only spotted him once: on a fan sticker of FC Lviv (or *Lemberg*, as the sticker called this city). He suffered the exact same fate as the Trespassers sing about in *Death to Fight Death*: "No *streets will be named after our nameless graves ...*"

Just like in besieged Sarajevo (*pod opsadom*, under siege, was the title of their concerts and albums), music in Ukraine is also moving underground. Even the philharmonics and jazz are becoming underground, and rock concerts are organized at Kiev metro stations, I was told by the locals or read on posters around the city. I watched clips of people in the clumsy practicality of improvised shelters spontaneously starting to sing either folk, patriotic, or famous rock songs. Refrains of many of these latter ones have also become encouraging political or military slogans. On the other hand, I was surprised that I could find not one store or even just one aisle dedicated to Ukrainian music — of any kind, ethnic, pop, classical, rock, or alternative. I somehow feel closer to physical than to online albums; I love to read the lyrics, see who worked on it, scan through every information on the recordings, etc. Just like I do in the bookstores, I also love to browse through shelves with music, study the albums, and Google additional information. As I could quite easily order their records online, it was more of a side quest for me to try and find (and, ultimately, fail) albums of Ukrainian metalcore attraction Jinjer, regular guests at all metal festivals around the world — they have also been touring abroad. Or Poshlaya Molly, a Kharkov pop slash emo slash synth-pop attraction. ("You really do listen to all sorts of weird sh*t," people often tell me while rolling their eyes — and I usually say "Yeah, happy to.") Or the lovely wackos that are the dark-cabaret Dakh Daughters from Kyiv, whose music and performances effectively and wittily combines various musical genres and languages. And even more those of the silent legends of stoner rock, Stoned Jesus, with their doomily slow, almost psychedelic riffs that I was reminded of by a friend. Since then, I have often played their musically and lyrically really convincing *I'm the Mountain* and *Bright Like the Morning*.

Further deepening my general feeling of surreal, my Kyiv host invited me to come to the National Opera of Ukraine that hosted a musical on 20th-century Italian history through their *canzone*. The play titled *The Ball* was conceived and organized by Italian director Matteo Spiazzi — due to the war, he has been doing everything through Zoom. What a show that was! The local performers were confident in acting and dancing in short scenes and in singing music from Calabrian and Puglian tarantella to Amanda Lear, from Celentano to Patty Pravo — in flawless Italian. The house was packed, the audience engaged, the war seemed to be somewhere else, somewhere infinitely far away. And yet, it wasn't — that was another mirage. It was waiting for us behind the closed doors. I later read that one of the dancers scheduled to perform, Vadim, was killed by a sniper on the front, just before the premiere.

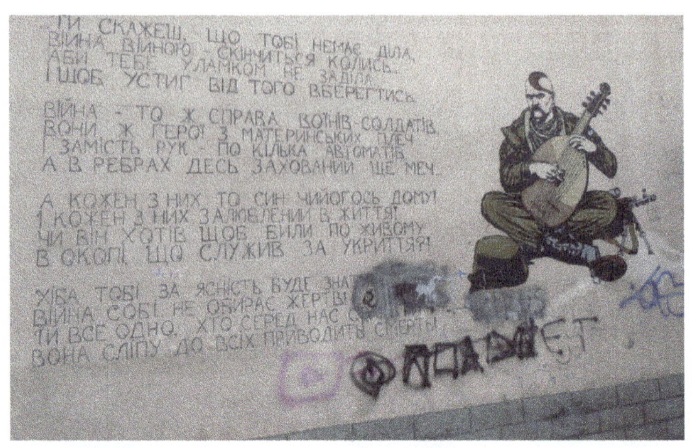

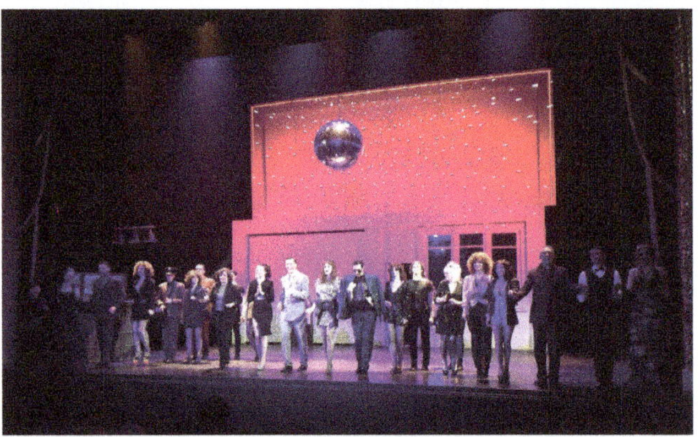

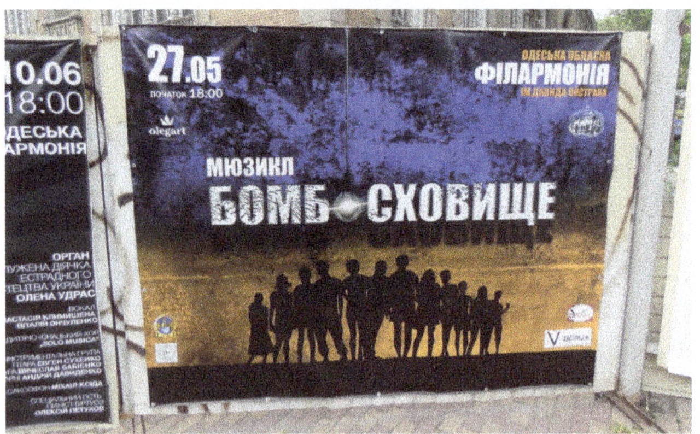

Top to bottom: Cossack playing a traditional Ukrainian instrument, the bandura, sitting next to a machine gun, with an anti-war poem by a young Ukrainian poet, Zoryana-Zlata Palamarchuk, Lviv, May 2023; Kyiv Operetta Theater, Kyiv, May 2023; Billboard for the musical "Bombshelter," Odesa Philharmonic Orchestra, Odesa, May 2023.

This brings my last three essays on the new literary, visual, and music art created under the influence of the war in Ukraine to an end. Considering their differences, do these forms of art have any common, intertwining characteristics? Any dominant genres, repeating motifs, similar ways of expressing feelings, related narrative compositions, general stance — and common ideological connotations and political reach? Because of their abundance, breadth, and intensity, they might be difficult to find, but it is worth a shot. Here goes: they mingle the first-person, autobiographical emotion with the wider social framework, and the aesthetic elements with documentarism and authentic testimonies — a docufiction approach. There are many chronicle- and journal-style recordings following the activities from day to day, from week to week, from month to month. Furthermore, as expected, these works often feature two dictions: a patriotic one (in a classic Tyrtaeus way, they praise their country, compatriots, leadership, history, and, yes, their armed forces, too) and a fighting, agitating, if not agitprop one. An old Balkan saying (that I first heard when I was in the army) goes *When flags fly, all reason is in the trumpet*, meaning that all reason is gone or focuses on the war. As a rule, cultural events at home and also abroad, on tour, end and sometimes begin with patriotic appeals and vows. Like in any other war, many artists volunteer or are recruited into armed forces; their pictures in uniforms regularly appear in various media. Others perform their patriotic programs in public institutions, schools, hospitals, military barracks, and, of course, on the front.

Along with the encouraging and the patriotic pushes, the majority of these works is also marked with lyricism, an intimate anguish of *what now?*, an astonishment at the tragic events that command, overtake, and scar people. The works often emphasize that all but the few more careful ones were surprised by the war; blindly believing in the good, they overlooked and ran over a few more than obvious *red lights* ("[H]ow naïve we were then …" writes Zakharov). Either referencing the spring of 2014 or February 2022, stories often begin with an initial shock and phrases such as *I never imagined …* or *my friends and I first thought that this senseless crisis would soon be over … or we couldn't imagine the coming catastrophe.* Their neighbors were supposed to move *for a few weeks only* and asked them to water their plants and feed their cat — they would soon be back. At first, everything seemed like a nightmare, a *bloody fairytale*, to borrow the title of a Desanka Maksimović tragic poem of Nazi atrocities in occupied Serbia, and all they had to do was wake up. That *ours* would soon take over again and that everything would return to how it was. But it soon turns out that this is not the case — and war changes everything. The dichotomy before/after is therefore evident: a discontinuity between the *previous life* (which carries no nostalgia, as it is often seen in post-Yugoslav case!) and *life now*, at war.

Another characteristic of many of these works is that they reveal how, at the beginning, the opposing sides were intertwined: there was no clear frontline, there was no way of knowing whose projectiles were flying above their heads, and there were only guesses as to who sent the uniformed youth that suddenly appeared at their door. I was told that many of these works mix Ukrainian with Russian language. They contain many details from the dramatic activities on the front or behind it, military vocabulary, as well as descriptions and cryptic codes (and abbreviations) for weapons, *ours* and *theirs*. On the one hand, the stories are full of anger, even hate: mostly directed at Putin's supporters and soldiers, who are despised as *Orcs* (referencing *The Lord of the Rings*), *drunken gang, bullies, madmen,* *"volunteers," terrorists, little green men.* Especially painful is a sudden collaboration of former friends, neighbors, and acquaintances, *a treason.* Only "here, in the middle of hell," writes Zhadan, you feel "how much you had and how much you've lost."[2] On the other hand, these stories are processual, with an extremely subjective, intimist tone: their protagonists find themselves forced in a difficult situation and overcome their fear and themselves to become something else. In a transformation of ruptured existences, they sincerely admit their weaknesses and depression following the initial shock, their paranoia, fears, anxiety, breakdowns, retreats, also escapes and shame: in many of these stories, every character is often simultaneously the hero and the anti-hero. To paraphrase the refrain from an iconic song by Slovenian dark-techno attraction Borghesia: they carry *hope* and they carry *fear.*

As is the almost a norm in art during the extremely tough times, the works abound in wider historical and political reflections, as well as clearly expressed one-sidedness. As could be expected, there is no reservation concerning errors or even evildoings on their own side. Existential reflections abstracting the concrete circumstance of war and the (self-)critical insights into their mistakes will certainly appear years from now — just like they did in the Balkans in the works of Slovenian writers and partisans Edvard Kocbek and Vitomil Zupan, Serbian film director Živojin Pavlović, etc. Absent is another thing so characteristic for East- and Central European art: the bitter, dark humor, the Aesopian ideas that subvert the authority of various totalitarian environments (state, church, army, bureaucracy) through laughter — quite understandably, war is no joking matter. Furthermore, people who had never expressed themselves creatively before are now grabbing hold of a pen, paintbrush, guitar, spray can, microphone, or any other medium.

Literal shrapnel of war events offer an unfortunate stimulation and painful inspiration to express their feelings, anxiety, anger, love, and courage. One of such new artists I found on my journeys is Ruslan "Pihota" (*pihota* is the Ukrainian term for infantry), who, before joining the frontline forces in February 2022, worked in a publishing house in Kharkiv. Over the following year he collected and published a few hundred caricatures and short black-and-white comics into a small but thick booklet entitled *Ukrainian Military Comics* (2023), which sketches life in the trenches, various military situations, and broader social and geopolitical issues in a witty way. Harsh first-hand experience lends authenticity to what is depicted and is committed to a DIY aesthetic of efficient simplicity.

The next characteristic might surprise some of you but, consciously or not and in varying degrees, this entire totally eclectic collection of authors of literary, visual, and music works mostly can and does differentiate

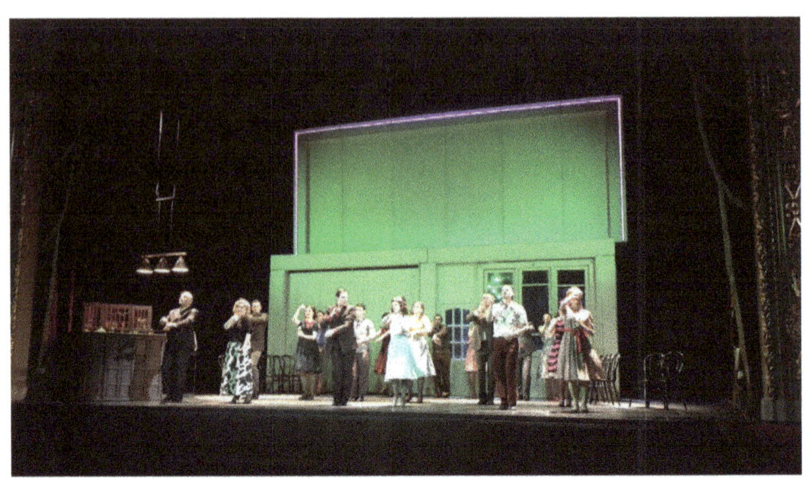

Kyiv Operetta Theater, Kyiv, May 2023.

between Putin's democratic dictature, *democrature*, which rules Russia today, and Russians as a nation and their culture. This is confirmed by the Tbilisi graffiti that I found on the summer streets of Georgia this year: *Putin is not Russia.* Angry outbursts can, of course, be found, and so can extremists who hate everything that has a whiff of Russia as they automatically connect it with the Great-Russian ideology and practice — from the tzarist, Russian Orthodox, and Bolshevik versions to Putin's incarnation today. And yet in Ukraine I found no appeals to kill Russians, no such extreme hate, no pamphlet akin to *Kill!* by Ilya Ehrenburg, Soviet writer and propagandist. (A reminder: "Count only the number of Germans you have killed. Kill the German — this is your old mother's prayer. Kill the German — this is what your children beseech you to do. Kill the German — this is the cry of your Russian earth. Do not waver. Do not let up. Kill.") I haven't even seen it in political graffiti, which are by definition the most direct, harsh, and rough. All these interpretations of war are mainly anti-Great-Russian, directed against Putin, against Patriarch Kiril, against *Russian occupiers* and their vassals — and not indiscriminately anti-Russian. Yes, there is anger, helpless rage, yes, there is rejection and exclusion. But apart from exceptions, there are no generalizations, no senseless score-settling. And finally, on the one hand, these works project the very obvious position of an innocent victim that is *our side*, what I described as self-victimization. Yet on the other side, they just as much radiate optimism, motivation: a wish, a readiness, and consequently an engagement in the resistance with the ordinary narrative figures of the *barehanded nation that overcomes a greater power*. These works therefore never include resignation or retreat — quite the opposite: they encourage. However bitter pain and loss makes them, they encourage.

To summarize this summary of literary, visual, musical, and other cultural interpretations of the war in Ukraine, their loose mold could be described with the words by Tamara Duda: "*Chaos, Anarchy* and *Courage*."[3] "Poetry does not have howitzers, cruise missiles, or cluster bombs," claims Ihor Pomerantsev, formerly emigrant author, "but it has high-precision words against which guns are powerless."[4] And again — I could not shake that feeling of *déjà vu*, which I must have mentioned a hundred times; the already seen, already read, already heard, already played, already lived during the times of war in the former Yugoslav territories in the 1990s. I have also often thought of the convincing diction in the wide specter of Yugoslav partisan art, which has been innovatively and acceleratingly researched in the past ten or fifteen years here at home and also abroad. But with one important difference: this latter art put a great emphasis on class and revolution, as well as on the emancipation of subordinate groups (especially women, peasants, the young), which is something that I don't see in the contemporary Ukrainian art. Nationalism doesn't question social injustices; but freedom without social justice is no real freedom.

NOTES

1 Krasovytskyy, Oleksandr. *Tomorrow*. Folio, Kharkiv, 2022. 125.

2 Zhadan, Serhiy. *The Orphanage*, 2021. 299.

3 Duda, Tamara. *Daughter*, 2021. 210.

4 Pomerantsev, Ihor. *State of War*, 2023. 155.

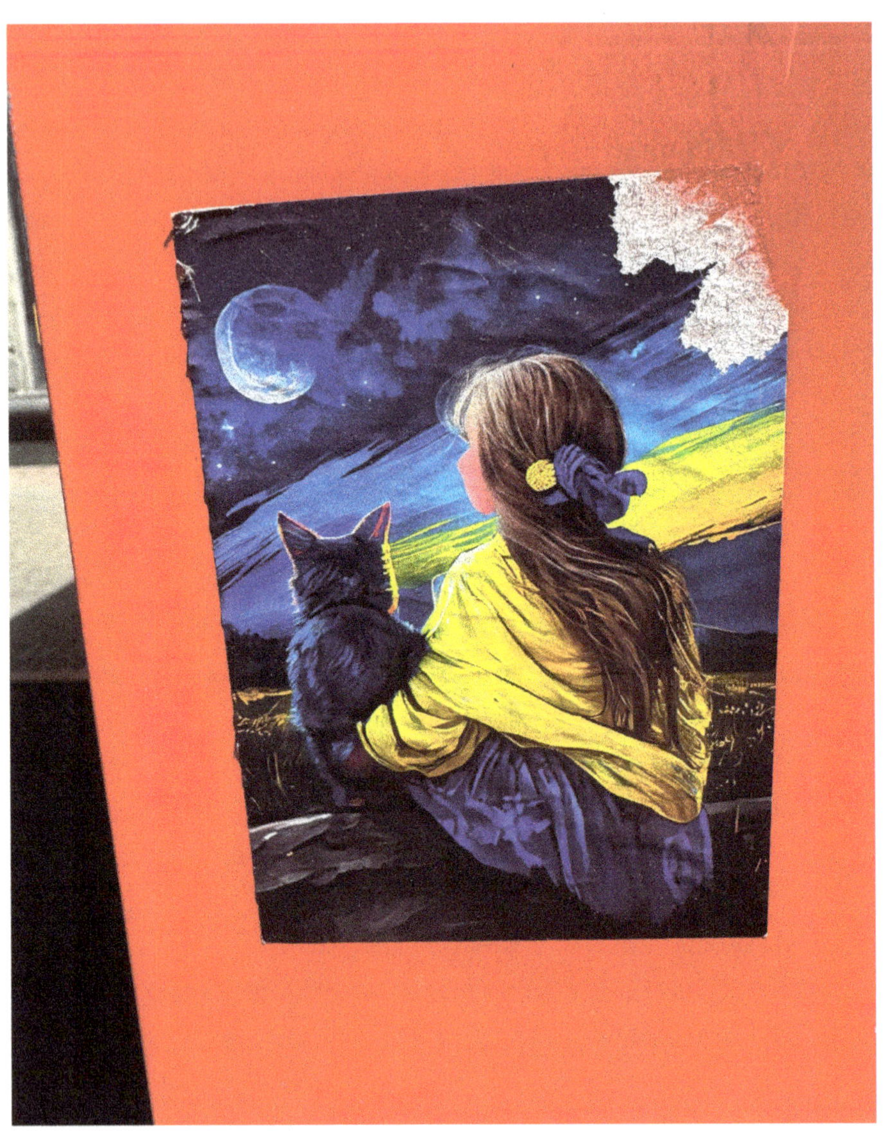

Kyiv, June 2024.

X

CONSEQUENCES OF WAR

"Have you ever thought of moving — for your kids if nothing else?"
"Not even for a moment. If I moved, if everyone moved,
they'd get what they want. When trouble starts, you can't just
walk away, my grandma taught me."
Talking with a Ukrainian professor,
mother of three, May 2023.

On my Ukrainian journeys, I have so often heard, seen, read, and encountered this stance that simultaneously holds the passion of anger and heroic contempt, bravery, and hope. No despondency, defeatism, no bitterness — but defiance, stubbornness, spite, a dedication to resistance, toughness, life. As if people fought fear with concentration, uncertainty with relentlessness. I saw wrath — but it didn't depersonalize. Instead, it gave purpose to being. Resist to exist. A lot more of the *optimism of the will* than of the *pessimism of the intellect*, I was reminded of Gramsci. In a previously mentioned interview from the beginning of the war, Kurkov unequivocally stated that "you just have to keep on living and do whatever you can in the circumstances. It does give you this kind of energy. And a conviction that it is possible to fight against a force of evil that is bigger than you are." He also began his diary with a question and an answer: ""Have you ever tried to remain optimistic during catastrophe and tragedy, during bloody military operations? I have tried and will continue to try."[1] On page three of his own diary (2023), Zhadan promises: "All our concerts will come later,

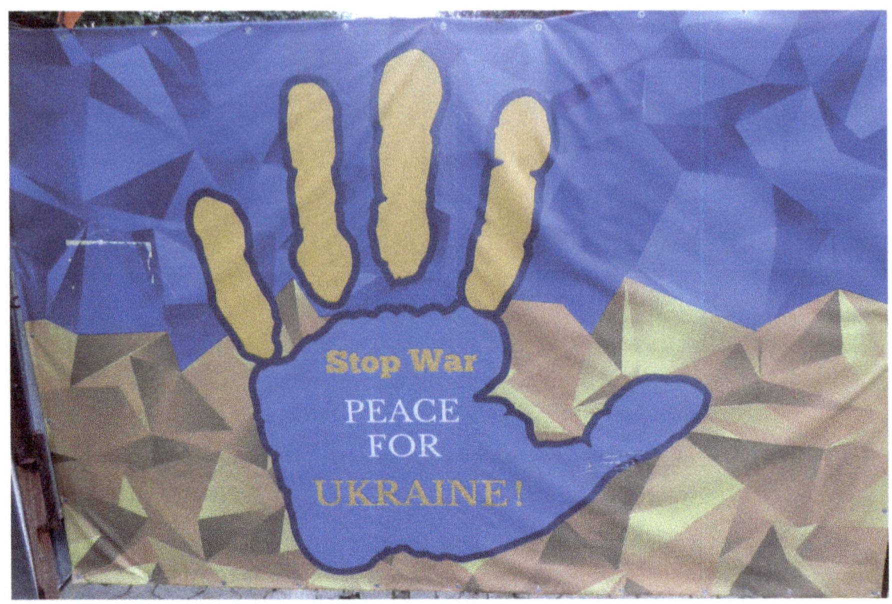

Uzhhorod, May 2023.

after we win." Street signs in Kyiv are already inviting future guests with the slogan *Kyiv is waiting for you after the victory!* (with a thank you note to the Ukrainian Army). Due to the lack of time, I just skimmed a bilingual brochure written by different scholars about the future of Mariupol, now in hands of the separatists, entitled *Mariupol Reborn: A Vision for Rebuilding Mariupol* — I still regret not buying it. Talking to my hosts, they generally concluded with *and when the war is over* — or the more confident ones with *and when we win.* "Technical advantage on the side of Russia, morale on the side of Ukraine,"[2] as Lampreht summarizes their dedication, being that they are attacked and are defending themselves. It seems that the smokier the bombs make the present, the more rockets and drones drown it out, the clearer the Ukrainian people see the future.

This is why a gift from my Odesa editor came as no surprise: he gave me a ceramic bottle in the shape of a rooster — liquid (alcohol, what else!) is poured in the hole in the tail and comes out from the beak. This beautiful product of folk art now guards my DVD stand. A rooster is a symbol of life — this one, that much more. On top of a wardrobe in a bombarded town of Borodianka in the Bucha region, one such bird miraculously survived the destruction of the entire building and became a unique symbol of Ukrainian resilience and resistance. This *Ukrainian Phoenix*, as it came to be known, has flourished in wartime popular culture, often presented as a diplomatic gift.

And yet ... and yet I couldn't help thinking if this bold conviction is a loud reaction to the quiet despair of an ominous present and the fear of a bleak future? When at the worst, courage can hold in short term — but how long can it remain at this level? At this writing, war is in full swing and bare existence is the first and the most important matter. But seeing that I spent time with people who are full of hope and cannot wait to see the better future that they strive towards, my mind often went to the cases from the Balkans. They are sadly not good. During the war of his time, Kocbek warned of this "duality of peace and war," this "duality of illusions and the weight of the coming disappointment."[3] I remember the excitement over the peace that my Bosnian-Herzegovinian friends told me about after the signing of the Dayton Agreement in late 1995. Today, this euphoria amounted to absolutely nothing, to washed out dreams, scraping by, these same people tell me. As it was obviously easier to survive the war in hope than to live in peace without hope, they are raising their children to prepare either for war or for emigration or for poverty. Not much of a choice.

The winners of the transition — the nationalist political elites, the oligarchs, the tycoons — can but reinforce their power with new protagonists: arms' dealers and other war criminals. Then there is praetorianism. Not to mention how many mines and other means of destruction will remain in the towns and on the fields and how many guns stored at home waiting for someone to lose their mind. Not just from Ukraine, people are still fleeing also *victorious* Croatia and *heavenly* Serbia, ever since the war-marked 1990s. I read that since the last census ten years ago, a half million fled each country. Similarly, in what are now the *European* countries of Estonia, Romania, Bulgaria, and Poland. It's probably redundant to add that those migrating are mainly young and educated people, the *spring* of these countries that are increasingly turning into a *teenage wasteland*, to borrow lyrics by The Who.

In his post-war Blue Ballad (Plava balada) from 2000, Serbian protest singer-songwriter Djordje Balašević bitterly summarized the devastating grip of today's dominating ideology and concrete politics of ethnonationalism and neoliberalism:

[And] then came priests and guns and crooks,

And the whole world warped,

Those who made it were predators and liars and entrepreneurs ...

And just over two decades later, the lucid Bosnian-Herzegovinian poet Selma Asotić in *Lesson on War*:

it never ends.

after the gunfire and the general comes

the intellectual, not necessarily in that order ...

[...]

it never ends.

after the gunfire and the general

comes the investor ...

We know all of this, we have seen it before — but when I'm talking to my warm-hearted new and old friends from Ukraine, I'm hoping that I am wrong. Winning the war seems hard enough on its own, but how to survive the peace after? Based on these Balkan experiences, I don't wish to kill their dreams in an already difficult situation or suggest that, at the end of this tunnel, there is perhaps another tunnel, followed by another and another.

Constantly challenged by the unpredictability of events, I still try to think differently, optimistically. First, there is hope that, based on the current military mobilization, they will in fact be able to move closer to a more inclusive, civil, democratic society, not towards a suffocatingly tribal and at the same time hermetically caste-ridden one. And, again first, as it is of the same importance: that they will attempt an equally key task, the construction of a socially fairer Ukraine. During my travels and outside them, I was constantly listening to and reading the urgent phrases for *decolonizing* Ukraine, its fight for freedom — with which I totally agree. But not once have I heard how urgent de-tycoonization, the restitution of the stolen wealth, the righting of social wrongs, and prosecuting corruption, nepotism, systemic crime, and also nationalism is; no fight against the negative practice of transition. Decolonization must be led by social reforms aiming toward solidarity and a fairer society. Failing to do so leads to new internal tension and conflicts.

The perspectives of Ukraine seem like those of the regions of the Balkans, but also of Central Europe. For a good century now, external superpowers have been delegating all three of them the ungrateful and unvoluntary roles of the *crossroads-bridge-fort* between one world and another. The home elites follow this direction meekly and with a perverted servitude. Just like the Balkans and Central Europe, Ukraine is also being pushed to somewhere in between, to an impossible position *in the middle*, to a *passage* between two extremes, to a state between *East* and *West*, between *Europe* and *Asia*, between despotisms and democracies, between civilization and barbarism, between empires and independence, between peace and war. And every in-betweenness is a stigma, no doubt about that. In the Balkans, this saturation with (an unfortunate) fate is called Balkanization, a negative ideological construction of this part of the world. In Central Europe, it is called *tragedy*, as Milan Kundera would say, an *impossible dilemma*. In 1869, Slovenian essayist and editor Fran Levec claimed only two things were possible: that we would either become Russians or Prussians. The Balkans and Central Europe are seen as two parts of the world where "everything starts or ends with a war, so there's no surprise there," as Polish author Andrzej Stasiuk wrote in the introductory pages of his novel *On the Road to Babadag*,[4] or "where every discussion ends in conflict" as Lyubka writes in his novel.[5]

Through our entire recent history — and, of course, now — Ukraine is also being dragged into this devastating position *somewhere in between*. Ukraine is supposed to be *the gates of Europe*, as Plokhy (2021) titled his book; other titles include *Borderland* (Reid 2015) and *Europe's Last Frontier?*. Plokhy believes that for Ukraine, "its claim to independence has always had a European orientation, which is one consequence of Ukraine's experience as a country located on the East-West divide between Orthodoxy and Catholicism, central European and Eurasian empires, and the political and social practices they brought with them."6 I have also read that Ukraine is no more than the *foyer of Europe*. The previously mentioned anthology *Ukraine's Many Faces* (2023) contains a string of chapters bearing titles with the symptomatic between: they claim Ukraine to be *Between Empires and National Self- Determination, Between East and West, Between Empires, Between the Holodomor and Euromaidan*, etc. Following the titles, the content is based on a presupposed notion of in-betweenness without a critical approach. In his 2022 novel, Lyubka also agrees to the division between *Europe* and *Ukraine*, but humorously surpasses it in the choice of the manner in which the latter will finally enter the former. In his inauguration speech, the February 2010 presidential election winner, pro-Russian Viktor Yanukovych, proclaimed that "Ukraine Will Be a Bridge Between East and West." I remember this *Wall Street Journal* article well, the quote was on page 12, I have cut it out and keep it in my archive. For him, Ukraine has European identity, but with strong historic cultural and economic ties to Russia as well and can benefit from both. The more Russia is Orientalized, the more liminal Ukraine is becoming.

In such a blocked, rigid, essentialist understanding of conflict times, a bridge rises from its horizontal state into a vertical rampart, a fort. Ideologists define Ukraine as a *bastion of European civilization* or *Europe's shield*, as I could often read in literature, see in visual presentations of Ukraine online and on billboards. *If we don't stop them*, I read, Europeans are next in line after the Ukrainians. No wonder then that, after my lecture, one of my Ukrainian students — similarly to many coming from former Yugoslav

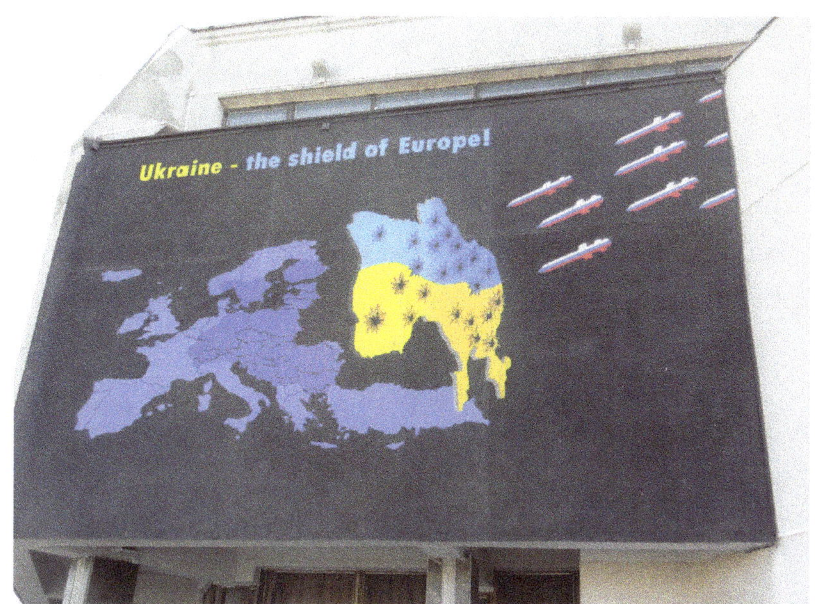

Kyiv, May 2023.

republics before him, or, recently, Georgian ones — told me in an informal chat that he has "never been to Europe" but would love to go study there.

These determinist notions — not just the one expressed by my student; his is just a logical interiorization of them — are not only extremely wrong but also and especially dangerous. Today, the (pro-)Putin side insists that Ukraine is a *collateral damage* of the imperialist ambitions of the West, especially the United States; the pro-Western side insists that it is the *collateral damage* of Russian imperialist ambitions. In short: pawns in the game of chess played by two declining former superpowers. But anyone that has even remotely heard of Van Gennep's theory of the rites of passage knows that the in-betweenness, liminality, fluidity, is not an objective state, a necessity, but an extremely key political fact managed by those who govern the transition. The judgement that someone is *in between* comes from the haughty position of the one who believes to *be somewhere*, that they are the new center, the Archimedes' point, the *sun of their solar system*, if you allow me this platitude; and that others, more or less remote to them, are *on the same path*. Just like they do in the Balkans, the external centers of political, economic, and military power are essentializing Ukraine into one of three roles (one less grateful than the other): first, it is a crossroads of different worlds; second, it is a bridge between them; and third, it is an *antemurale*, a fort, a bastion that defends one against another. But Ukraine never stands alone as a protagonist and a leader of its own fate. Ukraine's liminality is an invention of others rather than of Ukrainian people themselves; it causes dependence on the will of others while stigmatizing, passivizing, and burdening Ukraine. Repeating this in-betweenness is a self-fulfilling prophecy that damages the one that takes on this stigma.

In contrast to these damaging notions and consequently, policies, the people I spoke to in Ukraine are completely clear about what they want. I didn't find them anywhere *in between*, not at all hesitant. No indecision that would lead into resignation, no confusion caused by fatalism — but a lot of anger. And anger, so Kocbek expresses, is "exasperation in regard to a certain goal" and "mediates between reason and hate."[7] While hate closes, anger inspires, opens, constructively transforms into resistance and persistence. Such forceful consistency to persevere can only be given by an actual life ordeal and not by previous principles fostered in peace.

I have asked myself countless times — this is the worm that is living in my brain ever since it inhabited my mind during my travels: how would I feel in their skin, how would I react to all this? Would I manage to have their resistance and persistence? What would I do if the people I love, if I was being bombarded? How would I react to the omnipresent militarism, if I dislike weapons and the army? I can't stand any of this, like I can't stand people in uniform, especially after hearing for the first time at the beginning of the 1980s the eponymous song mocking them by Slovenian heavy metal group Pomaranča. How would I react to the growing suffocating nationalism dressed as falsely more acceptable *patriotism*? I find every nationalist equally foreign; those closest to me, the Slovenian ones, who puff their chest in my name even though I don't want them to, are the worst. Infinitely more interesting than someone's *national identity*, I want to hear about her/his world view, their cultural preferences, their favorite band living in their ears rent-free, the book that is currently on their nightstand, or the film they have watched the most. I agree with my friend, a dead poet who disclosed — I can't remember what shameful situation we were talking about, perhaps the 1991 erasure of people in Slovenia, the attitude towards refugees, racism towards *čefurji* (racial slur for those Slovenians who come from former Yugoslav republics), the rehabilitation of the WWII quislings — that he only feels a belonging to his nation when he is struck by the shame over the evildoings certain people perform in his name.

I could see how right he was on the faces of my friends, colleagues, and acquaintances from those militant countries that have recently *spread democracy*, that have conquered territories that were supposed to *belong to them since forever*, that have carried out ethnic cleansing of *newcomers, wastrels*, that have terrorized the *Axes of Evil*, that have fought new crusades, etc. They are, of course, all anti-nationalist, anti-imperialist, and clearly against their authorities of the time and against executioners implementing their policies. Those were not their wars, not their bloody campaigns ... And yet ... And yet I felt — with some of them confiding in me — how difficult it is for them, despite this being neither their doing nor their responsibility. As if their surroundings — both the one of their *fatherlands* and the new land — is quietly reminding them of it. It doesn't, of course, but reproaches, especially the unfounded ones, hurt. I hope that they haven't felt this in my company: we know and meet each other based on everything else apart from our nationality.

The main challenge that I have heard and pondered upon on my travels is how to fight ethnic chauvinism and not be ethnically chauvinist; how to fight militarism without militarization; how to fight autocracy without limiting democratic rules; how to fight pompous propaganda without blowing up a counterpropaganda; how to fight ruthless words of power with words that would disarm them. Is it possible to resist the barrage of violence without using violence; brute force without using brute force; hate without hate; persistent exaggeration with just as persistent search for the truth even though it might not always be in our favor? One of the witnesses in Tamara Duda's novel says: "I shall sum up my piece like this: it's for those who think that war won't affect them, as long as they stay neutral. When war has already creeped up to your front door, it affects everyone: people both on the left and right, nationalists and pacifists, patriots and people who don't care what flag they live under."[8]

A new context, different circumstance, and a historical volte-face therefore put the a priori, pre-war principles to the test. A radical situation demands radical response. What to do when you are caught in the storm that first and foremost completely shatters your ivory tower? When there is a war situation that you never chose? Can you go over it, past it, can you escape it, ignore it, can you merely haughtily judge what is happening? Can you afford this? How to deal with your own powerlessness in the face of war? Not just in this desperate situation in Ukraine but always, these questions lie as wide open as the book you are holding in your hands, only forcibly. "What is to be done?" as phrased by Chernyshevsky and Lenin.

Here are the two symptomatic answers to these questions. In August 2023, Ukrainian security services began persecuting Ukrainian peace activist Yurii Sheliazhenko, executive secretary of the Ukrainian Pacifist Movement. On the one hand, he explicitly condemned the Russian attack; on the other, he called for the fighting to end and a dialogue to begin. He stood for non-violence and negotiation as the method of solving conflict, advocated for the recognition of the mistakes of both sides, and rejected the militarization of local society and education. He was following the principles written in the *Peace Agenda for Ukraine and the World*, adopted by the Ukrainian Pacifist Movement on the International Day of Peace, 21 September 2022. The agenda also states that "[i]t is wrong to put yourself on the side of any of the warring armies, it is necessary to stand on the side of peace and justice. Self-defense can and should be carried out by non-violent and unarmed methods" and ends with: "War is a crime against

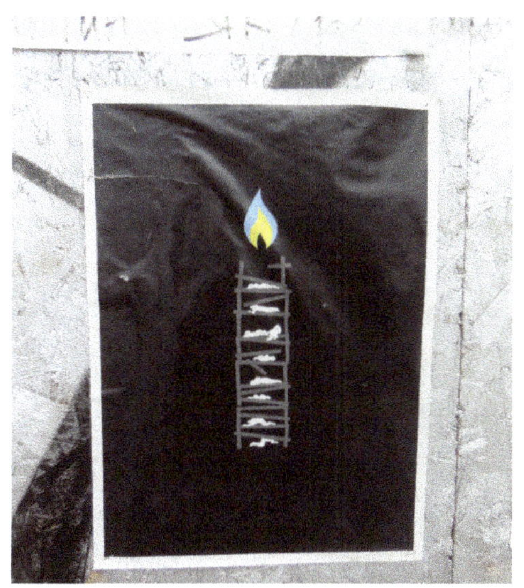

Left to right: Odesa, May 2023; Kyiv, May 2023.

humanity, therefore, we are determined not to support any kind of war and to strive for the removal of all causes of war." In his engagement for peace, Sheliazhenko worked with the neighboring Belarus and Russian peace organizations as well as many other international organizations that have since started collecting signatures and doing other activities in his support. His apartment was searched in August 2023 and authorities placed him under house arrest until February 2024. At the moment (spring of 2025), the trial against him has begun. In a letter to his Slovenian supporters he says that he hopes to be acquitted, however he's well aware that there are several less good outcomes (e.g. probation) with the worst case scenario being five years of prison. In summer 2023, his colleague from the Ljubljana Peace Institute Brankica Petković reacted to his prosecution with: "Among all the enemies of Ukraine, Zelenskyy found an enemy in the peacemaker."

The second answer to the above questions can be seen in the fate of Ukrainian humanitarian activist, anarchist, a proponent of non-violence, and journalist Maxym Butkevych. He was brought to my attention by the visibly shaken author of my Ukrainian book preface while we were having coffee in Lviv. Fifteen years ago, Butkevych co-founded an NGO that has monitored human rights in post-Soviet countries and arranged political shelter for refugees in Ukraine; he was active at the United Nations as a refugee specialist for Eastern Europe and at Amnesty International. When the war began, he joined the Ukrainian army, explaining that he unfortunately had to stop with his humanitarian activities and defend what he found important in the given moment. In a few months, Putin's soldiers captured him, labelled him a *neo-Nazi*, charged him with *war crimes*, and sentenced him to thirteen years in prison. He was recently, in the last fall, released in context of a war prisoners' exchange between Russia and Ukraine.

This is, of course, not the first time that pacifists took to weapons and anarchists supported the authorities — however controversial some, including themselves considering their previous principles, may find this. I already mentioned the *Makhnovshchina*, the autochthonous Ukrainian anarchist resistance against any form of authority that it doesn't find their own: occupiers, tzars, or Bolsheviks. Resisting Franco, Spanish anarchists organized in their anarcho-syndicalist confederation CNT immediately joined the republican government of the Popular Front and took three important ministries. This provoked strong condemnations by the nationalists, but also by many on the anarchist side. However, faced with the choice between two evils, the Spanish clero-fascism and monarchism on the one hand and a secular republic on the other, they chose the lesser one. Especially at the beginning of the war, their participation in military operations was indispensable but also based on completely different, libertarian principles: self-organization, elected commanders, horizontal democracy with no political or officer hierarchies, direct action, etc.

Recent Slovenian history also offers a different, yet no less clear answer to these dilemmas: partisan resistance, which I still find to be an example of unique, unsurpassed courage. In the inductive level of argumentation, I follow cases: a professor teaching at my faculty, a member of two of my thesis defense committees, joined the partisans at the age of 15, immediately after the capitulation of Italy. His colleague and fellow fighter, the mentor of my dissertation, joined at 16, in the summer of 1942, i.e. before the battles of Stalingrad and El Alamein when the Nazis were at the height of their power: in the name-by-name warrant in Slovene collaborationist Rupnik's 1944 *Official Journal*, he was listed as *secondary-school pupil*. And my uncle, the younger brother of my other uncle who ended up in the mass grave of a Soviet prisoner camp: he was barely 17 when he escaped the Italian *labor battalions* near Livorno (where the *politically unreliable* were sent) to join the Gradnik Brigade and spend the entire war fighting German Nazis, Salò fascists, and their Slovenian and escaping Serbian helpers. *Apart from their chains,* all these poor youngsters had literally nothing to lose — that is why they won in the fight for a fairer world and emancipated.

Answers to these questions are never clear-cut, much less instantaneous. Every exact, ready-made, *principal* answer risks remaining an unfounded speculation. Back to the Balkans: the fates of Yugoslav ideological non-conformists of all nationalities and from all countries involved in the blood-bath call for comparisons. Some of them grabbed one-way tickets on the last Yugoslav Airways flights out; others opted for an internal exile; the third type simply died from grief at their fate; the fourth remained engaged at home until the end; the fifth persisted for a few years, then quit due to constant threats from nationalist hyenas, those in ties and those with baseball bats roaming the streets.

In this sense, the reaction of the Norwegian government and its premier Jans Stoltenberg (who is today a controversial proponent of a more radical NATO alliance) following Breivik's massacre of July 2011, carries enormous importance. In his eulogy, he emphasized that the correct answer to such evil is "more democracy" not less; "more openness" not concealment; "more humanity" not brutality — ending with "But never naivety." Barbarity is never the response to barbarity, nor is primitivism to primitivism; it is precisely in these heightened circumstances, in which radicals demand unity and call for Talion measures, that it is necessary to show that we are never all the same: neither *we* nor *they.*

It is impossible to say what I would do in such a situation as I am not — and sincerely hope never to be. A tentative answer would be a constant self-reflection of my own actions, not just my reflecting opponent's; self-limiting my reactions and not giving in to the opponent's logic, which irrevocably leads into a spiral of violence and lies. And locating and revealing the real culprits for the conflict instead of generalizing. I realize that this is easier said and written down than done but I am encouraged by a strong example for this, coming from my end of Slovenia. I always remember it when it comes to (post-)conflict societies. Despite being, just like every person from the Slovenian Littoral region, in the interwar and war period belonging to Kingdom of Italy (1918–1943), subject to radical Italianization and the accompanying ethnic humiliation, despite attending school in Italian language, and despite their names being Italianized — my father's entire village was even burnt down by a joint expedition of German Nazis and Italian (Salò) fascists —, my parents later never blamed the Italian people in general but only fascists. Never! They resented fascists, but not the nation as a whole. They taught their children to respect Italian culture, language, cinema, literature, everything Italian — but fascism. As a child and also later, I felt no ethnic poisoning; however, I did feel a strong political warning.

Finally, choice always comes down to individual judgement, decision, and engagement. I suspect that in such circumstances, I would make my choice after a thorough reflection, following my conscience, and doing it my way: figuratively speaking, fighting my battles, choosing my weapons, and pointing out the mistakes on both sides, on all sides. Halyna Kruk says that she cannot battle and that she must "fight for peace not in the first but in the last lines"[9] — she sees her engagement as serving with words; she helps those engaged in battles with words. And I am sure that I would not generalize and blindly judge everyone on the *other* side, just like I would not generally and blindly support everyone on the side that was supposed to be mine — like some people that I mention in these essays do. I am sorry, but affect is no excuse. I would choose what I would find best in that moment — bearing in mind that it is impossible to completely agree with the chosen side and amalgamate with it; that even people who are supposed to be *ours* make mistakes; and that anyway, I simply don't want to be completely *ours*. Taking a position and, yes, even taking sides does not mean renouncing its criticism.

I call this critical affection, a *spectateur engagé* position of an independent yet engaged observer, whose affection doesn't win over judgement. This was also the basic mental and emotional framework of this book of essays on the culture of war in Ukraine. I learnt about it as I went: while writing, while taking pictures, while attending various events, while engaging in short or in in-depth conversations with familiar or random people. Not for a moment do I imagine encapsulating it in all its immensely complex and painful reality. These are more its fragments, chips that rolled toward me as much as I rolled toward them. This is why the essays first and foremost contains my story, they are a narrative patchwork of my impressions and adventures from three trips to Ukraine, intertwined with those written, drawn, spraypainted, acted or sang out, recorded, etc. by people that I met live or through their works there, beyond the Carpathians, and here, under the Alps. War never has only two sides, nor does it have as many sides as the people involved in it — but as many sides as the people that have an opinion on it. This travelogue presents my reflections and photographs, my *thousand plateaus* of Ukraine, but remains very conscious of all the other *millions of plateaus*.

This book of visual sketches on the culture of war in Ukraine has strongly surpassed my initial wish of publishing my journal and is more than a document of (hard) time that I spent there. In those weeks and in the later months, I have become friends with these road records, I was reliving the situations that I would otherwise forget. They are a connection between both sides of my experiences, learning, reflecting, or even anticipating, my *heretical empiricism* to reuse Pasolini, my "human and extra-human, internal and external" to cite Kocbek who points to "both poles of reality": a growing internal intensity on the one hand and the unfathomable, shapeless, and unlived colorfulness of great days on the other.[10] Based on this, I draw conclusions — although the normally open form of an essay does not necessarily encourage me to do so. And perhaps the book has become, even as you read these lines, completely out of date, its conclusions wrong, its assumptions ridiculous. The situation is changing rapidly, any moment anything can happen; we are living surrounded by the tsunamis of events that are given no time to quiet down. To illustrate: when I started writing these lines, the infamous Prigozhin was still enjoying Putin's favor and supported him, alive and kicking — very much alive and kicking hard; in the middle, the two fell out; and by the time I got to the end, Prigozhin was dead meat, paying for his insolence with his life. Everybody but him knew that the fist of revenge would get him. In the summer and fall of 2023, Former Commander-in-Chief of Ukraine's armed forces Valerii Zaluzhny still firmly held his position, glorified from all sides; in 2024, when I finished my manuscript, he was replaced. During that time, in the past few months, two other brutal wars have happened: in Nagorno-Karabakh and in Gaza, and the one in Syria has just ended, however the tensions there remain still very high. In such a dynamic, all research is ongoing, every impression and reflection transient, every result no more than interim, their timestamp is ruthlessly temporary. But I nevertheless brought my book of Ukrainian vignettes to a conclusion.

Before I went to Ukraine, but mostly after, many people told me how brave I was to even attempt such a risky journey. A New York colleague wrote to me how it had a certain Sontag dimension to it. What bravery, I replied: of course, I was scared when distant detonations were heard; I was scared when it was quiet. I revealed how cowardly and relieved I felt all three times I crossed the border coming back. The only brave, the only truly admirable, the only real *Heroes*, to refer to the already mentioned salute, who deserve *Glory*, are all those people who stay there in the face of an uncertain present and an even more uncertain future. Gritting their

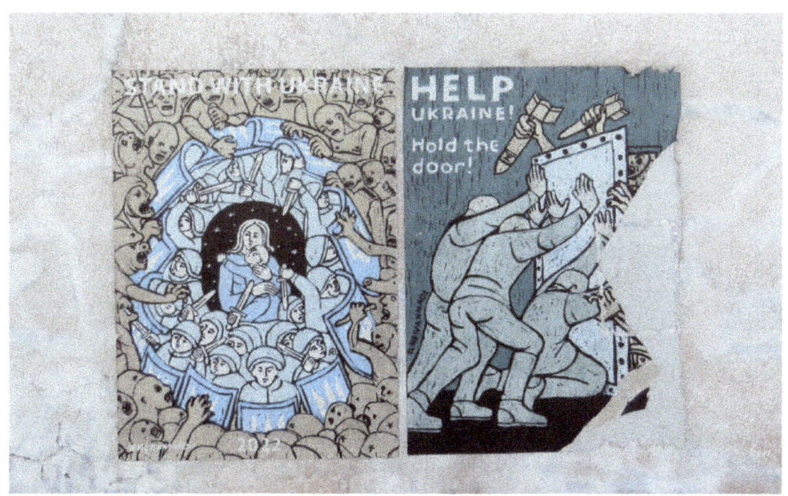

Lviv, May 2023.

teeth and clenching their fists, they remain optimistic and persist in bitter dignity. This is definitely the most important lesson that I learned from all of them.

NOTES

1 Kurkov, Andriy. *Diary of an Invasion*, 2022. 14.

2 Lampreht, Miha. *Kratka zgodovina vojne v Ukrajini*, 2023. 90.

3 Kocbek, Edvard. *Tovarišija*, 1972. 44.

4 Stasiuk, Andrzej. *On the Road to Babadag*, 2011. 8.

5 Lyubka, Andriy. *Carbide*, 2023. 192.

6 Plokhy, Serhii. *The Gates of Europe: A History of Ukraine*, 2021. 364.

7 Kocbek, 1972. 107.

8 Duda, Tamara. *Daughter*, 2021. 347.

9 Kruk, Halyna. Interview, *Svet je od nekdaj ujet v neravnovesje med vojno in mirom*, 2023. 19.

10 Kocbek, 1972. 25.

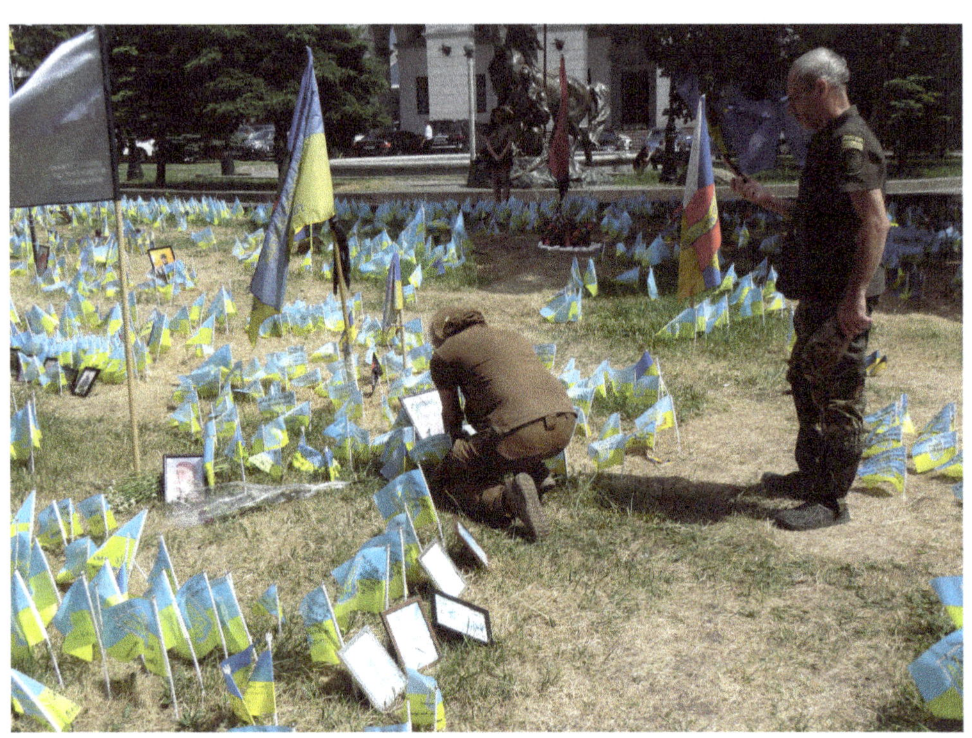

Maidan, Kyiv, June 2024.

In a state of war, any sense of relaxation is deceptive, even dangerous. My last night before leaving Uzhhorod, which seemed safe from Putin's projectiles, was marked by sirens, as if saying goodbye. Retaliatory strikes as Ukrainian drone attacks on Russian infrastructure the day before were successful, that's what I read in the news. Now, back in Ljubljana, I also wake up during the night, for no reason, there are no alarms. At home, night is still separated from nightmares. "What a rare luxury," I think sleepily, "to wake up with no war …" Only when you return from there can you see how peace is not to be taken for granted.

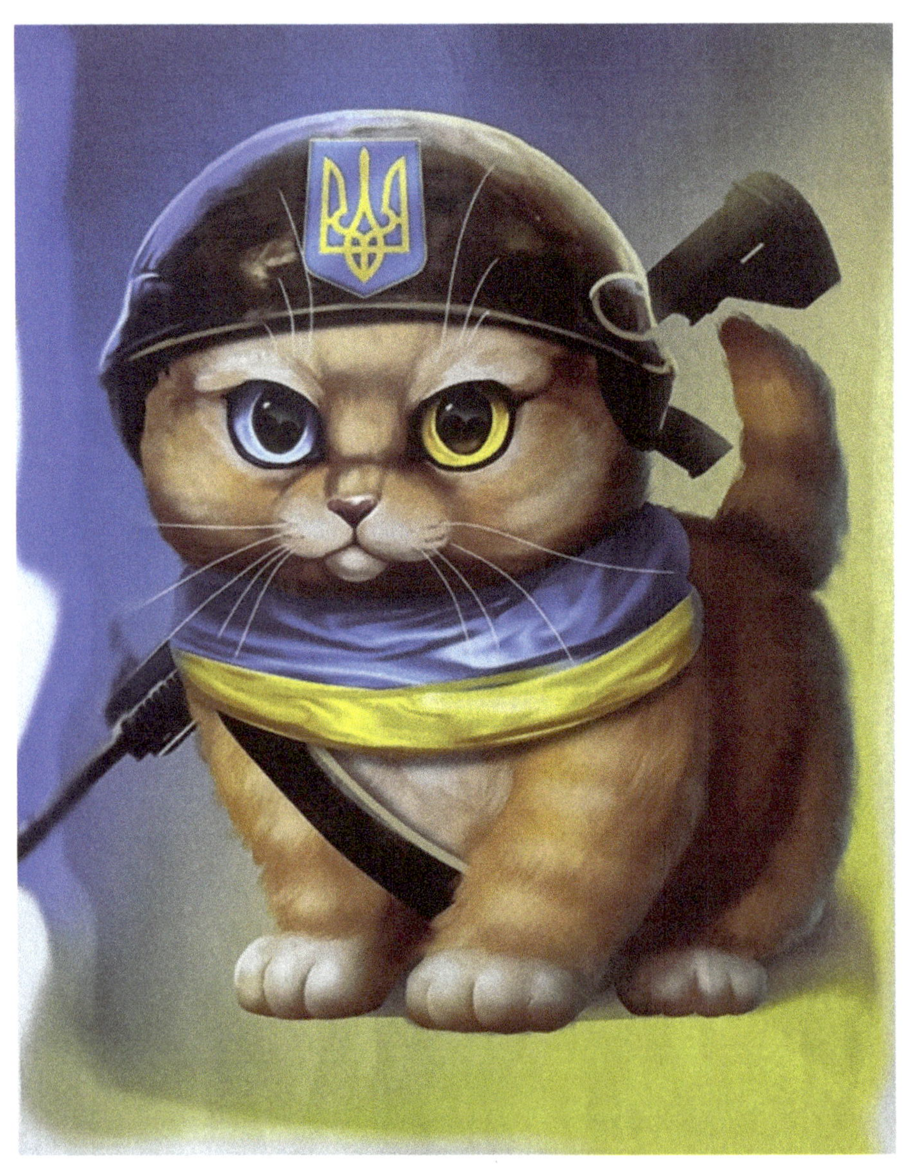

Poster, Drohobych, June 2024.

SOURCES AND LITERATURE

"Historical books made war more distant for me. In contrast, memory literature made it closer."
Paolo Rumiz, Like Horses Asleep on Their Feet, *150.*

Andruhovič, Jurij. *Dvanajst krogov.* Cankarjeva založba, Ljubljana, 2016.

Andrukhovych, Yuri. *The Moscoviad.* Spuyten Duyvil, New York, 2008.

Applebaum, Anne. *Red Famine: Stalin's War on Ukraine.* Doubleday, New York, 2017.

Asotić, Selma. *Reci vatra.* Nulta stvarnost, Sarajevo, 2022.

Babelj, Isaak. *Zgodbe iz Odese.* Beletrina, Ljubljana, 2019.

Babkina, Katerina. *Moj deda je plesao bolje od svih.* Blum izdavaštvo, Belgrade, 2020.

———. *Srećni goli ljudi.* Blum izdavaštvo, Belgrade, 2024.

Belorusets, Yevgenia. *War Diary.* Translated by Greg Nissan. New Directions, Cambridge, MA, 2023.

Bojanowska, M. Edyta. "Pushkin's 'To the Slanderers of Russia'. The Slavic Question, Imperial Anxieties, and Geopolitics," *Pushkin Review,* No. 21, 2019. 11–33.

———. *Nikolai Gogol: Between Ukrainian and Russian Nationalism.* Harvard University Press, Cambridge, Mass. & London, 2007.

Bulgakov, Mikhail. *The Master and Margarita.* Translated by Hugh Aplin. Alma Classics, London, 2012.

Chkvanava, Gela. *Toreadors.* Diogene Publishers, Tbilisi, 2013.

Colborne, Michael. *From the Fires of War: Ukraine's Azov Movement and the*

Global Far Right. ibidem Press, Stuttgart, Hannover, 2022.

Čolić, Velibor. "Na Balkanu narod tlačimo v vse." Interviewed by journalist Nina Gostiša. *Delo*, Ljubljana, 22 August 2023. 19.

Čolović, Ivan. *Politika simbola: Ogledi o političkoj antropologiji*. Biblioteka XX vek, Belgrade, 2000.

Dehtyaryova, Lina; Olashyn, Oleg. *Uzhhorods'kyy modernism: Mizhvoyenna arkhitektura*. Polygraphcenter Lira, Uzhhorod, 2018.

Duda, Tamara (Tamara Horikha Zernya). *Daughter*. Bilka Publishing, Kyiv, 2021.

Dugandžija, Nikola. *Svjetovna religija*. NIRO Mladost, Belgrade, 1980.

Fenghi, Fabrizio. *It Will Be Fun and Terrifying: Nationalism and Protest in Post-Soviet Russia*. The University of Wisconsin Press, Madison, 2020.

Gogol, Nikolai. *Evenings Near the Village of Dikanka*. Foreign Language Publ. House, 1957.

———. *Taras Bulba*. [eBook #1197], translated by Isabel F. Hapgood, 1917.

———. *Dead Souls*. [eBook #1081], translated by D. J. Hogarth, 1997.

Igort (Igor Tuveri). *Quaderni Ucraini: Le radici del conflitto*. Oblomov Edizioni, Bologna, 2022.

Klid, Bohdan and Motyl, Alexander J. (eds). *The Holodomor Reader — A Sourcebook on the Famine of 1932-1933 in Ukraine*. University of Alberta Press, Edmonton, 2022.

Kocbek, Edvard. *Tovarišija*. Mladinska knjiga, Ljubljana, 1972.

Komnenović, Dora. *Reading Between the Lines: Reflections on Discarded Books and Sociopolitical Transformations in (Post-)Yugoslavia*. ibidem Verlag, Stuttgart, 2022.

Krasovytskyy, Oleksandr. *Tomorrow*. Folio, Kharkiv, 2022

Kruk Halyna. "Svet je od nekdaj ujet v neravnovesje med vojno in mirom." Interviewed by journalist Nina Gostiša. *Delo*, Sobotna priloga, Ljubljana, 17 June 2023. 18–20.

Kurkov, Andrey. *Death and the Penguin*. Vintage Books, London, 2001.

———. *Diary of an Invasion*. Deep Vellum Publishing, Dallas, 2022.

Lampreht, Miha. *Kratka zgodovina vojne v Ukrajini: Leto zamujenih priložnosti*. Didakta, Radovljica, 2023.

Leidig, Eviane. "An Interview with Bellingcat Journalist Michael Colborne on the Azov Movement in Ukraine." *International Centre for Counter-Terrorism*, Haag, https://www.icct.nl/publication/interview-bellingcat--journalist-michael-colborne-azov-movement-ukraine, 29 March 2022, accessed 10 September 2023.

Ljubka, Andrij. *Karbid*. Translated by Janja Vollmaier Lubej and Primož Lubej. Društvo slovenskih pisateljev, Ljubljana, 2019.

Lyubka, Andriy. *Carbide*. Translated by Reilly Costigan-Humes and Isaac Stackhouse Wheeler. Jantar Publishing, London, 2023.

Lopata, Evgenia and Lyubka, Andriy (Eds.). *State of War*. Publisher Svyatoslav Pomerantsev, Chernivtsi, 2023.

Luciuk, Lubomyr Y. *Operation Payback: Soviet Disinformation and Alleged Nazi War Criminals in North America*. The Kashtan Press, Kingston, Canada, 2021.

Menon, Rajan and Rumer, Eugene. *Conflict in Ukraine: The Unwinding of the Post-Cold War Order*. The MIT Press, Cambridge, MA, 2015.

Michnik, Adam. *Skušnjavec našega časa*. Mladinska knjiga, Ljubljana, 1997.

Moussienko, Natalia. *Art of Maidan*. Kyiv Huss, Kyiv, 2016.

Nietzsche, Friedrich. *Onstran dobrega in zlega (Predigra k filozofiji prihodnosti). H genealogiji morale (Polemični spis)*. Slovenska matica, Ljubljana, 1988.

Palko, Olena and Férez Gil, Manuel (Eds.). *Ukraine's Many Faces — Land, People, and Culture Revisited*. Transcript, Bielefeld, 2023.

Pasolini, Pier Paolo. *Empirismo eretico*. Garzanti, Milan, 2014.

Pihota, Ruslan. *Ukrayinski viyskovi komiksy*. Disa, Kharkiv, 2023.

Plokhy, Serhii. *The Gates of Europe: A History of Ukraine* (Revised Edition). Basic Books, New York, 2021.

Pobožiy, C. I. (Ed.). *Imena Ukrayiny: 100 Mytsiv*. Universytetska knyha, Sumi, 2020.

Polenakis, Stamatis. *Stopnice v Odesi*. KUD KDO, Ljubljana, 2022.

Puškin, Aleksander S. *Pesnitve, pravljice*. Državna založba Slovenije, Ljubljana, 1970a.

———. *Pesmi*. Državna založba Slovenije, Ljubljana, 1970.

Reid, Anna. *Borderland: A Journey Through the History of Ukraine*. Basic Books, New York, 2015.

Rumiz, Paolo. *Kot konji, ki spijo stoje*. Modrijan, Ljubljana, 2016.

Rupnik, Anton. *Tretji Rim: Rusija nekoč in danes*. Znanstveno in publicistično središče, Ljubljana, 1999.

Schulmann, Ekaterina. "Ruski Hitler morda šele prihaja na oblast." Interviewed by journalist Aljaž Vrabec. *Delo*, Sobotna priloga, Ljubljana, 17 June 2023. 14–17.

Semena, Mykola. *Crimean Report: Chronicle of the Occupation of Crimea*. Mega-Press Group, Kyiv, 2018.

Semenišin, Marjana (Ed.). *Zgodovinske vezi kot temelj sodobnega partnerstva: primer ukrajinskih in slovenskih občin*. U-LEAD z Evropo, Kyiv, 2021.

Shevtsova, Lilia. *Russia: Lost in Transition: The Yeltsin and Putin Legacies*. Carnegie Endowment for International Peace, Washington, D.C., 2007.

Shore, Marci. *The Ukrainian Night: An Intimate History of Revolution*. Yale University Press, New Haven & London, 2017.

Smrke, Marjan. *Religija in politika: Spremembe v deželah prehoda*. Znanstveno in publicistično središče, Ljubljana, 1996.

Snyder, Timothy. *Bloodlands: Europe Between Hitler and Stalin*. Basic Books, New York, 2010.

———. *Black Earth: The Holocaust as History and Warning*. Tim Duggan Books, New York, 2015.

Stasiuk, Andrzej. *On the Road to Babadag. Travels in the Other Europe*. Translated by Michael Kandel. Houghton Mifflin Harcourt, Boston & New York, 2011.

Sturken, Marita. *Tourists of History: Memory, Kitsch, and Consumerism from Oklahoma City to Ground Zero*. Duke University Press, Durham, 2007.

Subotić, Milan (Ed.). *Druga Rusija: Kritička misao u savremenoj Rusiji*. Biblioteka XX vek, Belgrade, 2015.

———. *Napred, u prošlost: Studije o politici istorije u Poljskoj, Ukrajini i Rusiji*. Fabrika knjiga Peščanik, Belgrade, 2019.

Ševčenko, Taras. *Ševčenko*. Mladinska knjiga, Ljubljana, 1976.

Velikonja, Mitja. *Religious Separation and Political Intolerance in Bosnia-Herzegovina*. Texas A&M UP, College Station, 2003.

———. *Eurosis: A Critique of the New Eurocentrism*. MediaWatch–Peace Institute, Ljubljana, 2005.

———. "The New Folklore: Neo-Traditionalism as the Cultural Logic of the Post-Socialist Transition." Presentation at the conference *The Other Europe: Changes and Challenges since 1989*. New Haven, Yale MacMillan Center–European Studies Council, 11–12 September 2020.

Vollmaier Lubej, Janja. "Ukrajinske družbene spremembe v romanu Dvanajst krogov Jurija Andruhoviča." In: Alenka Čuš, Marcello Potocco, Lidija Rezoničnik and Nina Zavašnik (Eds.). *Družbeni in politični procesi v sodobnih slovanskih kulturah, jezikih in literaturah*. Založba Univerze na Primorskem, Koper, 2018. 139–151.

Zabuzhko, Oksana. *Fieldwork in Ukrainian Sex*. Amazon Crossing, Las Vegas, 2011.

Zakharov, Serhii. *DumPsteR: DumPsteR = Donetsk People's Republic*. Onova, Kijev, 2018.

Zhadan, Serhiy. *The Orphanage*. Translated by Reilly Costigan-Humes and Isaac Stackhouse Wheeler. Yale University Press, New Haven, 2021.

———. *Sky Above Kharkiv: Dispatches from the Ukrainian Front*. Yale University Press, New Haven & London, 2023.

———. *Vorošilovgrad*. Beletrina, Ljubljana, 2018.

Yekelchyk, Serhy. *Ukraine: What Everyone Needs to Know*. Oxford University Press, Oxford, 2020.

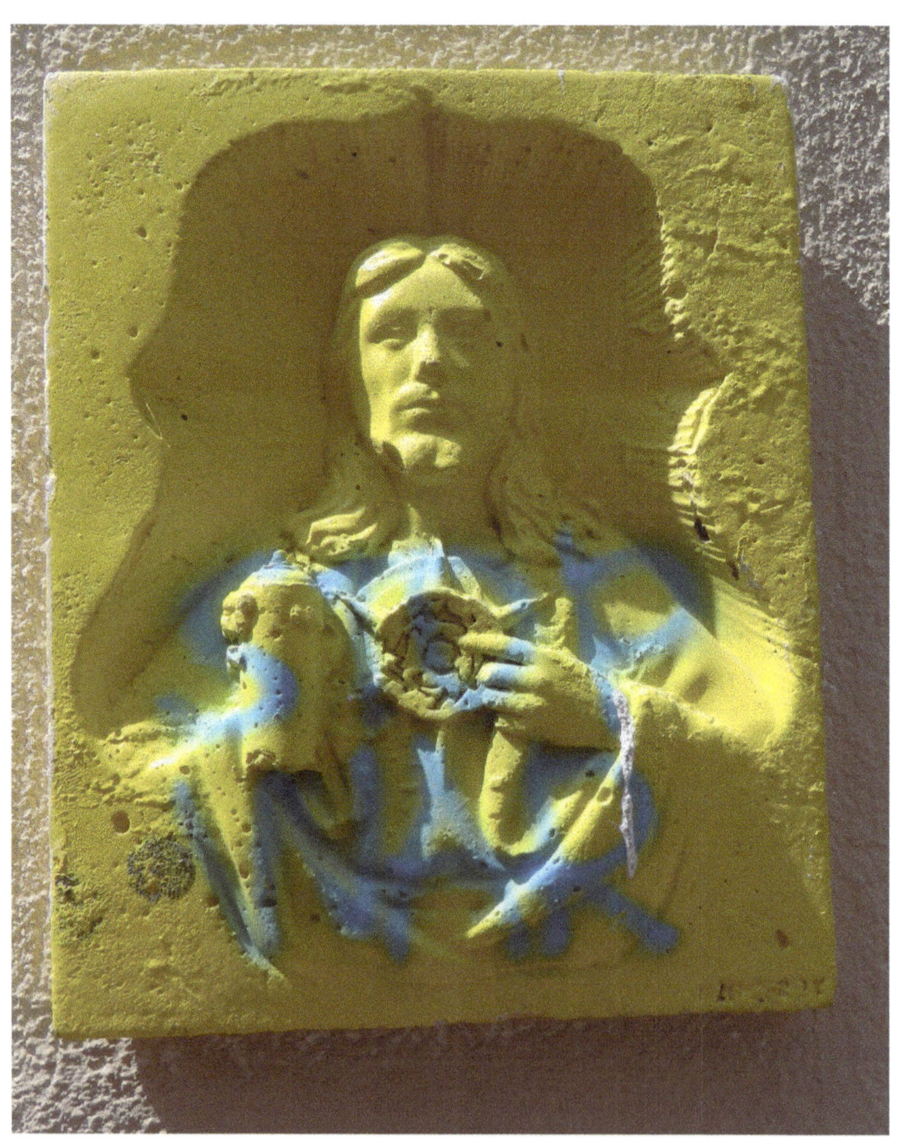

Lviv, May 2023.

ACKNOWLEDGMENTS

There are too many people that I would love to thank for their inspiration, encouragement, reflection, help, and experience on my travels. I shall nevertheless try. To Darja, Kateryna, Iryna, Vyacheslav, Viktor, Lina, Serhiy, Oleh, Olena, Hanna, Yuri, Taras, Igor, Nina, Asmati, Andrii, another Kateryna and another Daria, Sofiia, Ava, Maryana, Bohdan, Mateja, Ketevan, Mariia, Valentina, Mikhailo, and Stanislav — sincere thanks to everybody, each and every one! I am especially thankful to Tomaž Mencin, Oleg Golovko, Sofiia Syniaieva, Selina Staltner, Zosia Kais, Anna Di Lellio, and Lina Dehtyaryova. My thanks also go to Igor Bašin, Faris Kočan, Samira Kentrić, Rok Zupančič, and Andrej Blatnik for a critical reading of the first version of my manuscript.

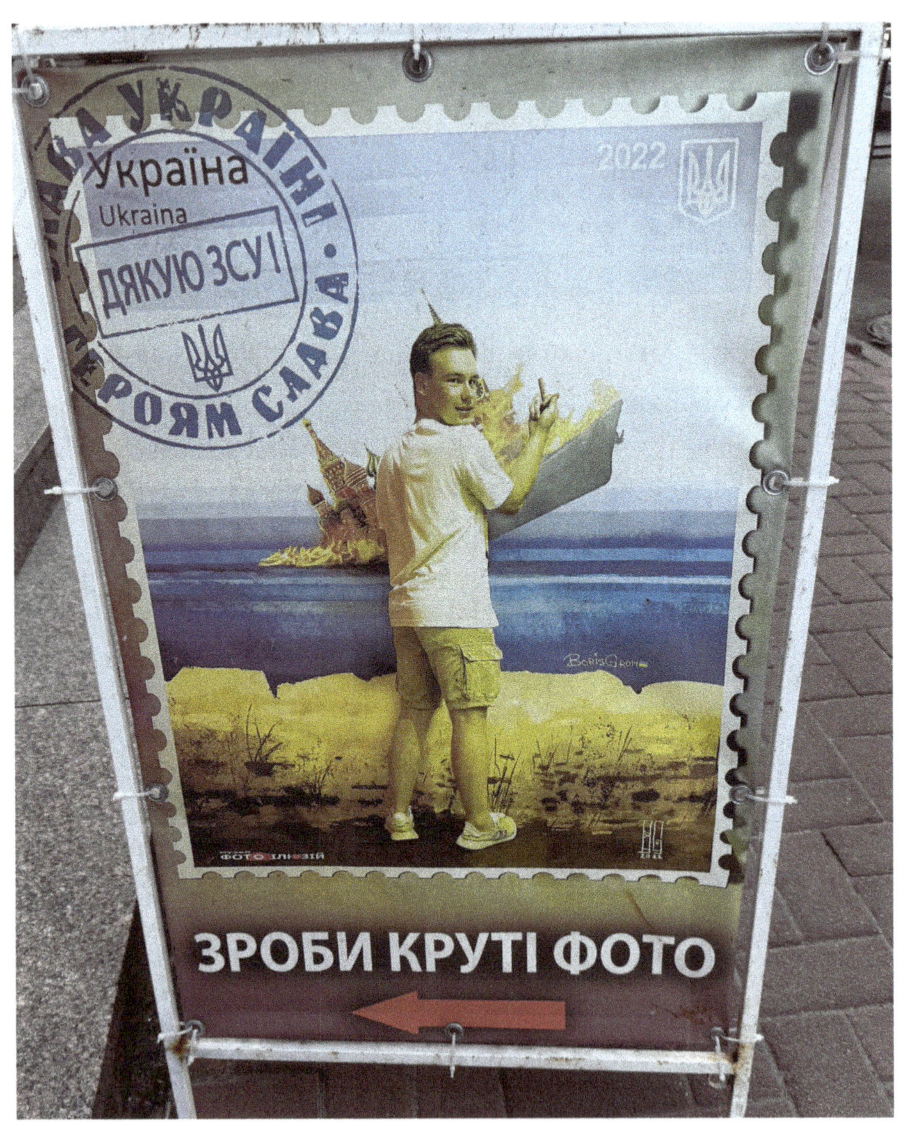

Kyiv, June 2024.

ABOUT THE AUTHOR

Mitja Velikonja is the author and coauthor of eight books. He is a Professor for Cultural Studies and head of Center for Cultural and Religious Studies at University of Ljubljana, Slovenia and has recently been a full-time visiting professor in Krakow, St. Petersburg, Rijeka, at Columbia University in New York and Yale University as well as Fulbright visiting researcher in Philadelphia, The Netherlands Institute of Advanced Studies, and NYU. His recent books on post-socialist graffiti and street art from former Yugoslavia have been translated and sold widely in the region, including in Ukraine, where he has been one of the only visiting professors to lecture and teach in the country during the war against Russia ongoing since February 2022.

This is Velikonja's second book with DoppelHouse Press; *The Chosen Few: Aesthetics and Ideology in Football Fan Graffiti and Street Art* was published in 2021 and was a finalist for a Next Generation Indie Book Award.